Stillwater Trout Tactics

STILLWATER TROUT TACTICS

BOB CHURCH with
CHARLES JARDINE

The Crowood Press

First published in 1989 by
The Crowood Press
Ramsbury, Marlborough,
Wiltshire SN8 2HE

British Library Cataloguing in Publication Data

Church, Bob
    Stillwater trout tactics
    1. Stillwater. Trout. Fly fishing
    I. Title   II. Jardine, Charles
    799.1'755

ISBN 1–85223–171–8

Typeset by Footnote Graphics, Warminster
Printed in Great Britain by Butler & Tanner, Ltd., Frome

Contents

Acknowledgements

My special thanks go to East Midlands Allied Press for putting up with me all these years. Many of the ideas for this book are based on my articles in either *Angling Times* or *Trout Fisherman*. They also helped me with the photographs.

My thanks go to Tony Pawson for his generous thoughts, Mike Peters and the Irish Tourist Board for photographs and to Jeanette Taylor for typing up the manuscript. John Wilshaw did the final editing.

My gratitude is extended to Fred Wagstaffe who brings trout fishing to life; to that canny hunter of big fish Alan Pearson, Datchet's Mick Bewick and to Peter Shelton whose scientific revelations are bound to spark off new developments.

My words are not enough to thank Charles Jardine for both his fascinating insight into the underwater world of the trout and his beautiful illustrations which depict the world of fly fishing as only a most talented artist and angler possibly can.

Foreword

'Fish the Bob Church way' was an easy slogan to coin, but only exceptional fishing ability has allowed him to live up to it. Inevitably when he fishes with a party or in a competition event Bob puts himself on trial. There is bound to be someone ready to try and prove his way is better and make critical comment if he catches more. Since there is no more active and dedicated a fly fisherman than Bob, he is continually popping his head above the parapet to be shot at if he fails to live up to his own high standards. Shot at he may have been, but never shot down.

I have always admired Bob's readiness to put his rod where his slogan is, showing year in and year out that he is one of the small group of leading stillwater anglers who have given England such a high reputation in this type of fishing. It is also delightful to see that his enthusiasm has never waned and to know that if you fish with Bob he will start the day full of confidence and excitement. Usually the confidence is justified and the day's action provides plenty of entertainment. Like all of us, Bob has times when little goes right, but unlike most of us, it is a very rare day when he is not catching well. His experience and ability cover all aspects of fly fishing on all types of water in all kinds of conditions.

Competitive events in fly fishing provide sociability in a sport which can be selfish and solitary, but more importantly learning and proving experiences. For my first fifty years as a fly fisherman I was much in awe of so-called 'experts', and it was disappointing to fish with one of them to find his reputation based on ability to milk others' ideas and express them in fine phrases, rather than on any personal fishing skill. Once I became involved in competitive events, however, not only did I learn more in a couple of years than in the previous fifty-three, but I soon discovered consistently good anglers whose methods were worth studying. High on that list was Bob Church.

Bob's reputation was firmly founded on his day-to-day fishing before he excelled in competitions. Competitive success has merely emphasised what a consistently good angler he is. Apart from the Home Internationals and many other stillwater events Bob has proved his versatility by performing well at World Fly Fishing Championships on rivers as well as on lakes. He was a member of England's first team in Spain in 1982 and two years later helped England to second place on the Tormes River, contributing much to successful team tactics as well as coming high himself. He helped the English team to win the championship in England in 1987 against twenty other countries. They won by a wider margin than any world cup has ever been won by scoring more than double the points of the runners-up Australia and more than triple those of third placed New Zealand and fourth placed Wales. In the individual, he himself finished third out of a hundred. Having already won gold, silver and bronze medals in world championships it was no surprise that Bob was selected to fish again in Tasmania.

From two world championships there were good illustrations of how Bob's tactical appreciation was even more important than his technical ability. The Tormes River trout were said to be catchable only on the dry fly, but Bob surmised that unusually cold conditions made wet fly fishing more appropriate, and a recent stocking made different fly patterns desirable rather than those so confidently recommended to us. Bob also helped the team to develop the new tactical method of fishing the static fly on the drift, which proved so effective at Grafham and Rutland, that his team left all the others trailing.

There are several reasons why Bob is an ideal man to write on the tactics of fly fishing. First there is his proven experience, then there is his high profile in the fishing world and his contact with other expert, practical anglers allowing him to assess and absorb the best of others' methods, as well as passing on his own. All this is complimented by his readiness to learn as well as instruct in a sport where something new is dreamed up every season (sometimes every month). Finally there is broadmindedness in recognising that angling preferences are an individual matter. Each angler has to decide for himself which legitimate type of fishing appeals to him, rather than being bullied by some small clique into accepting their particular method. Fishing is about individual enjoyment and one of the main attractions of fly fishing is that there are so many different ways of enjoying yourself. Bob has recognised that in this book, obtaining expert contributions on the tactics of particular methods which he might not enjoy himself, but which he accepts hold appeal for others.

For all these reasons, those who wish to improve their particular type of fishing will find much useful and authoritative advice on the tactics which are so important for consistent catching.

Tony Pawson
1989

Preface

How could I even begin to discuss the most important aspects of a seasonal monthly diary? The more I thought about it the more my early excitement waned. The last thing I wanted was yet another book on fly fishing. The book shelves are full of them as it is. Then it occurred to me that what I really needed was the aid of a skilled artist who could make it all come to life. He would have to be special and as I thumbed through *Trout Fisherman* magazine it all became so clear. Charles Jardine, best known perhaps for his river fishing expertise, was contributing a superbly illustrated series, depicting the scenes in a way no photographer could ever do. With his agreement, we set out to reveal what we know, in a month by month calendar of events. We decided to cover all the basics, but also to attempt a more advanced approach, facing any controversial issues which arose.

Suddenly I find myself at fifty-two years of age but I am happy to say that in fly fishing circles this is still comparatively young, the beauty of getting old being the wealth of experience gathered along the way. I feel sorry for footballers and the like who have to hang up their boots just when they know a thing or two. My old friend Frank Cutler is nearing seventy, but he fished for England twice in the Home Internationals at Bewl Water and Loch Leven and won two gold medals. In the same year his team came third in the Benson and Hedges with him taking top honours on the final day.

I find myself looking forward to each season with even more enthusiasm. At the moment I am totally hooked on the competitive aspect of the sport and I am really motivated to do my very best. So far fortune has been with me. Competition fishing has grown beyond all our expectations. Who could have imagined more than 760 teams all representing different clubs would enter the 1987 Benson and Hedges competition? Over the years I have used secret flies, lures and tactics to help keep me at the forefront of the sport, and the purpose of this book is to pass on all that I know. Good reading.

Introduction

Even the most expert among us can never guarantee catching a trout on fly tackle. However, there are times when you would find it difficult not to put fish on the bank – at small, daily-stocked fisheries for instance. When fishing such waters, I use tactics designed to select the larger fish from their smaller and more gullible peers, rather than fishing merrily on for a succession of unwanted stock fish. Thankfully, no matter how skilled the angler, the element of chance can make or break a day on the water. This quick-silver contest with Lady Luck is, of course, exactly what draws us back to the waterside time and time again.

The never-to-be-solved mysteries drive all serious fly fishers on in a search for more clues, even though they might suspect that the fail-me-never medicine for all waters and all conditions will never, I'm glad to say, be found. At best, we can only strive to improve our knowledge of a wide range of possibilities. Fishing techniques require more than just an understanding of theory. There is no substitute for the hours spent on the water in all sorts of weather and at all times of the year.

Very often, anglers will be unhappy with their results despite owning the most expensive tackle and having read everything there is to read. Usually a lack of success can be traced back to a poor casting style or an inability to handle a boat well in awkward winds. Even more likely, the fault lies with the retrieve. What should be seen by the trout as a flickering illusion of something edible will (through lack of thought) appear as just what it is – a highly suspicious bundle of fur and feather.

The longer you fish, the more obvious it becomes that many of the most successful fishers have a deceptively casual approach to their sport, usually catching more than the frantic but less skilled. Having said that, hard work and lots of it will put fish on the bank, but it's a tough way of enjoying yourself.

The old adage that you cannot catch fish unless your flies are in the water is as true today as it ever was. The late Dick Shrive, that very canny Northampton stillwater fishing pioneer, had many favourite sayings putting years of experience in a nutshell. One was that the evening rise usually began at about 10a.m. He knew that the all-important Chironomidae family began to stir deep down at about this time of the day when the newly formed pupae hovered in the depths, seemingly building up their strength for the final ascent to the surface. Later on, in the early evening, and if conditions were suitable, the pupae would emerge as the adult flies familiar to every stillwater fly fisher.

How do the trout react to this timeless behaviour? Of course, Dick knew that the fish began feeding on the feeble creatures well down and totally unseen by the angler scanning the water for signs of insect activity. To cash in on this early stage he would fish his home-made sink-tip line, pausing for a time to allow his artificials to join the real thing. This way he could catch fish all day long. If, by evening, he still had a fish or two to go for his limit, only then would he switch to a floating line and standard buzzer fishing techniques.

There can be no better proof of this feeding sequence than that first morning-caught trout. It will be full of still-wriggling pupae. Another Shrive gem was that it wasn't how far you could throw a fly, but how you pulled it back that made the difference.

In the main, our attention will be focused on either rainbow or brown trout with just the odd excursion after sea trout and salmon. A few anglers may be fortunate enough to have waters stocked with brook trout or even the hybrid cheetah or tiger trout. Some years ago attempts were made to cross rainbows with browns. A hatch was successfully reared and the promising results stocked into Ogston Reservoir in 1970. The much awaited hybrid, handsome as the youngsters were, was a complete flop. The anticipated growth rate never materialised and interest in the potential winner waned. In the quest for bigger, faster-growing and harder-fighting fish, many experiments have been carried out including the stocking of sea trout into Llyn Alaw on Anglesey. These super fish grew to four pounds or so but that idea came to nothing either.

More recently a few fisheries have been stocked with salmon – cage-reared fish 'migrating' down the motorways from Scotland's West Coast. There have been many arguments about the ethics of stocking fish which have been bred primarily for the table but more of this later. The perfecting of the sterile triploid rainbow has been a move in the right direction. Aveley Lakes in Essex specialises in stocking these jumbo trout and sport there has been tremendous. Mind you, at £30 a day for a four fish limit some think it too expensive. I prefer to think of it more in terms of paying for a day's salmon fishing. The smallest fish you'll catch will be four pounds and with luck you'll end the day with four grilse-sized trout.

At the moment, the British record for rainbows stands at twenty-one pounds four ounces. This monster fell to Scots angler D. Graham while night fishing on Loch Awe. Although the fish took a fly, it was offered on a bubble float and fixed-spool reel. The rainbow was thought to be an escapee from rearing cages in the loch. Even so, it had lived the life of a happy free-loader, scooping up pellets intended for the small captive rainbows. A similar situation is common on many of our bigger English reservoirs and as far as size goes it's just a question of time.

In 1987, a 27 pound rainbow was reared by Roy Ward at Avington but it died before it could be used for breeding. Several fish topping a score of pounds have been landed at Avington and I fully expect the record to break the 25-pound barrier before too long. But I'm sure too that it will be a fish reared and stocked at that size.

Any fish from a large reservoir topping five pounds is an exceptional fish having grown from a youngster of a pound or so on a natural diet. In the big natural waters, native brown trout breed quite freely having access to clean feeder streams. These tinkling brooks and burns are a world away from the silty, slow-moving rivers in the lush valleys flooded to form our major stillwater fisheries and while the food supply may well be abundant, the chances of natural breeding taking place are slim and certainly cannot be relied on.

Brown trout live a great deal longer than their American cousins, reaching fifteen years and more. The British record stands at over nineteen pounds caught by J. Jackson from Loch Quoich in 1978. Nearly all double-figure brown trout are taken on spoons or trolled bait which makes the big browns which did take a fly all that more special.

Rainbows have a lifespan of about five years which they spend very much in the

Stocking with good quality brown trout at Draycote Reservoir.

Taking stock fish from the rearing cages at Bewl Bridge Reservoir.

The impressive sixty-five boats at Rutland's boat station.

The dam wall gets busy at Grafham at the beginning of the season.

Trout fishing is very exciting and you can often expect an aerial battle.

fast lane. Once let loose into a fertile low-land reservoir they pack on weight at a gallop. The opening of the 1,500-acre Grafham Water in 1966 highlights this phenomenal growth rate. Stocked at just ten inches long, the same fish had been transformed into rip-roaring four and five pounders eighteen months later. Even today, Grafham can turn a pound stockie into a three pounder by September.

Blagdon was the first of the English reservoirs to stock with rainbows back in 1904 when it became obvious, to everyone's delight, that both brown and rainbow trout would coexist quite happily. If one was off the feed then usually the other would be on the hunt. There's no doubt that without the dashing rainbow, still-water trout fishing as we know it would never have developed. In 1924, Lt.-Col. Creagh-Scott landed an 8½-pound rainbow from Blagdon. This fine fish remained the British record until 1968. The record has increased steadily since then, to today's huge proportions. A twenty-five pound rainbow is on the cards, but where will it come from?

THE STILLWATER EXPLOSION

Where did the many thousands of dedicated stillwater fly fishers spring from? Like me, most had a coarse fishing background and this basic grounding in water-craft helped in the conversion to the fly. Those who trout-fish only in the coarse fishing season from mid-March to mid-June may then decide to put their fly gear away and return to tench and carp. This dual affection tends to dwindle after a year or two when they discover just what they have been missing in July and August.

If you must go coarse fishing, do try to fit in a trip or two in between. You will not

The late Cyril Inwood, one of the early masters of stillwater trout fishing.

Bob Church spotting fish while Sir Michael Horden fishes at Avington.

be sorry as reservoir fish are in the peak of condition in these months. The fly is at its peak too, with sedges hatching in greater numbers as the summer goes on, providing the cream of our sport – casting to rising fish full of life. If you are a devout bank fisher, then try to concentrate on the last two hours at dusk, and pick a sheltered bay where the fly is hatching in profusion in shallow, weedy margins. Then you can fish nymphs, wet or dry flies with confidence. Stay with the trout a little longer. You will not be disappointed.

Make your fly fishing more interesting by travelling around the fisheries. I have a soft spot for the west of Ireland where the immense limestone loughs of Conn, Corrib and Mask beckon me with their beautiful wild brown trout. When I can, I try to enter the World Wet Fly Championships held each year on Lough Mask in August. Around five hundred fly fishers contest

four days of eliminators, the final being fished by the surviving hundred and twenty anglers. In my opinion Mask is the most wild and challenging trout water in Europe. Scattered with a myriad of islands, its great depths are punctuated with rocky shoals and reefs lurking just beneath the surface. Drifting over these limestone knife-edges provides the finest fly fishing you will ever experience. If you ever consider a holiday in Ireland it is best to hire a boat and an experienced local boatman. These men know all the most productive areas and are well aware of the ever present dangers.

One year, I was drawn to fish with a local shopkeeper and our ghillie for the day was to be Michael Arness from Ballinrobe. Mike had lived in England for fifteen years before returning home to set up his own plant hire business. One of his last jobs in England was digging out the 600-acre Draycote Water near Rugby – a mere

Fund-raising competitions are attended by numerous celebrities.

puddle when you consider that Lough Mask is over seven times the size of Rutland Water at a mighty 22,000 acres.

Despite August being the dourest month on Mask, the festival attracts fly fishers from all over the world. To qualify for the final is a proud achievement in itself and this is all I could ever hope for. Our party included English International Peter Thomas, photographer Peter Gathercole and Brian Bromley from Wolverhampton. I noticed that mayflys were still about in good numbers together with sedges. The mayfly is more yellow than olive and sedges are brown or almost black. The huge sedge which the locals imitate with the Murrough and the green one imitated by the famed Green Peter, were few and far between.

During the first eliminator the two Peters caught fish but just failed to get through. Brian and I were lucky enough to get over this first important hurdle. In the final I was drawn to fish with Irish International Mike Gilmartin from Sligo. Our boatman was the very experienced Noel May. Noel has a favourite area towards the canal outflow where he knows every rock and he put our boat right among the dangerous, but fish-holding, shallows. My very first cast produced a good brown, over a pound, on a Goat's Toe which threw the hook after cavorting about in the big waves. Little did I realise how important that fish was to be. Mike boated one a little bigger on a Mallard and Claret, followed shortly by one for me which accepted a yellow and green mayfly pattern.

It is the done thing in Ireland to head for the nearest island for lunch, no matter how important the competition. To our surprise, we discovered that very few fish had been taken, the wild fish not taking at all to the sudden angling pressure. Lunch put away, Noel suggested a drift known as the Black Rocks. I was now fishing with four flies – a normal thing with local anglers. As we rounded a wave-swept outcrop, a large trout soared from nowhere to snap up my mayfly. I paused as it turned on the fly and with heart in mouth lifted the rod. It weighed three pounds and to say I was pleased would be an understatement. We rose a few more but sport was dour to say the least. But, as always in competitions, large or small, you must keep plugging away with confidence that sooner or later something must happen.

Come the weigh-in, empty boats were the order of the day. Several had managed a single fish or perhaps a brace. German angler Kurt Menrad had scraped a brace like me and it looked as if the result was between us. He pipped me at the scales by just over an ounce. In a field of that class, I came away delighted and was an outboard motor prize the better off.

Any fears that trout fishing might be ruined by competitive fishing have proved groundless. I would go further and argue that such events have been a marvellous boost to the sport. It would be interesting to see some figures on the national growth of organised fly fishing clubs and associations. Fifteen years ago there were just a few. Now there must be hundreds.

FIND YOUR FISH

American sport fishers, with their plugs and spoons, have developed what they call structure fishing which they employ not only for trout but for other sporting species like small-mouth bass. We should take note of what they do as their style can be easily applied to our own methods. My own results over the past twenty-five years have proved beyond any doubt that this is so.

Their highly successful method is based on the location of any prominent underwater feature. Where do rabbits live? Certainly not in the middle of an open field but in a hedgerow. Thus river anglers look to the head of a pool or to its nooks and crannies where a fish might lurk, and pay scant attention to wide, open, featureless stretches. In a still water, such hidey-holes could be weed beds, submerged hedges and ditches, boat jetties, towers, shallows surrounded by sudden deeps and especially the line where shallows plunge into depths. Locating a trout by seeking out its likely habitat is vital. If you cannot find them you surely will not catch them.

Location is the starting point for all that we do. Boxes stuffed with every fly under the sun will be useless scraps of feather if the fish are not there. Sometimes only quite small areas of even the largest fisheries will hold any trout. In the case of Rutland Water this means the bottoms of the two giant arms where the water is shallow. We are speaking now of the better fish, not the newly introduced stock fish which tend to be found wherever they are put in.

There is definite proof, gained from experiments at Rutland Water, that brown trout feed heavily at night and in the early mornings, on the shallows, before retiring to the depths for the daylight hours. Fisheries Officer David Moore and I became convinced of this feeding pattern after discovering large shoals of brown trout lying quite stationary thirty feet down in seventy feet of water. David first found this concentration of suspended brown trout while experimenting with a new depth sounder. The trout pin-pointed almost to the foot, we took a good number of them to over three pounds and all were stuffed to the gills with the sort of food you would only find on the shallows.

The amount of light is the key factor governing trout movement for much of the season. The more light, the less fish will be found high in the water or on the

Emlyn Hughes landing his first trout under tuition from Bob.

The ultimate in a competition.

shallows. Remember that sunlight in June, July and August will have a more adverse effect than it would both earlier and later in the year. The effect on darker, peaty lochs is less than on clear-water lakes. The darker and more overcast the day the higher the all-important *Daphnia* will be in the water column. If it is gloomy and windy too then they will be concentrated in great clouds on the downwind shore line. There are no prizes for guessing where the trout will be.

The spawning urge really gets the trout moving from the sanctuaries in the depths on to the shallows. In large natural lakes, trout will move into the mouths of the feeder streams first. Happily this happens at the season's end, in October, and so big catches of spawn-carrying brown trout are avoided. Trying to put one of the really big stillwater trout into the net is an exciting challenge requiring a high degree of dedication. Fishing in April and May probably gives a better chance of connecting with a big brown when they are in tiptop condition.

However, late on in the season, both species behave in a similar manner, turning their undivided attentions to the massive shoals of coarse fish fry. The bank-bound fly fisher's best chance of connecting with one of these big fish is a dawn start. Loch-style fishing can be forgotten and lying at anchor over known fish-holding spots is the boat angler's best bet.

In 1934, this Irish angler used very basic tackle but still managed to land this 18¾lb brown trout from Lough Mask.

The full waterproof gear.

Most anglers wear a waistcoat.

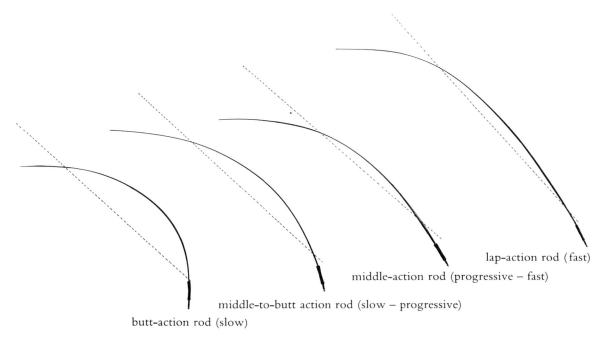

lap-action rod (fast)

middle-action rod (progressive – fast)

middle-to-butt action rod (slow – progressive)

butt-action rod (slow)

The dotted line shows the constant plane, giving a better idea of the rod's area of action.

CHOICE OF EQUIPMENT

During the past twenty-five years the popularity of stillwater fly fishing has risen by leaps and bounds and the tackle shops are filled with a bewildering array of gear, all of which the beginner will be convinced he must have. In truth, much of it is designed for special techniques so even if you are feeling financially flush, do not rush out and buy the most expensive rod in the shop. The chances are that it will be designed for a kind of fishing outside your present level of skill or interest. Far better to select versatile equipment at middle-of-the-range prices to begin with. You would be surprised just how many beginners take up the sport and buy on impulse only to regret their rashness when experience has proved their expensive folly.

The First Rod

The choice of the first rod is vital. Assuming you are going to fish the bigger reservoirs in the main, with just the odd visit to smaller waters, I would not hesitate in recommending a medium-actioned rod, nine and a half feet long. Forget all the nostalgia about split cane – it is far too heavy. Fibreglass rods too, are not really worth a second thought. The only sensible choice is carbon fibre or those with the addition of boron. I find some Kevlar rods too rigid and breakages have been high, so steer clear of them. It is true to say that even the cheapest carbon rods are better than anything made in glass or cane. The cheapest cost around £35 and the very best are about the £90 mark. Buy a rod in this bracket and you should have a tool that will serve you well for years.

The variations in rod actions are a matter

Casting sequence. The rod is flexed and the first haul is made with the left hand.

When the line straightens behind, the left hand feeds line through the rings.

Now the forward motion is begun and the left hand hauls down again.

The haul finished, the timing needs to be just right for releasing and the line shoots out over the water.

of personal choice. Rods are no more than an extension of your arm, so the one that feels comfortable has to be the one to choose. Rods range from light, crisp-actioned sorts which take very light lines, to specialist eleven and twelve footers used for loch-style fishing from a broadside drifting boat. Both these are not for normal bank fishing however, and will not concern the beginner as yet. It is better to go for something which can handle lines rated between seven and eight. Such a set-up will enable you to make the long casts often necessary for successful reservoir fishing.

If the line is too heavy, the rod will be overloaded and the line will flop down heavily, sending any self-respecting trout running for cover. Most beginners do better with a medium or even a fast-actioned rod. Certainly the stiffer rods allow more line speed to build up when false casting which, in turn, means longer, smoother casts.

The rod bought, you must get down to the business of putting a line on the water. Some find casting difficult to pick up, while others find it quite easy. You do not even need water. A field or your local recreation ground will do fine. The aim is to cast consistently well. A really good caster is not conscious of what is happening. It just happens.

Casting is all about rod power, line speed and timing. The line must straighten out behind then power forward to land smoothly on the water. Sounds easy doesn't it? And so it is, as long as you stick to the basic rules and stay relaxed. The correct stance is with one foot slightly forward so that you can rock backwards and forwards to distribute your weight during the casting sequence. This becomes more important as you cast a longer line. Get the technique right from the start and it's just like riding a bike. It helps if, rather than just thrashing about, you keep what you are trying to achieve firmly in mind,

which of course is getting the fly out to the fish.

To begin, draw a few feet of line from the reel and pull it out through the rings. Lifting the rod quickly and smoothly, the short length of line will fly out behind you. Wait for a second until it reaches its full extent before bringing the rod forward at the same speed. The line will fall in a straight line in front of you and that will be your very first cast. It may have been very short, but distance will follow naturally if you stay relaxed and persevere.

Choosing a Reel

The reel is less important in fly fishing than in any other branch of angling. Reels have changed little over hundreds of years. Some may have a more complex drag system but otherwise little has altered. A variable drag is useful when playing big fish but most experienced trout anglers play the fish by holding the line and only use the reel to take up slack line. The single-actioned Rimfly has been the still-water fly fisher's work horse for decades. They are tough, straightforward and totally reliable. What more could we ask for? The Leeda LC is a great reel too, and will only cost you about £20.

It is quite rare to play a fish off the reel as it is far easier to keep a trout rocketing towards you, stripping in the line by hand than winding in, your hand a blur. A danger when using a reel to play a fish, is that it can 'slack line' you by powering away and then, without warning, coming straight back towards you. The sudden loss of tension is quite enough for the hook to fall out. But there are dangers in stripping in line by hand too, as I found out to my cost in a Benson and Hedges match. I had played a trout, of nearly five pounds, close to the boat when it suddenly dived. Swivelling round to keep in contact, the loose line

A large-diameter reel, like the lineshooter, helps to avoid line tangling.

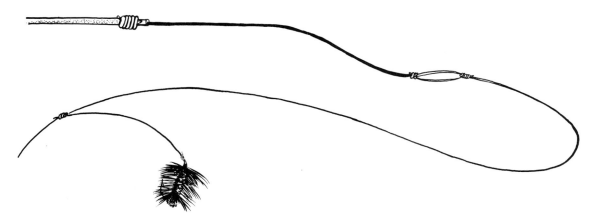

How to connect your leader. Note the permanent loop to which each new leader is attached.

caught around my foot. Everything went as tight as a bow string before the nylon parted. So, if you do play fish by hand make a habit of putting the slack line on the reel as soon as it touches the bottom of the boat or the ground.

The Fly Line

The wide selection of lines we have today means that we can reach fish wherever they may be feeding. All the talk about densities and profiles is bound to baffle any beginner but really, there is nothing to it. When I took up trout fishing in 1963 we only had silk lines. If you wanted them to float you greased them up regularly. As soon as you neglected this chore they sank.

Modern lines are about thirty yards long and in either double tapered or weight forward profile. A cheap one costs about £7 and the best, about four times that amount. The first and most important line to buy has to be a floater. It is more versatile than it sounds as it can be used to fish dry flies, wet flies and nymphs sub-surface, and lures in all sorts of ways. A weight forward Number 7 or 8 is a wise choice. Where you seek distance always go for forward taper lines. Double tapered lines are used where accuracy and delicate

presentation are the prime considerations.

A slow-sinking line is important in summer when you need to fish three or four feet down to reach the level of fish feeding on nymphs and *Daphnia*, so the beginner will need one of those without any doubt. A line which sinks a little quicker is the one to use in the early season, from the bank, when there are good numbers of fish to be caught within comfortable casting distance. So that is another one to consider.

If you can afford it, buy a new floating line at the start of each season. We tend to use them a great deal and they do show the signs of harsh treatment after a few months. A cracked and chipped line takes yards off your casting and will not be pleasant to use.

The Leader

Let's begin with those required for general bank fishing. When you are lucky enough to have either a following wind or one blowing from left to right you can get away with a much longer leader than you could in more adverse conditions.

The only permanent part of the leader is the thicker butt piece – a two foot long length of heavy nylon fastened to the fly line with a Needle knot. If you form a

A deep net and large-diameter frame are essential for the safe landing of big fish.

loop, about two inches long, at its end from then on all the various permutations of leader lengths and strengths can be added with another loop. A typical all-round leader is put together by adding two yards of six-pound nylon to the butt piece and then the same length again, using a Water knot, leaving about five inches as a dropper. Then add a further yard with the same knot. You should leave short spurs of nylon about five or so inches long at these joins to form the droppers. With this simple leader you will be able to fish a weighted nymph on the point, something like a Wickham or Invicta on the top dropper and perhaps something drab such as a Pheasant Tail nymph or Stick Fly on the middle position.

You can use exactly the same leader through the summer, the only change being a drop down in nylon strength. The more experienced a fly fisher becomes, the longer the leader he can handle without tangles. It's worth remembering too, that we must shorten everything when attempting to fish into the wind.

1 A Fly Fisher's Entomology

My great fishing friend, Charles Jardine, covers this subject in great depth and in fisherman's terms.

It was more than 25 years ago that the chalk-rich downlands of the south of England offered me, a complete beginner, a fly fishing philosophy which has endured, remains utterly enthralling and shows every sign of becoming more involving. Days spent, in the company of my father, on a diminutive chalkstream first fuelled my desire to understand not merely the trout but the world in which it lived. Like most young people, I greeted this new-found crusade with great alacrity. The ensuing time lapse has been kinder to me than it has the streams I fished as a boy. Most are now either polluted or abstracted – graveyards for a modern civilisation's discarded trappings. Trout, minnows, sticklebacks and other creatures have now to share their shrinking habitats with bits of cars, bicycles, tins and other household waste.

Understanding trout requires time, patience and a certain enquiring mind. This has lead me to investigate the food needed for their survival. Over the years, there-fore, I have become engrossed with the creatures which share the trout's domain – insects and even other fish. Writing about the trout's diet requires a certain amount of metaphorical tightrope walking – it is so easy to 'fall off' and make a bad deduction or an incorrect assessment. The trout themselves do not help. So often they will change diet to other organisms one may not be able to identify. This we have to leave to the eminent men – biologists and qualified entomologists. But, and it is a big 'but', we, as fly fishermen, can play our part.

There is a simple equation I would like you to consider: water = weed = insects = trout = angler = trout = insect = fly choice. One can even subtract 'weed' but where would we be as fly fishers by subtracting the other parts? So often anglers are content with trout = angler = catch and, as laudable as this policy may be, it leaves a gaping hole in our approach with a fly rod and shortcomings when considering tactics. Indeed, far better that we add to the equation 'bait' fish, jointed-limbed creatures such as shrimp and hoglouse and molluscs such as snails.

Bob Church with Bernard Cribbens spooning a fish for tell-tale signs of its diet.

Let me say from the outset that you do not need to be a genius to evaluate the trout's diet. Indeed, ignorance can be bliss. A prime example of this occurred over 20 years ago. The mists of time have made the exact timing hazy, but the incident and place are as fresh as if it were yesterday . . . Whilst fishing my father's river, I happened to notice some particularly attenuated wriggly things which looked as though they ought to catch trout, and which resembled my recently acquired Buzzers. Having just purchased these with my pocket money, I, like most keen beginners, wanted to use them almost immediately. The fact that I saw these creatures underwater meant, presumably, that this was precisely where my fly should be. How well I remember the two trout I seduced with them. I did not know it then, but I was, in fact, 'matching the hatch'. In other words, I was pandering to the diet of the trout. If only I had realised the significance of this. My subsequent fly fishing would have been a great deal less arduous as a result, especially concerning midge pupae on rivers.

So far, I have only mentioned rivers. There is a reason for this. Since time immemorial, generations of stream fishers have found it necessary to evaluate the trout's food forms and present these within the artificial constriction of our sport. This has led to a philosophy, which is, indeed, still being elaborated and improved upon, of almost 'pure' fly fishing, which is solely concerned with the trout's natural and imitable larder. This is not elitist, old-fashioned or backward. It is essential both for the outwitting and catching of a species that is at best fickle, at worst selective and often nigh impossible. Reservoirs and lakes are merely enormous watery extensions of this notion.

Of course (and this a personal opinion), I doubt if the Viva or Green Butt Tadpole will ever lose their charisma for the early-season lure fisher, nor the Whisky Fly or Leprechaun for the mid-season angler. But, why, I have always wondered, has the trout taken these flies? Gaudy lures leave me in a state of quandary. There seems to be no rational reason to this philosophy, yet I like to think that I understand the logic behind, for instance, a spotted back that has eased through the surface and engulfed my tiny pupae hanging motionless amid the other natural facsimiles. Quite simply, I was offering food, but more importantly, *how* and *where* the trout expected to see it. As I said earlier, insects = food = trout = fly fisher = fly. Mine tend to be imitative.

But how can one deduce the correct candidate? What does it look like? How does it behave? How does the trout react to it? What can the angler use to deceive the quarry? All timeless questions, some of which we have yet to find the answers for. Nevertheless, to give some idea as to, at least, a majority of situations, it would be a good idea to follow Bob's route of seasonal and monthly cycles, offering and highlighting specific species for each. June and September, in particular (but also other months), will be full of variations on one theme, but generally, one type of species will predominate. There may be a variation from water to water so, together with specific insects, I will include at least some local variation.

Lifestyles

Before the journey begins, it might be prudent to give both a written and illustrated breakdown of the major food types in relation to the trout, in order of priority. Without question, the most universally important character is the midge or, to give it its fitting title – Chironomidae. There can be few anglers who have not encountered

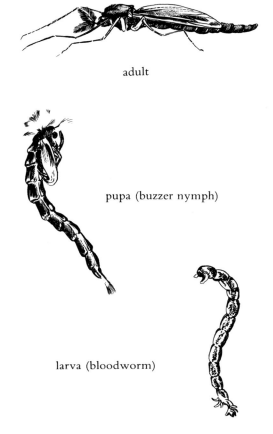

adult

pupa (buzzer nymph)

larva (bloodworm)

Chironomid (midge, buzzer) stages of development.

this non-biting mosquito-shaped insect during their angling career. Belonging to the order Diptera (flat-winged flies), it occurs on probably every water in the land to some degree or other. Its family is so vast that to list the infinite colour and size variation would take up the rest of this chapter. I would not presume to bore you!

Stan Headley, the great Orcadian fly fisher, wrote in *Trout and Salmon* of the importance of a bright green variety of midge which occurs on his northerly lochs. The Duck Fly, legendary in Ireland during the season's embryonic months, can also be

found in Scotland where it is known as the Blae and Black. The almost magical Grenadier so loved by the Chew and Blagdon anglers is none other than our old friend the Large Red or Ginger chironomid. Almost every water has its own pet variety. Indeed, some have been inspired by particular waters – the Blagdon Green Midge for instance, which, strangely, has caught more fish for me at Bewl Water than at its birthplace and the aptly named Grafham Racehorse, which I suspect is either a Large Red or Green Midge, that must measure all of one centimetre, perhaps larger. I say 'suspect' because, as its name implies, the creature has so far evaded capture, the emergence and resulting flight being so rapid.

These are just a few of the permutations available to the angler and trout. By and large, chironomids are small. Obviously, one needs a comparison, but sensible and imitative hook sizes start at std shank 10 going down to as small as 20 and, if one has a penchant or indeed, if confident, 24 and 26. Realistically though, it is seldom necessary to look to sizes lower than 18 in practicable fly fishing situations.

Before progressing, I must just add that many fly fishers refer to this group of insects as 'Buzzers' which is slightly erroneous. They don't all 'buzz' – the noise is generally made when egg-bearing females are making their way back to the water in colonies. I once heard this insect referred to as an 'olive' by an angler at a local water who added that fish were everywhere and going berserk for them. In some state of pandemonium, I hastily made a batch of pond olives (an upwinged species, more of which later) that evening. The following day I proceeded, with some degree of anticipation, and, it has to be said, a fair amount of confidence that I would 'match the hatch'. On arrival at the water I encountered quite the heaviest emergence of olive midge I have ever seen – not olive 'olives' at all. Luckily, at least some suitable patterns lurked in the recesses of my fly box. There is a moral here. Always trust your own observations rather than relying on hearsay from other anglers.

One has to know what one is looking for, however, and indeed, where to find it. In the case of the midge, this is rather less of a problem than with other fauna. Firstly, let me trace its life cycle. The chironomid begins life laid as an egg on the surface. The eggs can be in long strings or globular masses. These, after only a short period, start to contain a tiny worm-like creature which is, in fact, the embryonic larva. These physically wriggle free of the egg and descend to the lake bed. It is here that we, as imitative anglers, enter the scene. This period of development can last anything from three to twelve months, depending on the species.

At this point, the larval life can revolve around many permutations. Generally, it is to be found in waters ranging from three to twenty feet in depth. Here it will carve out one of many varied existences. Some larvae manufacture tube-like tunnels in the silt, often covering one aperture leaving the other for emergence, feeding entirely on the tunnel entrance's webb. Others create cases (rather like caddis), and occasionally, leave this sanctuary on feeding missions. Another variety, and possibly the most important in fishing terms, has a lifestyle which is free-moving and swimming. It is here that many of us have surely cut our entomological teeth, for who has peered into a water butt or perhaps a forgotten watering-can and failed to see the wild thrashing and undulations of bright scarlet worm-like creatures? These are none other than the bloodworm – chironomid larvae. This is rather a misnomer, for not all these larvae are bright red in colour. Indeed, they can vary from very pale buff through browns, encompassing many shades of green, as well as the well-known red variety.

Incidentally, the deep redness of many of these larvae types is caused by haemoglobin being present, assisting the creature's oxygen intake allowing it full range of not only a wide variety of habitats but also ones which are both dark and largely devoid of insects. This, in turn, helps the angler as it allows for fishing areas which would possibly prove useless with other insect-based patterns. The one striking feature of this stage of development, even considering its remarkably bright coloration, is its movement – a point Arthur Cove quite revolutionarily embraced, creating his now infamous and lethal 'Red Diddy'. A wonderfully simple concept, it is a thin, curved section of scarlet rubber band, suggesting the wriggling, lithesome figure-of-eight lashings of the natural with almost uncanny realism. Both S. D. 'Taff' Price and Peter Lapsley have further elaborated on this theme, utilising the now commonplace material red or green 'marabou' to achieve the same, perhaps even more sinuous, motion.

However, it is the next stage in the insect's life cycle which is perhaps the most important. Certainly, it is the best known – the pupal stage. Yet I believe it is not its sheer volume or colour permutation that makes its appeal so great. Chironomids can be found 'active' for nearly 365 days of the year and on most waters, and it is the pupae that can form the basis of a 'nymph' orientated strategy from the opening of the season to its close. Indeed, it is not unusual, even on quite cold days, to see some evidence of this creature. An instance comes to mind which occurred at the Rockbourne Fishery in Hampshire when, as a guest, I was invited to cull a few rainbows in December one year.

It was far from easy. Indeed, considering the lack of angling pressure, it was downright difficult. Then, at noon, a shaft of pale and disconsolate winter sun raised the water's freezing temperature, and with it, tiny black specks began to emerge on the surface. As if a switch had been thrown, trout began to rise. On closer inspection of the water, I found the little black specks to be tiny midge. The nearest sized facsimile that came to hand was a size 20, which, when placed against the natural, looked colossal. Nevertheless, it proved to be approximate enough to inveigle at least some of the rising fish.

Colours are diverse and sizes almost infinite, yet certain times of the fly fishing year will hold a very definite bias for one or two colours depending on locale. One of the soundest and most enduring axioms in fishing is 'get to know your water', and by heeding it you will most certainly begin to unravel various hatch colour sequences. Over the years, I have developed a modest little theory. Like all ideas, it is largely untenable, yet it does appear that the colder the weather, the darker the fly; and the coldest part of the spectrum is echoed therein (blacks, blues, dark greens, etc.). April, for instance, sees a predominance of black and grey. As the sun gains more strength, so the dark greens begin to appear until the water temperature begins to rise significantly in mid-May and June, when light olive predominates. In the comparative warmth of, say, July (occasionally June) water, so the fawns, oranges and browns begin to ascend. With the sun at its zenith in late July, August and early September, red prevails, until a point is reached when the colour begins to recede, slipping back into black and greys once more.

Certainly, this appears to be the case with midges and also in river upwings which can vary even within the same species. The Blue Winged Olive, for example, is much lighter in July than in September, when it can be a greeny chestnut brown rather than the mid-dark olive body colour of certain periods. Another exceedingly important factor is that some reservoirs, notably Rutland and Grafham, can take a great deal longer to warm up sufficiently to encourage certain hatches, unlike Bewl Water, with its tree-shrouded banks and comparatively smaller size. Also Blagdon, which is overall more shallow and warms up much faster, thus offering a different hatch sequence.

Why bother to attempt to understand this colour variation? Quite simply because the trout do. They instinctively know what to expect to see in a hatch of black midge and it is not a red one! Yet, there are phenomena which cannot be explained. Why is it, for instance, that trout will occasionally 'lock in' on a certain colour of fly, when the hatch is quite a different shade? Dr Shelton's contribution in Chapter 2 may give the angler, for the first time, a true picture of what the trout sees. I urge you to absorb his words.

For my own part, I passionately believe that trout can deduce colour, but in many tonal variations. Hence my fondness for pupae patterns containing an amalgam of colours – black being suffused with brown (hare's mask guard hairs, also, strands of red seal's fur); the olive – a blend of yellows and again, brown hare's fur, and a base of olive and so on.

The pupa's life span is short, by comparison with its larval stage, lasting between thirty and seventy hours, the majority of which are spent in ecdysis – the transformation into a true pupa in the accepted fly fishing sense. Occasionally, one can find pupae both in the water and in the contents of the trout's stomach which incorporate the still semi-larval state, often displaying a marked redness or green in the lower abdomen – a point which A. D. Bradbury, the Cheshire tackle shop owner and fly dresser, stressed in a range of very personal and innovative tyings many years ago. They are, incidentally, still very effective today. The late master, Richard Walker, also included this 'recognition point', if you like, by adding a few turns (butt) of fluorescent red to the abdominal end of his black midge pupa dressing.

However, it is on the, shall I say, 'pure pupae' (sic) that most angling attention has been focused. It can be traced back to Dr Bell, the revolutionary Blagdon angler, who not only discovered the importance of this diminutive species with regard to trout fishing, but could also, rightfully, be conferred with the title 'the father of reservoir nymph fishing' as a whole. His simple Black Buzzer has endured as has his Grenadier which are still very much in evidence in nationally diverse fly boxes. Interestingly, at the time, he was considered to be 'persona non grata' for using 'maggot-like things'. How things have changed! Perhaps though, it would be fairer to say that during the 1960s, Grafham gave 'rise' to the popularisation of this insect stage and the fishing of it.

Who can have failed to notice those brooding spotted submarine-like backs gliding through the surface film on calm evenings gorging on the trapped pupae? The languid 'head and tail' rise form is woven into the very fabric of our stillwater 'tapestry' of sport. As important as this area undoubtedly is, when considering midge pupae, there are other areas not only worth exploring but of marked importance. A great deal depends on prevailing weather conditions.

Once, when attending a lecture by the entomological enthusiast, 'Taff' Price, I listened in a comparative state of shock as he said he felt midge were often straight and pupae tyings should echo this, as my conception (along with many other anglers), was one of curvature. I now be-

lieve he was right – at least in a great many instances. The first thing that one has to bear in mind is that the pupa is a poor swimmer and must feel rather like a paratrooper drifting helplessly into a caldron of enemy activity, only in reverse, as all the time the pedantic creature is wriggling up from the bottom layers to the surface, it is at the mercy of the avaricious trout.

But, as mentioned earlier, I firmly believe it is weather conditions which suggest when an artificial should be employed to best effect and one occasion which calls for a curved style of dressing is a calm day, particularly when the air is heavy and full of moisture. The water's surface film or miniscus is extremely thick at such times. I recall a simple test from my formative years, when, at school, we were encouraged to watch a needle floating in a tumbler full of water; of course, the needle was heavier and should have sunk, but the miniscus kept it afloat. It is this factor that makes the surface film *the* place to be on still, calm or muggy days and evenings if midge are active.

Insects breaking through this barrier, which forms the division between air and water, has been likened to ourselves having to push through four to six feet of earth above us – a prodigious task and one the trout certainly wastes no time in ravenously taking advantage of. Nature is a wonderful arbiter, however, and will create times when midge find airborne transport far easier. These are generally when conditions are rough and the water's surface is broken up with wave action. Then the angler's midge tactics do have to be amended, for the critical depth is no longer the first half inch of surface film, but can be anywhere from two to twenty feet.

As well as being greedy, trout are practised and economic hunters. They will not bother charging after a 'golden fleece' if it is not in their best interests; instead they will dine at leisure during the midges' ponderous ascent to our dimension. This, I believe, is where the straight pupa is at its most effective. I can visualise now, shoals of rainbow scything through the hapless pupae as they rise through the layers. Indeed, there is enormous scope for fishing a very fast-sinking line such as a Wet cel Hi. D Extrafast and a team of pupae, from a boat, in open water, echoing this surfaceward migration. It is during such periods that pupae tactics should also be concentrated in a sub-surface two to four foot area.

Often the fish will be cruising without giving the slightest indication of their piscine presence, which leads me to think that certain shoals of trout hunt in different areas, albeit simultaneously. For instance, one concentration of fish may well be following the ponderous climb of the pupae from the lake floor, intercepting them either at this point or in mid-water, while a separate shoal will be picking off the straggling survivors in the upper stratas. Hypothetical, I know, but certain instances have definitely indicated these trout feeding divisions to me.

Finally, we come to the adult. For years this stage of the chironomid's development received little or no attention and what sport we have missed! Indeed, John Goddard, the eminent angling entomologist, felt they were the least important of the cycle, only to reassess the situation totally in *Trout Flies of Stillwater*. Now dry fly fishing is approaching almost cult proportions, the majority of which revolves around this adult stage. In reality, though, the midge's adult life is short-lived. For, on emerging from its pupal shuck, it will rest for only a matter of moments, until its wings are dry enough and transformation is sufficiently complete for take-off – only eight to twelve seconds after splitting its pupal thorax on the water's surface.

One can often see the struggles enacted whilst one is fishing, the shuck being ejected on the water combined with a frantic whirling of movement across the surface of the lake. How could any self-respecting trout not be drawn by the commotion! After skittering for a while, it will then drift up into the air and ultimately mate, the female venturing back to the water to lay the eggs for a next generation, some eight to twelve hours later.

Identifying adults is really quite easy – the body is long, fairly thin and clearly banded with a lighter colour. Also, unlike the pupa, it is covered with a fine filigree of abdominal hair. There are two wings, held closely to and often covering the abdomen and, as with all Diptera, they are flat and hyaline – that is to say, they have an almost clear, shiny quality. The six long legs are quite a noticeable feature, as they protrude from the bulbous thorax or head section, some attaining lengths of a good one and a half times the size of the insect's body. Also issuing from this noticeably chubby thorax (but only in the case of males), are a pair of moustache-like, fluffy antennae. Fortunately, most midges, regardless of colour and size, conform to this shape. The one exception I have found is the large green midge, which has much broader, almost oval, wings, as opposed to the more normal torpedo-like dimensions of other adult chironomids. Naturally enough, the adult's colours will echo faithfully those of the pupa, there seeming to be little variation from one dimension to another, excepting the Large Red and a few others.

Having given a brief description of the adult, I believe it is worth tarrying a while at this juncture, in order to 'dovetail' the adult's lifestyle into our fly-fishing strategies. As an 'ex-patriot' river fisherman, my instincts are still 'if it rises, put on a floating fly'. For years, I felt that perhaps I was wrong and somewhat 'antedeluvian'

– especially if midge were about. In retrospect, I believe I have been misled, for certainly now, along with many other fly fishers, the effectiveness of dry fly fishing is there to see.

Over the years, patterns have been developed to accommodate many adult midge instances, especially those of Bob Carnhill and his 'deadly' adult buzzer series which has accounted for legions of trout in many varying situations. However these, by and large, have been fished 'wet' mimicking the drowned insect, sunk by either wave action or viscious bank undertow and related currents. Subsequently, I developed a similar range of patterns, substituting the soft hen hackle for 'high riding' cock hackles, combined with light iron hooks in order to achieve floatability. I was, at the time, blissfully unaware of similar 'minor tactics' being fashioned elsewhere.

This new (to me at least) floating midge exercise worked better than I could ever have dreamed. Not only were rising fish beguiled, these diminutive facsimiles held enough allure to 'ghost up' unseen specimens to the surface. This instance, perhaps more than any other, shows how parallel concepts can evolve almost simultaneously. Grafham, and indeed other, midge-rich waters, have been following this same doctrine in one form or another for a number of years. This proves that the dry midge can be effective, *and* hold very definite attraction for larger than average fish.

In summary, I would merely add that a variety of patterns will work, ranging from the vague 'impressionistic' to 'calculated suggestion'. My own inclination is towards attention to detail, especially in instances such as a flat calm. These slavish adherences to the insect's dimensions, colour and size, I feel, are wholly commendable in the widest possible sense. I would

add, that not all situations demand such accuracy but feel that not to fish the dry midge, is to squander some of the cream of the reservoir's surface potential.

Having deliberated at such length on merely one reservoir creature, it is hard to know which of the myriad significant species to follow on with. Indeed a state of quandary exists, for the next, perhaps most obvious piscatorial candidate must surely be the Trichoptera, in other words, the Anglophile sedge, but, perhaps more appropriately – the caddis. And yet the trout may well disagree, for unlike the chironomids, sedges/caddis can be both variable and intensely seasonal. I think it would be consistent to continue this diverse subject from the trout's point of view. Seasonal occurrences are merely the 'icing and marzipan' on a much richer and more succulent annual 'cake', the ingredients of which are often the forgotten, the unnoticed and even the unseen. Let me start with the 'unseen'.

During the summer, occasionally even in early-season cold water, one 'animal' can dictate to quite extraordinary lengths, the trouts' location, depth, and even reactions. It is largely inimitable. The humble sounding water flea or grander, *Daphnia*, species hold this key. In fact it is a tiny crustacean, the largest being a mighty eighth of an inch long! This diminutive character lends credence to the axiom 'the best things come in little packages', especially if one adds 'when they group together and form vast, glutinous clouds'. Bob will be rounding on the esoteric value of the Pickwickian proportioned organism, especially for the mid-season 'thinking' lure angler. It remains only for me to offer a few personal thoughts about the *Daphnia*'s undoubted ability to fashion fly-fishing tactics.

The first real occasion I encountered its persuasiveness was during Bewl Water's second season. Quite normally for me, I

Daphnia *enlarged.*

arrived late at the lodge and, unable to secure a motorboat, had to resign myself to the rigours and dubious charms of rowing. Having sculled myself out with somewhat erratic, crab-like movements from the 'harbour' a sudden and ferocious squall was experienced. It was early June, grey, overcast and humid and, having struggled in less than elegant fashion towards the Nose, I decided enough was enough. Windaided, I elected to drift back to the sanctuary of the lodge. As the boat drifted 'nosedown', I began to notice the sullen water surface intermittently change with darker grey fleeting flecks, some two to four feet down. I threw out a drogue and cast to my right with a black leaded longshank nymph on the point, in harness with an orange thoraxed Pheasant Tail on the dropper. I secured six fish in eight casts, with this floating line set-up. On unhooking, each trout disgorged an orange jelly-like substance which was to be my first encounter with *Daphnia*, proving on numerous subsequent occasions, that it is not merely a lure angler's domain.

Looking back on that occasion, I realise that I had been, mercifully, in the right place at the right time in the right conditions, and that rowing is considerably easier with fish in the boat! Perhaps one of the most important points is that *Daphnia* are light sensitive. Given the day in question, one would reasonably expect to find 'blooms' in the upper layers fluctuating between two and six feet beneath the waves. In calm weather this can alter dramatically and encompass the actual film. However, problems exist during periods of harsh light and direct sun. This has the effect of literally sending the *Daphnia* on a crash dive in search of the cooler and darker areas of twenty feet or more. The angler is left with little option other than a 'seek and ye shall find' strategy.

Given intermittent cloud cover, I believe that *Daphnia* will rise to the surface when the sun is obscured, only to plummet smartly downward on the reappearance of directional harsh sunlight. During such instances, the fly fisher will necessarily have to change tactics equally quickly if he is to keep in touch with the predatory shoals of trout that rise and fall with these colonies of water flea.

Of course, it has been proven time and time again that trout are eminently catchable during this *Daphnia* preoccupation, scything open-mouthed, like basking shark through the hapless concentrations, literally 'souping in' the protein-rich harvest. It is certainly a period very much tailor-made for the lure fisher – a veritable 'orange madness', indeed, a 'green madness' seeming to prevail. This has led directly to the large bright orange and green lures so often used to seduce by colour rather than shape, mimicking the tiny crustaceans' green or orange hues. And yet, as laudable as this policy is, my nymphing philosophies appear not to be compromised, for I have found, by using orange or green thoraxed

Pheasant Tails or Arthur Cove's Orange Nymph (indeed, midge pupae in various colours), and the utilitarian Black Long Shank Nymph, one can pander equally well to the trout's dietary fads. The reasoning behind this is quite simple, for I believe that a trout's memory can be triggered, and offering a nymph it may well have fed on only hours previously, can bring about a conditioned reflex.

Daphnia, in the main, are seen very much as a boat angler's prerogative, yet there are frequent occasions when the bank-bound fly fisher can benefit from their appearance too, angling location almost suggesting itself through the *Daphnia*'s peripatetic motions, due to the wind's prevailing direction. For example, the windward area of bays and the often wind-battered corners of dams. Indeed, evening fishing, especially towards the end of May and throughout June can be determined, on many occasions, by the influences that the *Daphnia* bring about.

Last season, two 'nymph-orientated' friends happened to be fishing Bewl Water over rising fish which they swore were feeding on chironomids. It turned out, however, that the only two fish they managed to deceive that evening were both full to overflowing with *Daphnia*, making their original diagnosis only partially correct, due to the creatures' close affinity with the top area of water at such times. Their normal sparse and drab midge patterns proved inaccurate, though fished, quite possibly, in the right manner. This instance does indicate the need for very careful vigilance during low light and free-rising trout periods, for what you see, may not necessarily be the chosen food form – a very salient point when engaging *Daphnia*-feeding trout.

For all its importance, *Daphnia* is not only seasonal, being in evidence from May through to September, in fly-fishing terms,

but is also confined to certain waters and even then, populations will fluctuate. No one really knows why this should be. However, the following food forms are nearly endemic in every water in the land and, without question, sustain trout through the lean, insect-barren months of winter. They are, in fact, a stillwater mainstay.

Two such ebullient little characters are the freshwater shrimp (*Gammarus pulex/ lacustris*) and the American resident, *Crangonyx psuedogracilis*. These animals are not 'true' shrimps at all, being amphipods (jointed, limbed beings). Incidentally, the shrimp has fourteen limbs, a number of which are used for a good turn of speed and intricate manoeuvring. The modest difference between the two is movement and colouration. *Crangonyx* flits back and forth in upright mode and is clad in almost transparent blue/grey, whereas *Gammarus* tends to do everything sideways, and its colour can range from dark olive through lighter greens into fawns and browny pinks, even extending to golden yellow/ orange. There has been a fair amount of rancour over the last colour scheme. Some *aficionados* say that this is the mating colour, others insist that this tone occurs at the onset of disease and ultimately death.

I tend to favour the former school, for in a lake near my home in Kent, the chalk-rich water gives rise to almost epidemic populations of this amphipod. Strangely, this lake frequently dries up, which manifests several fascinating points. Firstly, the trouts' almost total preoccupation with shrimp, there being little other food in the chain. This, in turn, brings about another feature concerning the trouts' growth rate which is curtailed by nature's self-imposed drought, then made up for over a shorter span. A fish weighing between one and a quarter to one and a half pounds in April, can escalate to two and three quarters to

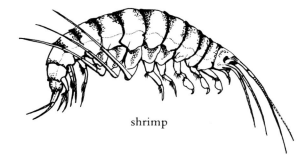

shrimp

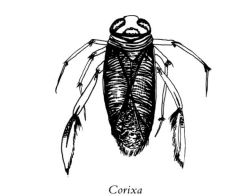

Corixa

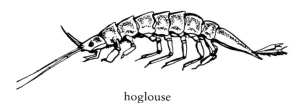

hoglouse

snail (wandering)

Ever-present food forms.

three and a half pounds in September. This is due almost entirely to shrimp feeding.

Almost without exception, these crustacea are a deep golden orange in colour. As the shrimp has no specific mating periods, it may well be that continuous breeding occurs to thwart the ever-present threat of 'dry-up' and the need to produce constant colonies. This is, however, largely guesswork, but it would indicate that the shrimp is very much alive in this golden colour scheme and not in 'death throes'. In any event, trout relish the delicacy.

This invertebrate can be found in just about any weeded area, even in acidic lake crevices. Indeed, it is not uncommon to find innumerable scuttling forms of between half and one inch on pulling up an anchor or bankside weed. This is, of course, the home of the shrimp and leads directly to the correct fly fishing area. So important, I believe its presence to be, that if confined to just one pattern for use on both lake and river, I would, without question, opt for the artificial shrimp, its uses and diversity far outweighing its dowdy appearance.

There are, of course, a plethora of artificials to choose from. They range from the absurdly, but nonetheless deadly, impressionistic Killerbug of Frank Sawyer (which I endearingly call my 'bedsock fly'), through to the equally persuasive Red Spot pattern of Neil Patterson, which I would never be without, especially on small fisheries, and culminate with the ultra-realistic Marabou interpretation of Peter Gathercole. If fished appropriately, all will catch trout. Their uses are wide and diverse, being general 'search patterns' as well as effective antidotes for cruising or observed trout. The criteria is that somewhere out amidst the lake, there will be a colony of shrimp and a strong possibility that trout, too, will be present.

Though slightly similar, the hoglouse

(*Asellus aquaticus/meridianus*), might, at first, appear a poor relation. True, it is lethargic in movement, dull in appearance and, somewhat unsavourily, feeds on rotting lake bed vegetation, yet it has real value to the fly fisher, one that is certainly overlooked on a great many occasions.

This relation to the common woodlouse can be found not only at great depths, but in comparatively large sizes, reaching one inch, further emphasising the scope for deepwater nymphing techniques. The hoglouse, water slater or (as the Americans call it), 'Sow Bug' does differ quite markedly, from the shrimp. It is flat as opposed to the rounded, compressed, plated shape of *Gammarus*. The colour differs also, the louse being mottled brown olive on top of a fawny tan base. But similarly to the shrimp, it incorporates two sets of antennae or feelers in the head area and two to the rear aiding its bottom dwelling habits. Size, too, averageing that of the shrimp (a third to half an inch).

Fishing strategy should broadly follow that used with *Gammarus*, both lifestyles being similar, only the deep water situation mentioned separating them. It is, however, more normal to seek the shallower areas and is, perhaps, more effective during the insect-sparse early-season period, whilst searching out quiet bays and shallow weeded areas of the reservoir. Trout often forsake the relative safety of deep water in order to harvest the sometimes dense crops of hoglice. This, of course, fashions our technique, requiring stealth, careful wading (to be discouraged in very shallow water), floating line, long leaders and slow retrieves.

One instance that serves to illustrate how shallow one sometimes needs to fish and how effective this dowdy crustacea can be, occurred on the vast Lough Erne one early May. I was in the company of local *aficionado*, Howard Black, who thankfully,

nay mercifully, knew the drifts and potential shipwrecking outcrops intimately as well as the fish and fauna. He encouraged me with uncommon alacrity to fish in what I felt, at the time, was to be my last exploit in this world. So close to the tiny island were we, that his insisted team of three Winged Hare's Ears, coupled with my tentative initial cast, landed inches from dry land.

From beside these cold, grey, tortured rocks, came the underwater flashes and swirls that only an angler who has fished Ireland knows – brown trout with the vivacity of rainbows, lunged and intercepted the tiny shaggy offerings with ferocity. The resultant drifts over water no deeper than four feet yielded nine pristine brown trout as wild as the grey sky racing over the Connemara Hills to the west, each one crammed with hoglice. Humble though the 'louse is, be certain always to have at least a couple of patterns in your fly box. It can be a definite case of a pauper turning into a prince. I can recommend Oliver Edward's pattern as well as Anne Douglas' version.

I suspect everyone has 'one of those flies', perhaps two, or, if very unlucky, more! – patterns that simply do not work even given a swimming pool with ravenous trout cheek by jowl. I have several – the Dunkeld, Peter Ross and oddly – as this ineffective phenomenon seems to exclude insect based patterns – the Corixa. Try as I might, the imitation of this ubiquitous stillwater insect will produce only limited success and then at decidedly odd times. This belies its very real value to the fly fisher. Though outwardly very dissimilar to the previous food forms, it does largely adopt the same habitat, enjoying a wide range of low lying rich reservoirs and relatively acidic upland stillwaters. Colloquially known as the lesser water boatman, it even enjoys the same areas, rejoicing around weeds and in depths of between two and six feet. It is also relatively active throughout the year.

It is probably one of the most readily identifiable reservoir species, most anglers being familiar with the bug's half inch (and smaller) size and appearance. It has a dark brown mottled shell back (in fact wing cases), pronounced red/brown eyes, creamy white underbody and six legs, two of which being the instantly recognisable oar-like paddles which enable its jet-propulsion from weed bed to weed bed, or surfaceward for necessary stores of oxygen.

Nature has played a nasty trick on the Corixa, however, for as fast as its ascent is (and it can resemble a fleeting bolt of silver through the water), in comparison, the descent is both laboured and erratic. Even more hazardous is the bright silver orb-like 'oxygen tank' it brings back from the surface, screaming its presence to any watchful trout. This, conversely, is good news for the fly dresser, offering legion recognition points to copy.

Corixa can often be witnessed flying, which they do over fairly large areas. This generally coincides with the mating periods of late May to early July. We do not know quite why this happens – perhaps it is to colonise other parts of the reservoir. However, and importantly for the fly fisher, we do know that the nymph endures as many as five instars (complete moults of nymphal skin) until maturity is finally reached. When these juvenile Corixa enter the instar stage, they are a creamy, off-white colour and, as far as I am aware, only Bob Carnhill has noted the significance, especially concerning periods through August and September when, traditionally, great colonies band together along the lake shores. This suggests two things. Either, the juvenile or nymph is joining the adults for the onset of winter or

another mating ceremony is entered into. These instances remain hypothetical. One fact does emerge, though. Trout join these gatherings as well, taking full advantage of an almost pre-packaged food source.

In summary of the Corixa, I can only add that its advantages for the angler, in terms of its ubiquity and valuable fishing opportunities, certainly at specific times of the year, far outweigh my incompetence with this particular artificial. It remains for me a bearable penance which I gladly endure, knowing that if I try long enough, something will happen in the end.

There are, of course, many other aquatic forms constantly present, ranging from the diminutive scarlet, spider-like Red Water Mite that is to be found lurking in fish-interesting numbers around stone and woodwork, such as dam walls and flooded woodland, to beetles and a conglomeration of other bugs, pupae and insects. To name them all and couch them in fly-fishing terms, would be to fill your fly box to overflowing, and many of them would be of doubtful value in all but the most extreme circumstances. Before mentioning the perhaps more familiar fauna, there are, however, two further candidates for special note. One has long been a firm favourite of the American angler and, I believe, may well unlock the door to some exciting deep water fishing for larger than average trout, especially brownies. I refer to the leech.

Though it may appear unsavoury, this attenuated creature's potential is very real. Trout not only eat it, they appear (in some instances), to be somewhat partial to it. There are, of course, more than one species of leech and it is doubtful if even a ravenous trout would tackle a horse leech which can attain lengths of twelve inches. It is more likely that smaller leeches will be eaten. These will conform, by and large, to either dark brown or dark olive and black shades and all use an undulating, sub-surface caterpillar-like movement across their chosen habitat. This is set amid the gloomy surroundings of the lake floor depths. They will venture into upper layers, yet I feel one must realistically see them as a bottom-dwelling creature.

The Americans, with their customary exuberance, have created many patterns to emulate this sinewy *Hirudinae* species. You may care to try either a Wooly Bugger, or one of Dave Whitlock's Eelworms, perhaps the straightforward Marabou Leech or even a Black Zonker. Certainly one of the best, well to be frank, the most innovative, has to be Schwibert's Egg-Sucking Leech that was first shown to me by Steve Parton. Even he felt it fearsome. It measured something in the region of eight inches of black rabbit skin and fur. To one end was a fluorescent red ball of about half an inch in diameter – one would need courage and possibly permission to fish this, but I am told it does work. In any event, I believe that a great many black lures that are fished in depths of over twenty feet may well be accepted as legitimate leech imitations, which lends at least some credibility to that Datchet 'horror' – the Dead Blackbird.

Over the years, I have come to realise that, sooner or later, if it appears in or on the water, a trout will eat it! Indeed, there have been some pretty extraordinary instances surrounding the fishes' catholic eating habits. Once, whilst fishing a carrier (small irrigation stream), that ran into the River Test, I noticed a good fish rising to mayfly under a bridge. After some adjustment and amendment to my casting, I managed to get a sufficiently good cast into its feeding lane. It rose and accepted my fly with unusual abandon. On arrival at my net, I noticed a long, sinewy, tapered string to the corner of the brownie's mouth. Intrigued, I dispatched the fish (a rare occurrence when fishing for river brown trout), and, on closer inspection and· post mortem, I discovered that the protrusion belonged to a furry body – the trout had eaten a baby rat. I fervently hope this is not a frequent 'hatch'. The thought of imitating mammalia fills me with utter dread. Nevertheless, it proves a point. For mice, voles, frogs and even snakes, are considered viable and imitative foodforms in the USA and elsewhere. I leave you with the option!

The last 'constant' major food form in this sub-chapter is, by comparison, mundane. The snail, in its many forms, is vastly important to the reservoir's food chain and diet of the trout. I have caught trout, both in the UK and Ireland, which have rattled audibly, such was the preoccupation with these Pulmonata. There are a plethora of different stillwater-dwelling species in this country, all of which will feasibly interest the trout at some point or other. The more common ones include the great pond snail (*Lymnaea stagnalis*), which measures up to two inches and may be of doubtful value, the ¾-inch common wandering snail (*Lymnaea peregra*), which is among the probable trout dietary candidates, the distinctive ramshorn (*Planorbarius corneus*) and the smaller keeled ramshorn (*Planorbarius carinatus*), and the white ramshorn (*Planorbarius albus*) measuring three-quarters of an inch and a quarter of an inch respectively.

This, of course, is a very small selection of the species, but most conform to similar modes of existence, feeding on algae in and around weed beds, often in quite deep water where they will munch merrily on organic debris, even fish eggs. The shell, though different in construction, does tend to encase a similar shape, the actual gastropod resembling its garden counterpart. It has horns on top of a quite large suction area which it uses rather like a foot to both adhere to objects and vacuum up organic debris into its radula (a toothed, sandpaper-textured tongue), which collects the delicacies to be planted and digested in the mouth.

It is their location, however, which affects

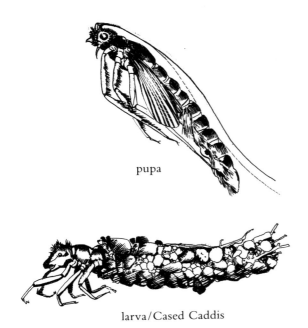

pupa

larva/Cased Caddis

Sedge/caddis stages of development.

our fly fishing approach. So often it is the sole reason for the adage 'slow and deep with a Black and Peacock Spider' during the inhospitable, early weeks of the season. For it is, as the aforementioned species, a ubiquitous, seasonal-resilient food item for the trout. There is one exceptional occurrence in its lifestyle which can dramatically mould fly-fishing tactics. I will be dealing with these in the section 'Important Interludes'. It does, however, remain one of those wonderful patterns for use when one is scratching one's head wondering which fly to put on.

This leads us to what can be best described as the 'super hatches' and, though these may at first appear cyclical, I feel that their influence spans a much wider period. Certainly, this is the case of the Trichoptera, colloquially known as sedge and often referred to as caddis. These will probably need little introduction as they are almost the harbingers of long, silken summer evenings, when the adults dance and pirouette across the darkening water's surface and bankside foliage, fading to indigo in the night shadows. Yet it is during the bleak, inhospitable opening weeks that their journey starts, for, stirring amidst the winter-rotted vegetation, entombed in a cold, grey waterscape, there resides the chameleon of the insect world – the cased larvae or caddis.

One would be forgiven for thinking that the familiar homes of tubular construction, dotted with bits of lake bed debris, are endemic to all species. Not so. Certain varieties of sedge will manufacture residences from different materials. This can give the angler at least an approximation as to certain colonies' locations. For instance, the larvae of the Great Red Sedge will utilise bits of leaf and weed, cemented into a tapered spiral shape; the Grouse Wing favours grains of sand and a slightly curved shape; Longhorn species, weed and sand tapered and curved; the Brown Sedge, two long twigs laid over a fine gravel base, and so on. However, all have one thing in common – they move ponderously and painfully slowly, with only the bulbous head section emerging, together with their six stubby, strong legs for propulsion. Some larvae are, to be accurate, free-swimming (*Rhyacophila*), whilst others fashion a silken anchor rope and attach themselves to rocks, posts and other stable underwater constructions. Both these types do tend to be river orientated species, yet observations would suggest at least some form of free swimming species do exist in stillwater. Both I and Brian Harris, have witnessed large green larvae in Bewl Water.

This may be 'gilding the lily', but what is certain is that caddis imitations such as Stickflies, Long Shank Goldribbed Hare's Ear or Harris's Marabou-tailed Stick, all work during the early months and, indeed, throughout the season. I feel it is lure fishing to some degree, for to mimic the slothful, trundling caddis would require a figure-of-eight retrieve to last some eight to twelve hours! I have not the patience. Thankfully, our erroneous stabs at imitation are met with approval from the trout.

On pupation, the larva will spin itself a trapdoor over the case and metamorphose within, changing from the sombre larva into the often brightly coloured pupa. Within this time span, lasting anything from a matter of days to several weeks, wing buds will grow, legs will lengthen and antennae will form. When sufficiently evolved, the pupa will burst free of its incarcerations, entering a watery world where it will either crawl along the bottom for hatching on dry land, or, more importantly for the trout fisher, lethargically swim up to the surface in a stop/start mode of rising and falling undulations. It is during such times that the greatest predation occurs.

I wish I could be of some help in identifying pupae with the resultant adult. It appears that this is problematic, even for practised zoologists. Suffice to say, that by carrying a variety of suitably shaped, sized and coloured examples, most situations can be covered. The pupal form has long found favour with the fly dresser, starting with Dr Bell's still effective pre-war Pupae pattern, extending to John Goddard's series in the mid-1960s and culminating in, what I feel are now 'state of the art' accurate, renditions by Paul Jorgensen, the great American fly dresser, Gary La Fontaine the caddis *aficionado*, and our own Gordon Fraser. All three have created lifelike and 'killing' versions which should be carried in hook sizes of std 10 to 18 in colours ranging from pale fawny yellow through to amber, encompassing the greens such as sea-green, and extending to dark olive, also brown.

This year, an interesting theory emerged whilst fishing with Arthur Cove. He said he felt the pupa was active for a considerable time before ecloding to the adult form, adding that this can take up to three weeks or

more. Arthur is seldom wrong, and this would extend the pupa's uses over a much greater period. Another factor concerning the pupa is its position, similar to the midge pupa, in the surface film. This area can lead to perhaps some of the best sedge fishing of the year.

Generally, sedge emergences coincide with the settled weather conditions, even in rough weather, the hatching period of afternoon and early evening usually combines with moderating wind strength. Thus, the surface tension (miniscus) will be at its most dense, giving rise to the familiar insect struggles for life. I believe it is no accident that James Ogden's perennial Invicta is then at its most deadly – mimicking the natural's state of dishevelment. At this juncture, the pupae splits its sheath-like skin along its entire upper length by internal pressure, the ensuing mêlée being a tangle of unopened embryonic wings, gangly legs and curled antennae. This is echoed perfectly in the Invicta's ragged appearance – a point that Steve Parton has also included in his range of Sienna, Green and Orange Sedges. This ragged tangled appearance is an important recognition factor for both trout and fly dresser.

Finally, the adult emerges, laying justifiable claim to its Trichoptera lineage. It is roof-winged, of which there are four – two under- and two marginally longer overwings, slightly hair-fringed. These, in turn, cover a tail-less (nine) segmented body, ending in a comparatively small head which is mostly taken up with a hair-surrounded eye. Two noticeably long antennae either sweep forward or curl backwards over the wing, depending on species. Most fly fishers will be familiar with this appearance, but may not realise that some varieties enjoy an afternoon emergence (these tend to be smaller and more hirsute), while others hatch more familiarly, in the evening. This, of course, does have great bearing on tactics, making dry fly fishing viable for a longer period.

There are a multitude of caddis species aflight in this country, a large proportion of which are important to the stillwater fly fisher, but thankfully a 'top ten' does exist. These are, in my humble opinion, the third-of-an-inch Grouse Wing (*Mystacides longicornis*), the Great Red Sedge or Murragh (*Phrygania grandis/striata*) measuring a succulent three-quarters of an inch to an inch, the various Silverhorns (*Athripsodes sp.*), a third to half an inch, Silver (*Odontocerum albicorne*), a half to two-thirds of an inch, Caperer (*Halesus radiatus/digitatus*), three-quarters of an inch to an inch. There are, of course, many more, but I believe it would serve little use to extend the list, for I have found that when trout are feeding on these often hyperactive 'V' waking forms, they are decidedly catholic in their tastes, the caddis' airborne struggles proving to be the trigger factor.

This, in my experience, obviates the need for ultra-close imitation. In fact, I now use, almost exclusively, the Troth 'Elk Hair Caddis'. It floats, wakes and masquerades as an adult sedge to a tolerably close degree, and it certainly proves attractive to adult-searching trout in a great many conditions.

The finale, or egg-laying stage of the caddis' life, has largely been overlooked, but provides vast scope both, strangely, in the 'wet' sense – some sedge species actually diving under the water to lay their eggs (oviposit) – and the more accepted 'dry' spentwing characteristic, when the female is either in her exhausted death throes or completely vanquished. In the latter cases, the four wings are outstretched and, importantly, *in* the surface film. The first instance of the female's 'last rites' brings about a wonderful contradiction, inasmuch as a leaded streamlined dry fly seems to be the best choice!

My experiments over the years have led me to realise that there are very definite times and places when the second instance of the spentwing should be deployed. I seek out (generally in the dawn period), any build-up of the previous evening's thick surface film. This, in turn, has led me to such places as bays, windward banks and dam walls. The use of fairly accurate spentwing tyings is beneficial and, on some occasions, essential to success. Indeed, having mentioned the impressionistic Elk Hair, I feel it important to add that, at times of flat calms, one should also carry some realistic examples of adult resting sedges such as Tentwings.

I suspect that everyone has a favourite species – one that sends the angler into raptures on its appearance. My pulse quickens when I encounter the first olive of the year. I fully realise that they are not nearly as important as, say, caddis or midge, yet the 'armada' of tiny grey upright, yacht-like wings, setting sail and coursing across the wavelets, somehow seems to herald fly fishing in its purest sense – perhaps it is the river fisher in me. There are, in comparison to other food forms, remarkably few of the Ephemeroptera to interest the trout on still waters in this country and, though widely distributed, they emerge in rather small colonies when talking in terms of specific species such as the Large Summer Dun (*Siphlonurus lacustris/alternatus*), the Claret Dun (*Leptophlebia vespertina*) or the Autumn Dun (*Ecdyonurus dispar*), even the regal mayfly (*Ephemera danica/vulgata*). Yet, where the mayfly does occur, notably on the Irish limestone loughs, it does so in vast numbers (I will cover this more thoroughly in the section 'Important Interludes').

Some species, however, enjoy very wide and dense populations, notably the pond olive (*Cloeon dipterum*) and the lake olive (*Cloeon simile*). For the southern angler, the April appearance of the Sepia Dun (*Leptophlebia marginata*) must fall into this category, as does an old friend (though you may blanche

Agile Darter nymph

nymph at point of emergence

fully-emerged dun, or sub imago

Pond and lake olive upwing stages of development,
depicting a typical Agile Darter nymph.

at its inclusion), the diminutive *Caenis*, collectively known as broadwing, though perhaps more appropriately entitled the 'angler's curse'. Thankfully, all follow a similar emergence pattern: egg – nymph – dun (sub imago) – spinner (imago). The first division between species occurs in the nymphal form, the different shapes pertaining to different lifestyles and species.

The mayfly nymph is classified a 'bottom burrower' and is, of course, only useful to the angler when emerging prior to hatching. The Stone clingers (Autumn Dun), again because of their reluctance to move, also belong in this group, as do moss creepers. Laboured swimmers (Claret Dun) and silt crawlers (*Caenis*), however, can be efficacious although they play a secondary role to the most significant group – the agile darters (Large Summer Dun, pond and lake olives). These, as their name indicates, lead a fairly vivacious existence, generally flitting from weed bed to weed bed, appearing never to stay still for more than a few seconds at a time. Broadly speaking, this particular group conforms to a similar colour scheme of drab browns, through dark olive to almost transparent light olive yellow. In order to determine these various groups, I have provided an illustration which will, perhaps, serve better than words.

I will continue with the agile darters, for they offer true fishing potential. As mentioned, their life revolves around the shelter of weed beds, where they live out an existence which can last between three and twelve months. Just prior to emergence, colonies will become even more agitated and darken noticeably in colour, even the embryo wing pads following suit by expanding slightly in readiness for imminent adulthood. Thus, like all ecloding insects, their perilous surfaceward journey begins. No one is completely certain how the nymph knows when this exodus should begin or why so many should undertake it simulta-

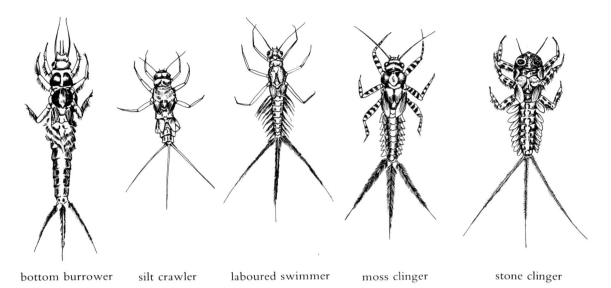

bottom burrower   silt crawler   laboured swimmer   moss clinger   stone clinger

Nymph types. (Agile Darter shown in previous drawing.)

neously. Perhaps the answer lies in baro-metric pressure or light intensity. Whatever the reason, they do so with the utmost precision.

All species of upwings seem to have this ability. Thus, hatch sequences are important and one should be vigilant, especially from late May to early June from about 11 a.m. onwards and then again in September. These times seem to herald the major emergence of both pond and lake olive. (They can occur throughout the season, but these periods are the major instances.) Once again, it is the top inch of water which is the critical fishing area, though a pattern fished in and around weed beds is always a fine strategy.

The nymph of the upwing is not exempt from the rigours of kindred hatching species, in turn, making a floating or emergent nymph one of the most potent weapons in our armoury. This deadly delay during eclosion can last for what must seem infinite seconds before the nymphal skin splits, due to internal body pressure, and the adult fly emerges, its wings creased and useless along its body. More precious seconds are lost while its wings dry and become erect to enable take off. Trout will, once again, be awaiting these hapless creatures' struggles, ready to accept nature's bounty. Some years ago I was introduced to an American pattern which has become the mainstay of my 'film fishing' and is known as the Floating Nymph.

The wings dry on emerging and the upwing can now lay claim to the title dun or sub-imago, becoming almost instantly recognisable. It is now that its short 24- to 36-hour adult life begins, which will en-compass courtship, metamorphosis and mating (this group only being able to feed in the nymphal form). The change in appearance between sub-imago and imago is one of nature's masterpieces. The com-paratively drab, grey appearance of the dun transforms into the shining, pristine clarity of the spinner. It is at this point that the fly mates (on dry land), the female returning to the water to lay her eggs and ultimately die. This stage is known as the spent spin-ner and should be among the most impor-tant in angling terms. I have found it less so. The *Caenis* apart, both pond olive and lake olive spinner patterns have seldom ever been employed, though I do carry them in my fly box. Indeed, the times when I have used this spentwing pattern could be counted on my hands. *Caenis*, together with the other vital spinner 'fall', the mayfly, will be dealt with in the section 'Important Interludes'.

It occurs to me that not everyone will know the difference between the Sepia Dun and the pond or lake olives. The Sepia is very distinctive, being clad almost entirely in chocolate brown colouration. The four wings (two large and two smaller hind ones), are fawn, but appear as dark as the body due to the very heavy dark brown veining. It may also be separated from many species by having three tails which are the same length as the body (half an inch) as opposed to the 'olive's' (both species mentioned) two.

The pond and lake varieties can, at a glance, look almost identical, as both are approximately the same size (a third to half an inch long). Even the body shades of browny-grey olive can look deceptively similar, as can their wings, both being a light, gun-metal grey and, unlike other members of their family, numbering only two, similar to *Caenis*. The tails of the dun are perhaps the most distinguishing feature – in the pond olive these are quite markedly ringed, in the Lake variety, a uniform grey. The eyes are another outstanding feature, the lake olive's being soft green flecked with brown, the pond olive (female) quite distinctively showing a faint red line across these oculi. (Males of upwinged species have their eyes, which are quite large, situated to the top of their heads, whereas the females' are smaller and to the side.) It is doubtful, however, that trout carefully note these intricate differences. In the light of this, may I recommend one dry fly pattern to cover both species, carried in sizes 14 and 16 – and a Greenwell will suffice admirably.

This concludes a brief synopsis of the major reservoir occurrences, but I would like to continue and explore, month by month, their relationship both to the trout and the angler, pinpointing more specific instances.

Important Interludes – Month-by-Month Stillwater Occurrences

March

I cannot think of a less auspicious start to conduct a journey through the seasons. Aquatic life will be at its lowest ebb during this period, and, due to the water's cold state, be somewhat comatose. In fact, there will be little glimmer of life at all. However, if urged and winter solstice non-fishing blues are getting the better of me, I would expect to find the odd snail, shrimp, hog-louse and Corixidae active in last year's decomposed and frost-bitten weed beds. I would probably look to the midday period when the day will be at its warmest, half expecting at least a sporadic hatch of tiny black midges (chironomid). After this, I would merely resign myself to the axiom 'hope springs eternal'.

April

Things should be better now, but only marginally. Fly fishers have to face the stark reality that water temperatures may be at their coldest, with only the hardiest creatures 'afoot' especially during the opening weeks. Slowly but surely, though, the sun will exert its influence, the dormant weed beds beginning to bud in youthful green. There will be a modicum of urgency now from the perennial water creatures of shrimp, Corixidae etc. The black midge may form the first line of attack, however, especially round the warmer periods ranging from 11 a.m. to 3 p.m. They are small though, and I would stress the need for careful observation and hook sizes of 14 and 16. Also on the midge front, there will be the semblances of more substantial trout food in the form of Blae and Blacks/ Duckfly and the occasional Grey Boy. All these will gather more momentum as the month progresses.

There is one villain that seems to hold great attraction for early season trout – the Alder larvae, which could be best described as the despot of the underwater world. I remember Brian Clarke mentioning the great diving beetle larvae (*Dytiscus marginalis*) as being the Genghis Khan of the insect world. If that is so, then the Alder must be likened to Attila the Hun! In fact, it is advisable to keep one's fingers away from this beast. Even humans aren't exempt from its vicious, pincered attack. Trout, however, experience no such problems and autopsies have proven that they show a definite liking for this creature. It sports a single long and hair/gill-fringed white tail, an abdomen of mottled brown over buff, again fringed with white gills to the side and a similarly marked thorax, combining with six powerful, cylindrical legs.

Its lifestyle, like that of so many insects at this time of year, revolves around the bottom areas and it conducts itself in ponderous movement. The adult emerges towards the end of this month and is, without question, a Dr Jekyll to the larva's Mr Hyde. The sombre dark brown/black, sedge-like (roof-winged) hatch species is utterly passive and, strangely, I have yet to see it taken by a trout, unlike the larva. Authorities would have it otherwise. I leave you with the choice. Patterns should include, for the larvae, Carnhill's Alder Larvae or Stuart Canham's rendition, both tied on size 10 longshanks and, for the

adult, a size 12 dark sedge pattern should suffice.

Mid April Onwards

This is an appropriate time to explore the hopefully sun-warmed shallows where one might reasonably find caddis, shrimp, hoglouse and Corixidae, artificials of which are always worth a 'wetting'. Sometimes, even a dry imitation of these insects is decidedly useful.

Before leaving this month, one character can be of enormous significance especially during windy conditions, though I feel it more important on the smaller fisheries than on larger reservoirs. No April would be complete without the undulating colonies of Hawthorn Fly (*Bibio marci*), rising and falling above the delicate spring blossom. It is rather similar to a shiny, black chironomid in shape, endowed with a housefly's thorax. Its most recognisable features, though, are two long, straggly rear legs which can be its downfall when blown on to the water, offering the angler the opportunity of some exciting, albeit brief, dry fly fishing, though I would recommend that an artificial should be fished *in* rather than *on* the surface.

May

Now we come to the merry month of May, which, in Britain, over the last few years, has been a far from accurate description, April exerting its cold water influences on this month, spoiling what should be the beginnings of an insect 'carnival'. Nevertheless, hatches do appear with traditional regularity and the patterns mentioned previously might find even more empathy at this juncture. There is, though, an erring to the colour olive which tends to be dark at the beginning of the month and lighter towards the end, especially when applied to

Well-known angler, Trevor Housby, catches a fine rainbow trout on a Mayfly Nymph.

chironomids. However, with the gradual rise in temperature both from land and air, other organisms begin to stir, notably the pond and lake olives which should start to hatch around the third week, the nymph of which is useful from the second week onwards. If you happen to be in Ireland, these flies are often referred to as 'sooty olives', though I am still unclear as to which particular one this applies to.

Another important interlude occurs towards the middle of this month. It is the emergence of the olive/black tadpoles which one can see in vast colonies around many of our stillwater margins, especially the smaller lakes. This might at first appear of little consequence. I certainly find it hard to equate with true fly fishing, but even so, trout feed on them in a manner reminiscent of 'sticklebacking'. A cautious approach should be adopted, together with a suitable artificial such as John Wadham's marabou-tailed Tadpole or Bob Church's Black version of a Frog Nobbler – two patterns which are effective throughout the season and in a great many instances.

However, pride of place where it occurs, must be reserved for that 'Queen of the Water' – the mayfly. On leaving its tube-like nymphal incarcerations, this cream, tubular, feathery and brown-marked nymph struggles surfaceward. Its journey is pedantic and certainly more alluring (because of the wiggles), than most other food forms. It is during their ascent that great colonies meet a premature demise. The trout intercept them anywhere between the bottom and top layers, yet, once again, I look to the top inch of water for the bulk of my sport. Both Irish wet fly patterns (I feel these to be marginally incongruous, but nonetheless effective), and floating nymphs have persuasive ways.

Once at the surface, the fly discards its comparatively dowdy nymphal costume for what must be one of the most distinctive adult guises in the fly-fishing world; on drying, the wing unfurls to produce

Here, Trevor Housby admires his catch from Dever Springs, Hampshire.

two large and two smaller hind wings that span some two inches and have a soft yellow fawn base, over which travels a maze of heavy brown veins. The body is a rich yellow cream marked quite dramatically by dark brown, intermittent abdominal markings, both to the top (dorsum) and the underside (ventar). The head section or thorax is pronounced and heavily marked with browny orange plates. The legs, like the three distinctive tails, are dark brown. Because of the staggered nature of some hatches, trout will, at first, be almost intimidated by their sheer size. However, once sufficient colonies have emerged, 'mayfly madness' begins. I ought to add that the mayfly season can be quite protracted, some of the larger Irish lakes not getting 'underway' until well into June.

There have, over the years, been a plethora of mayfly dressings; I can only offer my own chosen selection, though these are merely a drop in the artificial 'ocean'. These include: Richard Walker's accurate nymph pattern, wet flies such as the Gosling and various Arrow patterns, combining with my own more realistic, Floating Nymph. I carry remarkably few dry flies. These are: the Grey Wulff, the Shadow Mayfly and my own interpretation, the Lively Mayfly, all of which cover the two predominant species of mayfly – *danica* and *vulgata*. Their difference in the natural state is so minimal, as to obviate the need for specific patterns. I do, however, carry spinner patterns to cover this most important cycle for, unlike the previously mentioned olives, the fallen and spent female spinners are among our fly fishing legends. Very often, great rafts of this ivory-bodied, heavily black-veined winged, hapless creature in its final performance are sighted. Trout can become ultra selective when engaging the spinner, necessitating the use of realistic patterns such as Neil Patterson's Deerstalker or my own Fallen Spinner.

June

So it is we move to June – very often an extension of May, with the same influences, and indeed, fly hatches. These May overtones can extend into the second week, sometimes beyond, but essentially, June is *the* fly fisher's month. The reservoirs should now be fully alive with industrious little insect bodies. June also heralds the warmer tones by virtue of the fact that midge will be incorporating yellowy olives, oranges and ginger into both their pupal and adult forms. It is also very much the month of the Gold Ribbed Hare's Ear which, fished either dry or semi-submerged, will cover multifarious situations.

One might also begin to see a few caddis hatches, especially Great Red, Silverhorn and Longhorn certainly towards the end of the month if not before. With such a proliferation of foodstuffs, all being as important as each other on particular days or in certain situations, it is difficult to be specific. One thing which might occur is 'preoccupation', i.e. the trout only accepting selected species, shunning all others. Two insects can incite this frustrating situation which has the potential for turning good anglers into prospective golfers! They are, if any introduction were needed, the tiny bright green midge (which I believe to be *Chironomus viridis*, affectionately known in some areas as the 'Green Wiggly'), and the often unseen (as its name would suggest), Phantom (*Chaoborus sp*). These do not occur, you will be glad to hear, on every water. Both, however, can be seen as a friend, not foe, as long as a certain dictum is followed. It includes floating lines, long leaders and delicate presentation, coupled with the confidence to fish flies as small as size 20 when the situation demands.

Phantom flies, similarly to chironomid species, go through an egg – larva – pupa –

adult cycle. The first and fourth area possibly having little or no significance, the second stage is merely a transparent bloodworm or midge larva and can be of only small importance. The pupa however, is eminently fishable, it having at least a modicum of colour (buff orange) in the thorax. These tiny, semi-opaque organisms tend to hang at various water levels, their quarter-inch bodies remaining in such levels for up to eighty hours before hatching. Trout can become infatuated with their form and, I would think, react in a way similar to when dining on Daphnia. An imitation, therefore, is a very sound policy and I can recommend Peter Gathercole's interpretation.

The tiny green midge, which can appear almost fluourescent lime in colour, is approximately the same size, but more often smaller and has a habit of being at its most profuse when algae start to rise from the lake bed. I have certainly found that this diminutive chironomid is relished by the trout. Autopsies I have conducted, both on Rutland and Bewl Water have revealed quite bewildering numbers. Imitatively speaking, I have found a size 18 bright green, sparsely dubbed pattern to work extremely well, and also a Pheasant Tail nymph incorporating a fluourescent green 'hot spot' thorax in either 16 or 18, to be effective.

July

July is rather problematic. Weather conditions tend to dictate both fly hatches and fishing times, but it does give me the opportunity to introduce the multi-faceted order Odonata, which encompasses the Dragonfly and, perhaps more importantly, the sub-order Zygopetra or damselfly, the nymph of which appears to be fashioned from the over-zealous imagination of a science-fiction author. Though not present

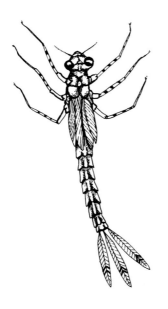

Damsel nymph.

on every water in the land, where it occurs it produces some of the most enthralling fishing of the entire season.

It is most in evidence from mid-June onwards with a cycle running: egg – larva – nymph – adult. The egg, having been adhered to a suitable platform such as a reed stem, hatches into the brief larval stage from where it almost immediately enters an instar (moult), becoming a juvenile nymph. From this point, it begins its twelve-month cycle, gradually darkening as it grows to the familiar slender, stick-like being, moulting ten times in the process. Its omnipresence around weed beds would suggest that it is a suitable candidate for imitation throughout the season, yet it is the bankward migrations starting around May and reaching crescendo in July which offer the best opportunities. They are lithe, athletic swimmers, propelling themselves quite quickly via jets of water from beneath their three, large, paddle-like tails (tracheal gills). This has the effect of accentuating its seductive wiggle. The damsel nymph seems to make its bankward exodus during a period from early morning through to midday, often favouring areas lined by grassy meadows or long-stemmed plants, where it can crawl from the water and change into the striking and elegant, winged damsel adult. Of all the species available to the angler, the most universal will probably be the Common Blue (*Enallagama cyathigerum*) which (in nymphal form), can attain lengths of up to two inches.

I have found the adult damsel less than useful, especially on large waters, though it appears to be an ideal trout candidate. However, I am assured by that big fish/small water expert, Bill Sibbons, that trout will take a blue imitation. He feels that fish cannot differentiate between water and air when chasing the blue female adults. His longshank Blue Nymph, fished at very fast rates just underneath the surface, has caught him many a weighty 'bag' which appears to confirm his theory. Before moving away from the damsel, it might be important to add that certain waters, even certain areas, seem to bring about both light and dark nymphal variations. Trout can show a marked preference for one or other, so it is a good idea to carry various shades.

I have been putting off the awful moment – *Caenis*! Its mere mention turns strong men to jelly and all because of a diminutive Ephemeroptera dressed in three tails, a cream body and a dark brown thorax with delicately rounded opaque wings. Nevertheless, it creates one of July's events and one which can truly be memorable. The Caenis starts as a small, sombre, dappled brown nymph, ferreting around muddy bottoms, which, to be fair, is of little consequence. There are patterns, I believe their uses are minimal. The same too could be said of the dun, which transforms so quickly to the spinner (imago) that one can actually see the sub-imago skin being shed.

The sad thing is that trout love *Caenis* spinners, and will zigzag, open-mouthed through the spent egg-laying insects with such gusto that even their direction can be totally unpredictable. Despite this, artificial patterns *do* work. All one needs is a certain amount of patience, a size 20 or better still size 22 close copy imitation, a de-greased leader, a fine tippit, accurate casting and a ready source of libation in case of failure. If your nerve holds, you will eventually catch a fish – maybe several. You may be inclined to use a large lure but I urge specific imitation at such times. It *will* bring its rightful rewards – eventually.

July also boasts other similar floating fly opportunities, though in more civilised proportions – the mounting if not crescendo-like caddis (sedge) activity. Species found in June will still be very active. Entering the fray will be Grouse Wing, Large Cinamon and Black varieties and where present, they will offer scintillating opportunities, both with dry patterns and nymphs/pupae, either hatching or in the ascendant.

August

August can be odd, either heralding the winding down to autumn, and the resultant recurrence of spring species, or providing its own individual high spots. The early weeks can often be scorchingly impossible, with only the idle 'buzz' of bees and the comatose drone of sleepy beings to break the sweltering, sun-bleached landscape's lethargy.

Conversely it can be exhilarating, producing some of the best imitative fishing of the year. Our old friend, the midge, will be about in colours of red, orange and ginger, with the odd olive for good measure. A few upwings may be present, as might the caddis especially the large and distinctive Caperer. There is, however, one particular, ever-present invertebrate that can provide extraordinarily good fishing during this period. It is the humble 'sloth' of the reservoir world which has a tendency, at this juncture, to go on 'drift about'. I refer to none other than the snail.

We are not absolutely certain as to why great colonies migrate to the surface and drift with the reservoir currents, though it could be due to the need to breathe, absorbing more oxygen at the surface. One might go further and suggest that because this phenomenon coincides with fairly hot weather, it may be an exodus in search of more favourable and efficacious areas due to their more familiar surroundings shrinking and stagnating through evaporation. Whatever the reason, trout are swift to seize this relatively unexpected feeding bonus, and they can become as preoccupied as when *Caenis* feeding. I have come to the conclusion that this occurrence revolves around the exploits of the wandering snail (*Limnaea pereger*).

Strangely, although accurate floating patterns such as the cork bodied Cliff Henry pattern and Bob Church's Black Deer Hair pattern would both seem perfect remedies, it does appear that, once again, a certain 'orange madness' will prevail. Whether this is due to the mollusc's shell showing an orangy brown when viewed against light, or whether trout merely find the colour synonymous with snail feeding activity, we don't know. However, an orange dry fly or Cove's Orange Nymph can often prove the fish's undoing when 'fished through' populations of snail. There are many more instances which occur in August, but perhaps these 'dovetail' more appropriately in the following month.

September

September is, without question, my favourite time of the year. It offers us an alternative 'Harvest Festival', if you like, but of the aquatic kind. It is as though species of all kinds combine to give thanks for summer bounty and proliferation, and assemble to thwart the onset of winter, in one vast celebration. So prolific can some days be, that it would appear that every food form mentioned previously in this chapter will be emerging or, at least, active. Strangely, trout seem less inclined to preoccupation, adopting a more general feeding manner. They too, one supposes, feel the onset of the leaner times, only weeks away.

With this multiplicity of organisms, several achieve star-billing at this autumnal concert. No September would be complete without *Tipula maxima*, the buff inch and a third bodied, gangly-legged cranefly or, as it is colloquially known, the 'daddy-long-legs'. This veritable giant is only a small member of a family of 250 (or more), some of which – notably, the brightly marked, black and yellow bodied *Nephrotoma maculosa* and *crocata* – are of interest to trout and the dry fly fisher throughout the summer months.

Craneflies are often seen as terrestrial creatures and though this is true of *Nephrotoma* species, *Tipula*, the largest, starts life after the egg has hatched, in 'Eeyoresque' surroundings of 'gloomy, rather boggy and sad places' especially those immediately surrounding reservoirs. Here the large (two inch) larvae, swathed in off-white, reside and though probably a rarity to trout, can, I am assured by 'Taff' Price, be taken in imitating-worthy numbers, especially when the banks receive a big wave, washing the creatures out to the main body of water.

The adult is a familiar sight with its trundling, twice knotted, long legs, a buff body, two thin Diptera-shaped wings and a pronounced rounded thorax. Once again, nature has played one of her more nefarious jokes, which must be construed as a fly fisher's bonus – the daddy is an extremely poor aeronaut, a strong wind rendering it ineffectual, incapacitated and at the trout's mercy. This often drives them to the awaiting surface film where the legs will adhere to the thick watery substance, pinioning it, as though ensnared in a spider's web. Thus, the legendary daddy fishing begins.

Fishing an imitation, as a natural, can take many forms. One widely practised method utilised in both Britain and Ireland is 'dapping' and, rather similarly to the mayfly method, incorporates the use of a live offering. I have an aversion to this, though legitimate, and I find the use of an artificial every bit as successful as a be-hooked natural. The interesting point most fly dressers and notably, the late Richard Walker, depict in their artificials is the trailing nature of these legs. But I would urge the use of a pattern, in some instances, with the long legs projecting around the fly. This 'resting' mode seems to be more effective when fishing from the bank.

Be warned! Not every year is cranefly year. They do seem to suffer from fluctuations due, I suspect, to different wind directions and changes and also climate variations. Years which see this fly in proliferation, are generally those with lengthy periods of humidity during July and August. Strangely though, artificials can be remarkably successful even when few natural flies are about, making the phrase 'a daddy for all seasons' really quite appropriate.

No September, indeed no reservoir season, would be complete without the mention of small fish or, to use the Americanism 'bait fish'. They are a significant part of the food chain and one which appears to manifest itself more towards August, positively exploding in September. Size, of course, plays an important role in any fly-fishing policy and no less so than when tackling fry feeders. The river angler doctrine of an accurate and delicate approach combining with an artificial that is roughly the right colour and shape, but stressing the correct size, rather sums up the tactics one should employ when fishing the 'fry'. Subtlety is very much the game plan and, if we look at July, when the vast shoals of immature fish swarm the margins, one can note that trout engage this food form with all the stealth and imperceptible guile of a practised hunter, leaving only tiny traces of rise forms and almost indiscernible underwater movements as evidence. The same could be said of stickleback feeding fish.

Everyone's popular conception of ravenous war parties hunting like pack wolves (if it happens at all), will happen during this month. Yet even here, a certain subtlety prevails which Bob will be covering in his chapters on tactics. This only leaves me to describe the types of fish one might encounter. So much depends on the waters you elect to fish, of course, species varying from place to place. A 1980s phenomenon depleted our major reservoirs of most of the perch stocks, which are only now returning to anything like normality. Ruffe or pope, suffered a similar fate, and both species could be seen rafting around many a shoreline. Although this offered remarkable fishing at the time, it left a big gap in the stillwater food chain, which has led to other fish gaining perhaps more importance than they had previously. The ubiquitous roach and the hybrids of rudd, bream and roach combinations, together with minnows and sticklebacks, all have their role to play, both as 'sacrificial offerings' to the ever-present trout and as imitable food forms. I believe the most useful to be the silvery, effervescent roach or the stickleback, though bream also have a very definite part in the proceedings, especially in the deeper areas of our reservoirs. It is

here that I find the use of larger than average flies, including enormous white tandems, wholly justifiable. For, is not imitating a small fish as valid as, say, a midge pupa? This, of course, does not include the mindless use of brightly coloured concoctions. It is a strategy based on pure imitation.

September, indeed the latter part of August, is also the time for Corixa and if a fry pattern fails to work in and around margin weed beds and fish are seen in the vicinity, there is a very real possibility that they are harvesting the Corixidae 'crop' and tactics should be fashioned to meet this instance, especially the immature, cream variety.

I mentally 'cut off' at the end of September – this is probably the river fisher in me. By comparison to the other months, October is almost sad and disconsolate, the fly fishers' year having run its course. There is, though, a very strong chance of an Indian summer and they seem to be more prevalent now than ever before. In many ways, they bring about a continuance of September, with the same instances occurring. However, the ever-present threat of short, sharp frosts, together with shortening daylight hours, tend to render aquatic life less active. There is, of course, the very strong possibility of midge, which will be clad in their spring-like colours of dark green and black; also the familiar pot pourri of snail, shrimp and hoglouse, but even their attractiveness to the trout seems to wane, like the late afternoon sun.

Oddities

This diverse and exciting journey through the insect kingdom, would not be complete without the odd, albeit rare, occurrence of certain food forms which can, on their day, prove to be the only thing of interest to trout. Many of these creatures are land based or terrestrial, often blown from neighbouring land masses and trees and into the reservoir food chain. Insects such as coch-y-bonddu, soldier beetles, lacewings, moths and a host more, will all, sooner or later meet an ignominious end on the lake's surface and, possibly, in the trout's mouth.

One specific creature can incite almost total trout feeding preoccupation – the ant. During those hot, sullen, lifeless days of July and August, one often sees the spiralling gyrations of feeding birds high above the water's surface, and though this may suggest midges, it may also be the prelude to a 'fall' of the flying adult ant. When it happens, you will not mistake it! How well I remember being becalmed just off the dam wall at Bewl Water one breathless August day. The ants descended in their thousands and were met with what seemed like similar numbers of rising trout. Specific patterns are *de rigueur* and should mimic the natural's fore and aft bulbous sections, one being the abdomen, the other the thorax, separated by a tiny 'waist' and incorporating two glassy, pale bluish hyaline wings. Body colours do vary, the most common being black, which is the common garden ant, or reddish brown, which is the wood ant. Trout are remarkably fussy when dining on ants and fly patterns should be fashioned in a life-like manner accordingly.

I must also mention another comparative rarity – the drone fly (*Eristalis tenax*), though I cannot speak from first-hand experience. (Instances of their importance have so far eluded me.) However, I still carry a few distinctive black and yellow bodied bee-like patterns, just in case. They are, in fact, waterborne. The larva can be found living on the lake floors, where it is dubiously known as the rat-tailed maggot. It is the adult fly which is the more important, generally when the female returns to the water on egg-laying missions during midsummer.

Having mentioned the damselfly earlier, it is only fair to briefly touch on the other, kindred, though less aesthetic, dragonfly species. As with the damsel, it is, I feel, more important in its nymphal form which follows an almost identical route to its 'cousin'. The opportunities of using imitations also fit into the same period and I do carry several variations based on its theme, but have never felt the inclination to use them. The fact that they are eaten by trout and are present in quite large numbers would suggest that I have been neglectful, but I have more faith in the sleeker damsel. The dragonfly nymph is tubbier and less tailed (three short spiky examples) in comparison, though in every other respect, it is ostensibly the same. After all, a fly box has to stop somewhere!

There are, of course, many other insects to concern and fascinate the fly fisher – various upwinged species such as Blue Winged Olives, even the *Heptagenia* species Yellow May Dun and Dusky Yellow Streak (both lovers of high rocky lakes), spiders, grasshoppers and perhaps others we do not know about, all, at some time will interest the fish. These are isolated instances and must be viewed as such, and though local knowledge would indicate that certain insects are vital to successful fly fishing, I reassure myself with the fact that there is rarely a day when a chironomid is not in evidence.

In closing, I would just like to mention some useful implements which, together with more normal fly fishing clutter, serve to make waterbound adventures that much more rewarding. A simple aquarium hand net of a size which can be fitted into either waistcoat or bag (and is available from any major aquatic store), will allow both flying and emerging insects to be captured. A collection of four to six plastic labelled phials should be used for retention of samples – *do not*, I entreat you, use the glass variety, as they shatter easily and as a result may well 'cut' short a fishing trip. Two of these should be dry, one or two containing a preserving solution such as alcohol or Formalin. I have used vodka, which worked, but proved to be expensive and tempting! One or two more should be reserved for holding nymphs or emerging species in water. A pair of tweezers are always useful, as are a notebook and pen for logging hatch species, density, area, time of occurrence and weather conditions etc. A magnifying glass is also very helpful. I personally use two types – a retaining jar with a magnified top, known as a 'Nature Viewer' and a plastic magnifying sheet measuring about two inches by four inches, called an 'Inscribe Pocket Lens' which can be obtained from most large stationers. All that one needs thereafter, is an enquiring mind.

Summary

I have attempted, in a small way, to introduce you to the diverse and fascinating world of trout food forms in the knowledge that I have not really done it sufficient justice or, indeed, covered everything there is to be found on our waterways. But, with each passing year, so my knowledge grows and by asking questions, even querying some former theories, the vast jigsaw is slowly beginning to fall into place. I would suggest that evidence of hatches can be found in the most peculiar places. Spiders' webs have often given me the information I needed for a successful day's fishing and hopefully it will not be long before you come to realise that the little wiggly black things are midge pupae, the little olive, darting beings, pond olives and damsel nymphs and the fluttering moth affairs, caddis. Indeed, a world will unfold in front of you, but, more importantly, become tangible and interactive with the trout and your fly fishing exploits.

I leave you with a quote from J. W. Hill's *River Keeper*. 'The proper fly, properly presented at the proper time, generally brings forth the proper result' (William Lunn).

MAJOR STILLWATER INSECT OCCURRENCE

	March	April	May	June	July	August	September	October	Size
Shrimp	A	A	A	A	A	A	A	A	½–¾in
Hoglouse	A	A	A	A	A	A	A	A	½–¾in
Corixa	A	A	I.A.	I.A	A	I.A.	I.A.	A	¼–½in
Snail	A	A	A	A	A	I.A.	I.A.	A	¼–½in
Leech	A	A	A	A	A	A	A	A	½–2in
Fish	A	A	A	I.A.	A	I.A.	I.A.	I.A.	
Daphnia		A (late)	I.A.	I.A.	I.A.	I.A.	A	A	
Chironomidae									
Larvae	A	A	A	A	A	A	I.A.	A	
Pupae						(*See* corresponding adult.)			
Black Midge (Duckfly Blae & Black)	E/H	E/H	A				A	E/H	¼in
Small Black	A	E/H	E/H	A	A		A	E/H	⅛in
Ribbed/Olive		A	E/H	E/H	A	A	E/H	A	¼in
Golden Dun			A	E/H	E/H	E/H	A		¼–⅓in
Brown				A	E/H	E/H			⅛–⅓in
Orange Silver		A	E/H	E/H	E/H	A	A		¼–⅛in
Large Red or Ginger			A	E/H	E/H	E/H	A		¼–⅓in
Small Red				A	E/H	E/H	A		⅛–¼in
Blagdon Grn		A	E/H	E/H	E/H	E/H	A		⅛–¼in
Caddis (Trichoptera)									
Larvae	I.A.	I.A.	A	A	A	A	A	A	
Pupae						(*See* corresponding adult.)			
Great Red			A	E/H	E/H	A			¾–1⅛in
Caperer				A	E/H	E/H	A		¾–1in
Large Cinnamon				A	E/H	E/H	E/H		¾in
Black Silverhorn				A	E/H	E/H	A		⅓in
Brown				A	E/H	E/H	E/H		⅓–½in
Longhorn				E/H	E/H	E/H	E/H		⅓–⅔in
Small Red			A	E/H	E/H	E/H	A		⅓in
Small Silver			A	E/H	E/H	E/H			⅓in
Grouse Wing				E/H	E/H	E/H	E/H	A (early)	⅓in
Brown					A	E/H	E/H	A (early)	½–⅔in

Ephemeroptera									
Pond Olive Nymph		A	A	I.A.	I.A.	A	I.A.		
Pond Olive Dun			A (late)	E/H	E/H	A	E/H		⅔–¾in
Lake Olive Nymph		A	I.A.	I.A.		I.A.	I.A.		
Lake Olive Dun			E/H	E/H		E/H	E/H		½in
Mayfly Nymph			I.A.	I.A.					
Mayfly Dun/Spinner			E/H (late)	E/H	E/H (Ireland)				1–1½in
Caenis Nymph			A	A	I.A.	I.A.	A		
Caenis Spinner				A	E/H	E/H	A		⅓–½in
Sepia (Nymph/Dun)		I.A.E/H		I.A.E/H					⅔–¾in
Claret			A	E/H	A				⅔–¾in
Plecoptera (Stoneflies)	Due to very localised emergence and activity, must be considered as a bonus and comparative rarity.								
Odonata									
Damselfly Nymph			A	I.A.	I.A.	I.A.	A		¾–2in
Dragonfly Nymph			A	I.A.	I.A.	I.A.	A		¾–1¾in
Hawthorn	I.A.		(late) I.A. (early)						½–⅔in
Phantom Midge			A	I.A.	I.A.	A	A		⅛–¼in
Ants				A	I.A.	I.A.	A		¼–⅓in
Alder Larvae	I.A.		I.A.	A					¾–1⅛in
Cranefly (Daddy-long-legs)			A	A	I.A.	I.A.	I.A.		¾–1¼in

N.B. This is an overall average grouping and does not allow for specific occurrences or different regional peculiarities which may be significant to only a few waters.

I.A. = Increased Activity.
A = Active in water thus open to imitation. Sparse hatches.
E/H = Specific hatching period of adult or species.

2 Science and Artistry in Designing Effective Fly Patterns

I have been so impressed by Dr Peter Shelton's scientific work that I asked him to cover a chapter on the angler/scientist link. The great thing about Peter is, he does not make his scientific facts boring. The exact opposite would be true. The subjects he covers here enable us, the anglers, to understand the trouts' behaviour far better and therefore plot their downfall.

For too long fishermen have concentrated on the artistry of fly design yet have given scant attention to the scientific principles upon which effective patterns depend. One hears anecdotal evidence that hot orange lures work well when the fish are feeding on *Daphnia* but the reasons for such success have remained obscure, and without proper scientific backing they are not likely to gain the attention that they may deserve. As a fly fisherman and a zoologist I set out to discover the scientific reasons for the success. A knowledge of the way that the

sense organs work is highly relevant when it comes to trout fishing tactics.

While humans consciously control much of what they do, that is not true of fish – much of their behaviour depends on reflex actions. The reflex movement can be simple, such as the tail-flick response elicited in fish by a tap on an aquarium window, or complex as in the sequences of behaviour associated with territorial fighting in male sticklebacks. The distinguishing feature of the reflex is that it is unconscious and once initiated will run to completion. Food gathering by trout falls very much into the category of reflex behaviour.

Some patterns of reflex behaviour are simple, inherent and instinctive; others are complex and learned. For many patterns of behaviour the reflex can be initiated by what students of animal behaviour call the releasing signal. Such signals can be quite simple. A model male stickleback will elicit aggressive territorial behaviour in a real male stickleback as long as the model has a

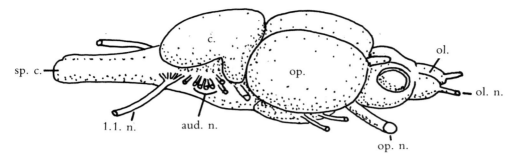

This drawing of the trout brain shows the very large optic lobes (op.) and thick optic nerves (op. n.). The prominent cerebellum (c.) is indicative of an active life-style. The olfactory lobes (ol.) and nerves (ol. n) are relatively small. Also labelled are: the nerve which carries messages from the lateral line organs of the posterior part of the body (l.l. n.), the auditory nerve (aud. n.) and the spinal cord (sp. c.).

red belly. The model can be a grotesque imitation bearing little resemblance to a real fish but as long as it has a red belly the response will be evoked. In other words the red belly is the releasing signal for aggressive behaviour in that species.

When it comes to feeding behaviour we are talking about a complex series of reflexes and then the releasing signals are not so simple. If they were we would have fishing methods and flies that are always effective and the unpredictability that makes fishing fun would disappear. That does not mean that we should not strive to find the best possible fly patterns that incorporate features likely to spark off the feeding reflexes. For complex sequences of behaviour the releasing signals may have to stimulate a variety of senses for the initiation of the appropriate behaviour.

The first requirement for the hungry trout is that it must be able to detect the prey. The senses likely to be involved include the auditory system for the detection of sounds, the lateral line system for the detection of water turbulence or local currents, the olfactory system which detects smells and taste, and the eye for detecting visual stimuli. By far and away the most important sense with respect to trout feed-

ing behaviour is vision. However, if the fly or lure can stimulate more than one sense in a way that is indistinguishable from the range of signals produced by the natural prey, then it should be more attractive than a fly that stimulates only one.

Let us discuss the various signals in the order in which they come into play. The alerting signal arouses the trout which then switches on to active searching with its sound and smell senses. We do know quite a lot about fish hearing and the way that sound behaves under water. Trout have a more restricted range of hearing than ourselves and tend to respond best to low frequency sounds. Whether or not trout can actually localise the direction of a sound source is debatable. In humans the ears are widely spaced and this improves our ability to orientate to a sound source. Fish ears are internal and are close together because of the narrowness of the head; they are often both connected to a single swim-bladder. For these theoretical reasons, and from results of laboratory experiments it has always been thought that fish have poor directional hearing. But experiments on directional hearing in fish are notoriously difficult to set up because of the complications of sound waves being reflected off the

a   b

Fly design can take advantage of what we know about movement perception. In the case of the Nobbler-style fly (a), the heavy head and marabou tail produce a particularly attractive type of motion. The eyespot adds to the visibility. To produce the undulatory motion, the centre of gravity should be well forward. With many patterns, including the Baby-Doll lure (b), this can be achieved using turns of wire behind the eye of the hook. Fishing with a long leader and a sink-and-draw technique will produce the best undulatory motion.

sides of the experimental tank. The best experimental chamber is a large body of natural water. Where better than the sea?

Recently, physiological recordings from cod auditory nerves and behavioural experiments in the sea have shown that this species can indeed orientate to sounds. It is yet to be proved that trout have similar abilities and in any case their ability to orientate to sounds is certain to be much worse than their eyesight. Nevertheless, sound-producing lures such as popping bugs can be highly effective. Why is this? One thing we do know is that sounds travel great distances under water. Thus, in coloured water especially, the trout will hear the lure before seeing it. So, even before the fish has made visual contact, it will have been alerted to the presence of possible food using another sense. I believe that a popping bug is effective simply because it emits the same sorts of signal as a natural struggling prey item like a small frog or injured fish fry. The advanced warning given before the fly is even seen can make this sound-emitting fly very potent medicine indeed.

It's worth considering which of the angler's activities a fish will also hear. Almost all sounds produced above water will be reflected off the water surface and however much you verbally urge the trout to take your fly, it will never hear you. At the same time, water-borne sounds are potentially off-putting to trout. While a relatively constant sound does not seem to upset fish, there is evidence from herring research that sudden noises or changes in sound level are likely to cause problems. We have all seen trout happily rising within feet of the boat under full outboard power. However, once you are moored, rattling anchor chains, banging about on the bottom of the boat and other sudden sounds are likely to scare fish.

What about the senses of smell and taste? Most fish, including salmonids, have an extremely good sense of smell and can detect the most minute traces of chemicals. As fly fishers we obviously cannot exploit this sense but it is worth noting that in many fish, food smells can provoke foraging behaviour in the absence of any direct visual contact. In still waters sources of smell are relatively difficult to locate. Eventually the source will be found, but it could take minutes rather than seconds. In rivers, fish locate an upstream food source by swimming against the current towards it. Field experiments have shown that the migratory salmonids use their sense of smell in identifying their home river. However, because fish localise smells rather poorly a fly doctored with an attractant is not likely to be very effective. Nevertheless, we can avoid upsetting the fish with unappetising or even threatening odours. We know, for instance, that sockeye salmon are alarmed by the smell of bear's paw. Other species are upset by extracts of fish skin. Thus, I would advise against keeping flies in old tobacco boxes

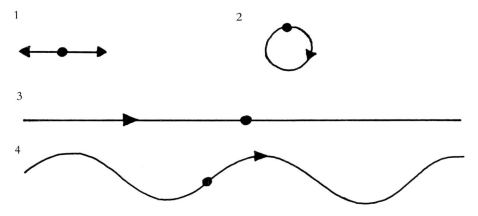

In laboratory experiments, oscillatory (1) or rotatory movements (2) do not stimulate feeding behaviour well. A unidirectional horizontal movement (3) is much better. This is improved if the bait has an undulatory motion (4).

or handling flies with fingers contaminated with midge repellent! There is no scientific evidence that they upset trout but why take chances when we know that their sense of smell is so acute?

Now we come to senses that can definitely be used to localise prey direction, the first being the lateral line which gives fish a so-called sixth sense. It consists of a large number of sense organs widely distributed over the body in the lateral–line canals. Contrary to opinion, fish cannot hear through the lateral line, which responds primarily to water displacements and localised current flow. Blind fish can locate and capture a moving prey using the lateral line to detect minute water movements caused by its struggles. The lateral–line sense is, if you like, touching at a distance. Such movements are large near to the prey but decline rapidly with distance, so the lateral line is useful in detecting prey at short ranges only. In blind pike, where experiments have been done to measure the effective range of the system, it turns out that the prey had to be within about four inches for accurate localisation to take place. Thus, as far as the trout is concerned and in all but the greenest of water, it is likely that the prey will have been seen well before it is detectable by the lateral line. Nevertheless, in that final approach, the trout will receive considerable input to the lateral line, and flies that create a lot of turbulence will provide just that extra something that can be the difference between a positive take and a near miss.

Vision is by far and away the most important sense for prey detection and anything we can do to increase the chances of the trout seeing the fly will increase our chances of catching fish. Experiments show that food items hidden in the bottom sediment are virtually immune from attack. Considering the immense numbers of chironomid midge larvae living in tubes within the mud, it is extraordinary that lake trout have never learned to grovel in the sediments. The explanation probably lies in the fact that the trout's gills are adapted for pure, sediment-free water and clogging the gills with mud would be a real hazard to the respiratory system. The consequence for the angler is that the visible pupal phase of the chironomid is much more likely to be on the trout's menu than the invisible larval bloodworm stage.

Some measure of the importance of sight

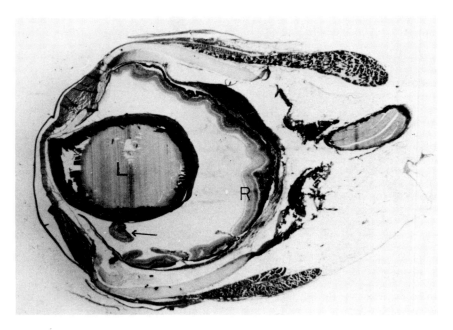

This section through the eye of a brown trout shows the typical camera eye arrangement. This fish lens (L) is spherical and can be moved back and forwards to focus the light on the retina (R). Such movements of the lens are achieved by contraction of a small muscle below the eye (see arrow). Normally, the eye is adjusted for near vision, so focusing on distant objects requires active contraction of the muscle.

is gained by inspecting the organisation of the brain. You will note that the two most prominent features are the optic lobes and the cerebellum. The latter is concerned with co-ordinating movement and its size reflects the active life-style of the trout. The optic lobes are relatively massive and are largely concerned with processing visual information and integrating it with information obtained through other sensory channels such as the lateral line.

Since the trout is so dependent on vision for prey detection, the more we know about it the better equipped we are. In particular we need to find out which sorts of visual stimuli are likely to elicit a feeding response. The fly should show up well which is achieved using appropriate colour combinations. This will be discussed later, after considering the detection of movement. Just as we are more likely to notice a

flying bluebottle than one that is settled, so the trout will see moving objects much better than stationary ones.

Laboratory experiments confirm that rainbow trout can detect moving objects 15 to 20 per cent further away than similar stationary ones. Organised movement implies life, which in turn can indicate the presence of threat or food. Consequently it is no surprise to find that the optic nerve contains many nerve fibres whose specific job it is to signal not shape or form but the presence of movement. Some of these movement detector nerves are specifically designed to participate in the detection of prey. Laboratory-based experiments show that there is one class of such movement detectors that responds only to small spots contrasting with the background. Some fishermen would regard the painting of eye spots on leadheads as a finicky detail. It is not! You can see from what I have said that such eye spots, with their black centre and white surround, are particularly visible because the fish brain has specific nerve cells tuned to detect the movement of such objects. Jungle cock eyes serve the same purpose and have proved effective over many years. This is not mere superstition or cleverness on the part of the fly dresser but fact based on scientific principles.

The question of what speeds of movement are likely to elicit the most vigorous feeding response in trout has not been fully answered. However, in other species, certain speeds are certainly more effective than others. Fish-eating species were found to respond best to baits retrieved at more than two inches a second. Species that fed on invertebrates were found to respond best to baits moved at slower speeds. It is likely that these findings can be generalised to the trout. For nymph fishing I must say that my success increased once I reduced the speed of retrieve. Just try measuring out two inches and then move the point of a pencil over that distance in one second. Remarkably slow isn't it? My own experience of fishing buzzers at the waterside is that as long as the fly is moving it is impossible to retrieve it too slowly.

I don't find lure stripping an attractive or relaxing form of the sport but I can see that in view of the above findings the rapid retrieve of a fish imitation may be the best approach for that style of fishing.

The next factor to consider is the pattern of movement and whether certain styles of retrieve are better than others. What produces the most attractive stimulus? While our eyes are more or less equally sensitive to movements in any direction, that does not seem to be the case for fish. This is probably because the visual world of the fish is constantly streaming by as the fish moves forward in still water, or as the current carries objects past the eyes. The

relevant physiological fact is that fish tend to have more motion-sensitive nerve cells that respond to horizontal movements than they do to other directions. Experiments prove that the kokanee or land-locked sockeye salmon gave the best feeding responses when the bait was moved horizontally across the visual field. Other patterns of movement including rotatory, or backwards and forwards oscillations produced very poor responses. The horizontally moving stimulus was found to be even more attractive when the prey also possessed pronounced vertical and lateral displacements.

This observation is fully consistent with my practical experience of fishing. I have often found that a fly weighted at the front produces more takes than one where the weight is evenly distributed. I remember a specific occasion where I had a suitably weighted Baby Doll. I took several fish and my companion asked if he could have one of mine. I gave him my last fly but it did not have that all-important weight at the front. He carried on fishless while I continued to take fish. Anecdotal evidence you may cry, but evidence consistent with what biologists have found to be the most attractive type of movement.

Undulatory motion is characteristic of many species of invertebrates including forms like leeches that are brilliantly imitated with the dreaded Dog-Nobbler. Midge pupae move with up and down flexions of the body and I have yet to see a buzzer imitation that successfully imitates that. However, if you can devise such a pattern – a touch of marabou at the rear and some turns of copper wire at the front – I think that would really score. There are other ways to produce an undulatory motion, and buoyant patterns fished with a sinking line can be deadly, so the next time you go on to the water forget about the steady retrieve and give your fly some life. Everything we know about how fish perceive movement and about how the naturals move will be on your side.

But do fish have colour vision and if so just what do they see? Since the visual systems of all predatory fishes are so important both biologists and fishermen alike are equally anxious to understand the factors that affect the fish's ability to see. That trout have good colour vision there is no doubt. Like us they have an advanced camera eye, and the retina contains both rods and cones. It is a sobering thought that

This high-power view of the brown trout retina shows the light-adapted state of the eye with the rod layer (R) shielded by migratory pigment. The cone layer (C) is responsible for colour vision. To reach the rods and cones, the light has first to pass through several layers of nerve cells (see arrow).

in fish this design of eye first appeared at least 300 million years ago and that we ourselves have inherited it from ancient fishy ancestors. In that time there has been ample opportunity for both present-day fish and ourselves each to develop all sorts of sophistication. Nevertheless, there are more similarities than differences between our eyes and those of fishes.

Exactly what a fish sees we will never know. The retina is merely a collector of light and the sensation of vision depends on processes that occur in the brain. Our brains are so different from those of fish that we can only speculate. However, study of the fish retina suggests that the eye at least, works in the same way as our own. The adult trout possesses three types of cone which are maximally sensitive in the blue, green and red parts of the spectrum. Thus the trout is capable of responding to light of different colours and it also has a set of non-colour coded rods that operate in twilight conditions. Like ourselves, fish can distinguish objects only if they differ in brightness or hue from the background.

In making an attempt at answering the question of what a fish sees, we should begin to solve the puzzle by asking how light behaves in water and what use can the fish make of that light. If we can answer those questions we can now ask how can we design a fly to maximise the chances of catching a fish. At the moment we have enough answers to make the process of selecting fly patterns a little more scientific and for what it's worth I will pass on what I know.

There are important differences between vision on land and vision in water. There is much less available light in water than in the air. One reason is that much of the light that strikes the water surface is reflected off it so that perhaps only half of the surface light actually enters the water. Further, the lower the sun's angle, the more light is

V	I	B	G	Y	O	R
I	N	L	R	E	R	E
O	D	U	E	L	A	D
L	I	E	E	L	N	
E	G		N	O	G	
T	O			W	E	

| 400nm | | 500 | | | 600 | | 700 |

The daylight spectrum of visible light ranges from short wavelength violet to long wavelength red. Not all wavelengths of light penetrate the water equally. At depth, this makes some colours more visible than others.

reflected and the less penetrates the water. So at twilight, when the light is fading, it is a fair bet that the trout is confined to using his non-colour-coded rod cells before we do. In other words, when there is still sufficient light for us to see colour above the water, the trout may already be seeing things in shades of grey. Under these circumstances the brightness of the fly will be more important than its colour because cone-cell vision does not operate at low light levels.

The next important point is that water acts like a colour filter and that light intensity decreases rapidly with depth. However, not only does the amount of light decrease but its colour changes. As we will see, the colours that the trout can see best are affected. Above water, the daylight spectrum ranges from short wavelength violet to long wavelength red light. The mixture of all colours of the spectrum produces white light. We see that white light consists of a mixture of colours only when it is refracted in a rainbow or passed through a prism. Pure water filters out both short and long wavelength components of violets and reds more rapidly than it does the blue light of intermediate wavelength. The proportion of short and long wavelength light remaining decreases with depth so that in deep water only blue light remains. Further, the water molecules scatter short

wavelength blue light so that in whichever direction one looks the so-called water 'spacelight' is blue.

Close to the surface, all the colours of the spectrum are present but quite soon the composition of the light is markedly altered. If the fly is close to the fish and both are near the surface, then the fish will be able to see a wide range of colours. These ideal conditions will be met in the average chalk stream where the water is relatively pure, the depth is not great and the steadily rising trout is not likely to take insects more than a metre away from his lie. In other words, the trout can select food items based on their colour.

Before discussing the problem of colour vision further black and white objects need to be considered. The former appear black because they absorb all visible wavelengths; the latter appear white because they reflect all visible wavelengths. Coloured objects absorb some parts of the spectrum and reflect others so it is an intrinsic property of coloured objects that they absorb less daylight than a black one and reflect less daylight than a white one. Compared with coloured objects, this makes black and white objects highly visible regardless of the colour of the illuminating light. Whether black or white is more visible in a particular situation will depend on the background. If the fly is seen against a dark muddy bottom the white fly will be most obvious. Similarly, seen against a light sandy bottom or close to the surface where there is plenty of light, a black pattern is the most visible. In mid-water, both should show up well. It is no accident that many very effective patterns feature black or white. Where black and white are combined, as in the teal-winged series of flies, we have a particularly potent arrangement which should give good visibility no matter what the background is like. There must be a lesson here that can be adapted for other types of fly. Instead of tying all-black patterns, add a white tag or wing. I don't guarantee anything, but surely getting the fish to see the fly is the first step in catching it. Of course, a white object in coloured water no longer looks white because the water selectively scatters and absorbs certain wavelengths. This has the effect that a white fly will take on the colour of the water.

The black and white patterns show how maximum differences in brightness between the fly and its background increase its visibility. The other way that objects can be made to stand out is if they are coloured to contrast with the background. In air the best contrast is achieved between so-called complementary colours. Red stands out well against a green background and orange is particularly obvious against blue. Now let's consider which colours are seen best in water of various colours. As we know, most colours will be available to the chalk-stream trout. However, in other types of aquatic environment not all colours are equally visible.

On reservoir water an algal bloom flourishes very early on in the year and yet by April the algae have often collapsed, leaving quite clear water. Although reservoir water will never be as clear as that in a chalk stream, it is at the beginning of the trout-fishing season that it comes closest to it. Here the filtering action of pure water means that at depth the light is quite blue. Obviously, a light blue fly will reflect a lot of light because there is a lot of blue light about. However, it will tend to match the water background colour and will provide a relatively poor colour contrast with the background water spacelight. Objects that reflect red and violet light will be less conspicuous than they would be in air, for another reason. Although they contrast well with the background they will radiate a smaller amount of light because light of

these wavelengths is selectively filtered out by blue water. At a distance reds and violets will tend to look blue/grey. The colours that are most visible will have to contrast well with the background light and be at wavelengths where there is plenty of light. In light blue water, these colours are either side of the light blue part of the spectrum and are indigo blue and yellow. The biological proof that these colours are seen well in clear water comes from the observation that many marine fish from blue coral-reef water have behaviourally important prominent patterns featuring deep blue and yellow. We can use this information in choosing lure patterns early on in the year. Those featuring yellow should still look yellow even at considerable depth and they should be particularly visible.

I remember one morning at Rutland a few years ago where we thought we had found the killer pattern of all time. That was the Black Ghost lure with its bright-yellow throat hackle and tail. Combined with a white wing and black body this makes for a particularly visible combination. For a couple of weeks that pattern accounted for a good number of trout. I feel sure now that our success was, in part, due to the visibility of the fly in those particular water conditions. The visibility of yellow in clear water can be exploited in other patterns. A yellow thorax to a Pheasant Tail nymph is well worth trying. Any fly featuring yellow and indigo should be particularly visible. Both elements of the pattern should retain their hue and both will contrast well with the background water spacelight.

Of course, in reservoirs, lakes and upland lochs the water colour varies and is often different from that in a chalk stream. In such waters, their colour relates to time of year and the amount of run-off from the catchment area. We have already seen that yellows will be particularly visible in the clear water at the beginning of the season. In late spring and early summer as the water warms, nutrient rich lakes and reservoirs support further algal blooms. The algal chlorophyll and accompanying so-called yellow substances produced by decaying plant material stain the water heavily. In such water the peak transmission is shifted to the green part of the spectrum. There are two colours particularly visible in green water. They also fall on either side of the region of highest transmission. Now it is blue/green and orange/red that are maximally visible. Once again, we do have biological evidence that these colours are important to fish that inhabit green waters. Think of the display colours of the male three-spined stickleback – red and blue/green. Another example is the red fin colour of the perch. A photograph of a perch at a depth of six feet in green water shows up the red fins clearly while other features of the fish merge into the background.

The presence of algae and yellow stain from decaying plant material greatly reduces the range at which any colour can be seen. Under these conditions it becomes more important than ever to select patterns that stand out well against the background. Whereas yellow was good in the early season it now becomes far less effective and will tend to merge into the background very rapidly as the distance between the fly and the fish increases. Now, one could do no better than choose any fly that has orange/red or blue/green in it. The effectiveness of hot orange lures in green water is often discussed and there is no doubt in my mind that its success is due to the fact that it shows up well. An orange or bright red thorax to a Pheasant Tail should be chosen in preference to a yellow one.

In the brown waters of a Scottish loch the water can be heavily stained with plant

breakdown products and the wavelength of maximum transmission is further shifted towards the red end of the spectrum. Once again this greatly reduces the range at which any fly can be seen. I was told recently by someone who had been diving in Loch Earn that it is pitch black at fifteen feet. Once again, at depths where light remains, there should be two colours that are most visible in such water. In moderately stained waters the colours likely to be most visible are greens and reds. However, where the water is very brown the situation gets a little more complicated. The heavy staining shifts the wavelength of maximum transmission so far to the right that now, one of the well-transmitted colours – it would be what is known as far red – is outside the range of wavelengths that the trout's eye can see. Consequently, in very brown water there is only one colour that will show up well to a trout and that would be green.

How can we summarise these facts and use them to best advantage? First of all, don't forget that the colour of the natural insect will change with depth because the quality of the illuminating light also changes with depth. If we want our artificial fly to look exactly like the natural at any depth or water condition, then we should use patterns that mimic the colours of the natural as closely as possible. As the artificial fly sinks in the water its apparent colour will change in the same way as that of the natural. However, if we do exactly mimic the natural colours we may sacrifice the visibility of the fly to the trout. Perhaps a better approach is to produce a caricature of the natural pattern that includes non-natural but highly visible colours. We can achieve this by substituting appropriately coloured tags, wings or thoraxes. The effect can be accentuated further by using fluorescent materials. Certain patterns include mixtures of colours each of which is most visible in a different colour of water. Gaudy salmon flies with mixtures of yellow, red and green are a good example and their success may in part be due to their visibility in a variety of circumstances. Finally we should never forget that black and white always show up well. Black is particularly visible against a bright background, white shows up well against a dark background and so a good combination of highly visible flies could always include a black top dropper and white fly on the point to fish the deeper water.

UNDERWATER LIGHT, COLOUR VISION AND FLUORESCENT MATERIALS

If we wish to evaluate when or whether fluorescent fly-dressing materials are effective underwater, then we have to take the bull by the horns and face up to the difficulties involved. Until I looked at this matter seriously I was uncertain myself about the advantages of fluorescent materials. I have been using fluorescent dressings in lures and in such successful patterns as the hot spot Pheasant Tail. Even so, I did not really know whether or not fluorescent materials were better than ordinary ones. Having studied underwater light and made measurements of the way light is attenuated as it goes deeper in the water you would think that I should know all the answers. It occurred to me that if I was unsure, then there must be a lot of anglers with the same uncertainty.

Discussions at my local fly fishers' club raised curious and often contradictory opinions. Some claimed that fluorescent reds were particularly good in the evening because there is a lot of ultraviolet light about, while others stated that fluorescent materials were no good because ultraviolet light does not penetrate more than a few centimetres into the water. I want to try and set the record straight here and show that there are good reasons for the sensible use of fluorescents. To do that the nature of colour, fluorescence itself, has to be examined and the way that light quality changes with depth and water colour. We also have to consider the trout's ability to distinguish colours.

Firstly, let us consider what it is that makes things coloured. Light comes in units called photons. Whereas white substances reflect photons of all visible wavelengths, coloured ones absorb at some visible wavelengths and reflect at others. For example, a yellow material absorbs violet, blue and green wavelengths (400–500nm) but reflects the longer yellow, orange and red wavelengths (500–700nm). The eye perceives this pattern of reflection as yellow. Similarly, other colours each have characteristic patterns of absorption and reflection. With a non-fluorescent material the absorbed light is degraded within the material in the form of heat energy. It is the reflected light that gives colour.

A fluorescent material also reflects photons of some wavelengths and absorbs others. However, with the absorbed light there is an important difference. Some of it causes the molecules to vibrate. Almost instantaneously the vibrations subside, at the same time emitting photons of a longer wavelength. Because of the chemical structures associated with the phenomenon of fluorescence, it is normally light of short wavelengths, particularly ultraviolet, that is necessary to cause fluorescence. That is what makes fluorescent substances so visible. Not only does the material reflect light in the usual way but also light absorbed at one wavelength can cause the material to emit visible light at longer wavelengths. This fluorescent light is added to the reflected light and leads to the typical glowing coloration.

The dependence of fluorescence on ultraviolet light is a clear disadvantage in conditions where there is little of it around. For example, an ordinary household tungsten filament electric light bulb emits very little ultraviolet and a fluorescent substance dependent on it would not work well under such illumination. By chemical modification of substances that normally fluoresce only in ultraviolet, engineers have been able to produce daylight fluorescent materials that fluoresce not only under ultraviolet but also at longer visible wavelengths. Such daylight fluorescent materials can be found in the catalogues of the suppliers of fly tying materials and they are particularly useful. They include such brand names as DRF and Glo-brite.

These daylight fluorescent materials work better than ordinary unmodified fluorescents that depend solely on ultraviolet. This is because the visible wavelengths, that can initiate their fluorescence penetrate lake water more effectively than the non-visible ultraviolet. In typical lake water, green light penetrates to the greatest depth and the ultraviolet at one end of the spectrum and the infra-red at the other, are both more strongly filtered out.

Although coloured daylight fluorescents can be excited by visible light as well as ultraviolet, that cannot be true of fluorescent white. White, by its very nature, has to reflect all visible wavelengths because if it did not it would be coloured. Since fluorescence is stimulated by absorption of light at wavelengths shorter than those at which reflection occurs we know that it is light outside the visible part of the spectrum that is necessary to cause a white to fluoresce. In other words ultraviolet light is essential for fluorescent white. The question now is at what depth does a significant fraction of the surface ultraviolet remain?

The answer is certainly worth knowing because white is so useful for making flies more visible. That is because white shows up well in all types of illumination. It is extremely useful in lures, and prominent white breather tubes on a standard buzzer pattern have proved their worth time and time again for me. Fluorescent white should be even better but is it? Also, if there is enough ultraviolet light to cause white fluorescence, then we can be sure that coloured daylight fluorescent materials will definitely work because they absorb at wavelengths that penetrate water better than ultraviolet. By considering the fluorescence of white dressings we will obtain the most pessimistic assessment of the advantages of fluorescents.

A truly white substance reflects all the light that falls upon it. In practice, because of impurities, even white substances absorb some light. Detergent manufacturers realised that you could more than compensate for the slight yellowness of white materials by adding optical brighteners that work by fluorescence. They absorb ultraviolet and re-emit blue visible light. After your shirt has been washed in the appropriate detergent it will, as the advert says, 'look whiter than white' because the total amount of light coming off the surface of the material exceeds the amount that would be reflected off an ordinary perfectly reflecting white material. With a fluorescent white material, not only does the eye see the reflected light, but non-visible wavelengths absorbed in the ultraviolet are re-emitted and added to the reflected light.

All this is fine when we are considering objects in air but what happens in water? There is one piece of evidence above all others that would convince me that a white fluorescent material dependent on short wavelength light would work under water and that is biological evidence that aquatic organisms are able to detect and make use of ultraviolet light. If they can, then there must be enough ultraviolet and short wavelength visible light to make a fluorescent white brighter than an ordinary white.

The answer to the question of whether aquatic animals can see ultraviolet light comes in two halves and surprisingly relates to the biology of the trout. It also involves important new information on colour vision in trout. First, the good news. Yearling brown trout have four types of cone cell in the retina and one of them has its maximum sensitivity in the ultraviolet part of the spectrum. This was demonstrated in 1987 by Dr J. Bowmaker of London University who together with a Dr Kunz made careful measurements of the light-absorbing properties of the four cone cell types. They also showed for the first time that the other three cone cell types were each sensitive to a different part of the spectrum and that there were blue-sensitive, green-sensitive and red-sensitive cones. In other words, if there was any doubt before, we now have conclusive evidence that trout have the machinery for colour vision and that young trout can see ultraviolet light. But now for the bad news. By the time a trout is two years old all the ultraviolet sensitive cones have disappeared from the retina.

How does this fit into our story and the question of the visibility of those fluorescent materials that depend on ultraviolet light? The first thing to be said is that as yet we do not know why young trout are sensitive to ultraviolet light. However, trout tend to spawn in the relative shallows of feeder streams and in their early life the young fish are likely to be found in water no more than a few feet deep. They are also predominantly surface feeders and are found in fast flowing water that is often relatively clear. We may conclude from this biological evidence that in clear waters

significant amounts of ultraviolet are likely to penetrate to the depths at which the fish are found. If that is so, fluorescent materials will also be more visible than non-fluorescent ones in the shallower, fairly clear water. However, in such clear water the need for always using fluorescent materials is not so critical. That is because, here, the abundant visible wavelengths that penetrate even better than ultraviolet, will make ordinary materials quite visible without the added fluorescent light.

The older, more mature trout of a fishable size have lost their ultraviolet receptors and this may be correlated with their known switch in feeding behaviour when they concentrate increasingly on prey items on the bottom. Also it may follow the tendency to inhabit deeper water, where it has always been thought that ultraviolet levels are low. The loss of a whole class of receptors by an animal at an early stage in its life is remarkable if it could still make use of those receptors. Does this mean that we are wasting our time in using fluorescent materials in deeper water? In order to answer that question we have to know how ultraviolet light is attenuated as it passes through the water. We also need to know what are the effects on ultraviolet transmission of algal blooms or the presence of brown peaty substances which are characteristic of the upland lochs. It is in just these conditions that enhanced visibility is so important but does the water coloration render fluorescents ineffective? We also need to ask whether daylight fluorescents compensate when there is a lack of ultraviolet light.

About one thing we can be certain: in pure water, physical measurements, as well as the biological evidence prove that surprisingly large amounts of ultraviolet penetrate the upper layers. In one study of clear sea water, at three feet up to 86 per cent of the surface ultraviolet was still found to be present. Because light levels fall off in a given way with depth, it is easy to calculate how much will remain at any depth. (At six feet 86 per cent of the ultraviolet light found at three feet would be present.) There would be less than one per cent at eighteen feet. The behaviour of ultraviolet in pure freshwater is likely to be similar. In other words clear waters allow fluorescent materials to work fairly well even at considerable depths.

What happens in lake water depends on its turbidity and greenness. Dr J. Calkins, of the University of Kentucky, has made a study of the way in which ultraviolet light penetrates all types of water and he measured the depths at which 37 per cent of the surface ultraviolet light remained. It was shown that in good conditions in Lake Huron, 37 per cent of the surface ultraviolet could penetrate to a depth of two and a half feet. That is quite a lot of ultraviolet and more than adequate to produce very noticeable fluorescence. However, things are rarely likely to be that good and when the water is discoloured the penetration of ultraviolet is fairly drastically reduced. In various other lakes and reservoirs that Calkins tested he found that the depth at which 37 per cent of the surface ultraviolet remained could be anything from two feet in Lake Michigan to about two inches in a very discoloured reservoir. From my rough estimates, in average conditions at Rutland Water, I suspect that about 37 per cent of surface ultraviolet would still be present at eight inches. A further eight inches down the amount of ultraviolet would be reduced to 37 per cent of what is found at eight inches and would be about 14 per cent. At two feet, two and a half feet and three feet, the corresponding percentages of surface ultraviolet would be five, two and less than one per cent respectively. What this means is that white fluorescent materials dependent on absorption of ultra-

violet or coloured fluorescents dependent upon short-wavelength visible light are likely to work well in the top three feet of the lake but below that, they may not be much better than bright non-fluorescent materials. For a fast-retrieved white lure on a floating line, there is a strong case for using fluorescent material because the fly is going to be at a depth where fluorescence will occur.

At depths of ten or thirteen feet, the performance of a material heavily dependent on ultraviolet such as fluorescent white is going to be a lot worse. Certainly for really deep-fished flies, some fluorescents may not be better than non-fluorescent ones. Nevertheless, many of the newer fluorescent materials are very bright in ordinary light even in the absence of ultraviolet. This is mainly because they can fluoresce with short-wavelength visible light. These are the daylight fluorescents and they work much better in green water than I ever suspected. The longer the wavelength at which the material emits fluorescent light, the easier it should be for the chemical engineer to arrange for the substance to absorb significant amounts of visible light. The oranges and reds are at the longer wavelengths and some of the materials that fluoresce in this part of the spectrum can be excited by blue and even green. Visible light as well as blue and green light penetrates better than ultraviolet so the enhanced visibility of orange and red fluorescent materials should be appreciable even at several feet in quite heavily stained water. This is good news for the fly-fisherman because if we want to give the trout the maximum chance of seeing the fly, it is the oranges and reds that we need to incorporate into our flies when we fish in green water. To see how good a range of fluorescent and non-fluorescent materials were in predominantly green light and in the total absence of ultraviolet I conducted a simple experiment. I took them into my dark-room and photographed them with an electronic flash and colour film. Then, instead of the electronic flash, I illuminated them with green light and took the photographs again (see colour section photos 13 and 14). Whereas the non-fluorescent materials had lost most or all of their colours, the fluorescent reds and oranges still showed up in their true colours.

These deductions are supported by recommendations on the use of fluorescent materials by sub-aqua divers. In the British Subaqua Club manual for 1972, the visibilities of various fluorescent colours in greenish coastal waters were evaluated. As expected, oranges and reds showed up well in green water, fluorescent orange was found to be good for horizontal fields of sight in shallow dirty water at ranges of five feet. Fluorescent yellow and ordinary yellow did not show up well. This is because yellow in general does not show up well in green water.

It is easy to repeat my experiment. Find a dark-room, get some transparent green plastic film or perspex and use it as a filter on a hand torch. A rough but less troublesome guide to how well a material will show up in the absence of ultraviolet is to look at it illuminated with an ordinary light bulb. You will be surprised how bright they are even under these circumstances. What we want to know is not whether a material is fluorescent or not but how bright it is in fishing conditions. Illuminating without ultraviolet may be the best method for assessing the likely brightness of colours under water where the ultraviolet and short-wavelength visible light is strongly attenuated and the material is absorbing visible wavelengths anyway. Of course, to establish whether or not a material is fluorescent you need to illuminate it with a small ultraviolet lamp. Then it will really glow. But don't forget that this only

tells you if the material is fluorescent or not. It does not tell you how bright it will be at depth in water. We should also remember that the maximum attainable brightness under natural conditions would be in direct sunlight above the water surface. So also take the material outside on a sunny day to make some sort of assessment. Then remember that under water it will look quite a bit duller.

So we know that it is mainly ultraviolet and short-wavelength light that makes things fluoresce. However, with daylight fluorescents even green light can be effective. In heavily stained waters of upland lochs the water is at times literally brown. At any appreciable depth in such water, virtually only the longer wavelength red light is left and the wavelengths useful to fluorescence, including green, have been almost completely filtered out. For that reason you will find that fluorescent materials do not work so well. There is evidence from divers that this is so. Once again, the British Subaqua Club *Diving Manual* tells us that 'in all except peaty water fluorescent oranges and reds show up with great brilliance at close range'. Nevertheless, it is in these brown water conditions where the sighting range is so poor that visibility is even more important. Even if the fluorescent material works at only a fraction of its maximum possible performance it will still be brighter than if it were not fluorescent. So, for green or brown coloured water, if I had a choice of fluorescent versus non-fluorescent, I would always choose the former because it certainly can't be less visible than the alternative and near to the surface it certainly will be more visible, however bad the water colour. In green water, I hope that I have demonstrated the value of fluorescent reds and oranges over conventional non-fluorescent materials. Even in trying peaty conditions, fluorescents should not necessarily be discarded; the effects may be marginal but it is these marginal effects that can make the difference between fish in the basket and a blank!

My thoughts would have ended here but then Bob Church told me that he had some fluorescent materials that literally glow in the dark. I was somewhat sceptical until I received a little parcel in the post. In my dark-room I was absolutely astounded by the light they emitted (*see* colour section photo 15). These materials are what is known as phosphorescent and they just have to be useful. They require a momentary exposure to light and then glow for many minutes afterwards. To see the glow to its full effect you need to go into a darkened room but even in a dark corner the ghostly glow is easily visible.

With an ordinary fluorescent material, the effect requires continuous illumination by light while with the phosphorescent materials, the enhanced visibility persists long after the activating light has been excluded. Somehow, the activating light energy is captured by the material and it is released in the form of light over a very long period. When I photographed these substances in the dark they glowed well for five or six minutes and although the effect had worn off considerably, they were still visible after twenty minutes. They come in a variety of colours and materials including Mylar tubing, Flashabou, and Phosphorescent Luminous Twinkle. The luminosity, however, lasts better in some colours than others. I found that the cream showed up for the longest followed by the green, yellow, orange and pink. The luminous orange in green water has got to be worth trying and when fishing really deep these materials will show up very well.

Coming back to conventional fluorescents, I must dispose of the question of what times of day or year are most favourable for the use of fluorescents. With whites that are strongly dependent on ultraviolet time of day does matter. It all depends on how high the sun is in the sky. Ultraviolet and short-wavelength light is filtered out by the atmosphere. When the sun is low in the sky the sun's rays pass obliquely through it. Consequently, more of the ultraviolet is lost before it reaches the earth's surface and the light becomes redder. In fact, for a given intensity of light there can be three times as much ultraviolet at midday compared with that at dawn and dusk. So, on a hot sunny afternoon in summer a fluorescent white is going to work at its best. However, even on a sunny day in summer, the depth at which it will work will be limited by the attentuation of ultraviolet. If the water is green take advantage of daylight fluorescent technology and stick on an orange fluorescent fly which will retain its visibility at a much greater depth than the white because it can be activated by green light.

Arguments about the sun's elevation also apply to the seasons. In spring and autumn the sun never gets high in the sky and the performance of fluorescent white will not be so good, but the daylight fluorescents should still operate much better than non-fluorescent materials. Now I'm off to tie up some more of my favourite patterns with the liberal use of fluorescent materials. I don't expect them to work miracles but common sense, scientific logic and the proven experience of many fly fishermen shows that I will not be wasting my time.

3 Techniques

As Alan Pearson knows the small fishery big trout scene so very well and has achieved much success while fishing these waters, I have asked him to cover this specialised chapter. Alan's knowledge has come through fishing at the major small fisheries as often as he can. On the way, he broke the rainbow record twice, now beaten. He still holds the brook trout record.

CATCHING BIG TROUT IN CLEAR STILLWATERS

It has long been accepted that in clearwater streams and rivers that are famous in trout fishing annals, the angler capable of using his eyes can frequently take above-average catches of trout, simply because he can visually locate his quarry and thus avoid wasting his time casting over fishless areas. This is not particularly difficult because of the relative shallowness of most such streams and the lightness of the gravel or sandy beds which are prevalent.

Generally speaking, the same principle had not been applied to stillwater trout fisheries, no matter how clear their waters may have been, and it is worthwhile considering why this should have been the case. Originally, most stillwater trouting in the UK was undertaken in the large natural lakes, often from boats, and the technique usually followed was a variation on a sea trout fishing technique; that of shortlining a team of wet flies from a drifting boat, usually fishing blind but whenever possible casting over rising fish. In a sense this was visual location, but it was the rise that was looked for, not the fish itself.

In the late 1960s, with the opening of Grafham Water offering a new concept of trout fishing at low cost for everyman, totally new styles of fly fishing began to be devised, and it was fortunate that modern technological advances made it possible for rods and lines to be produced that would permit these styles to be developed. Rods constructed from tapering tubes of glass fibre, then carbon fibre reinforced plastic allied with the new accurately weighted plastic-coated fly lines, encouraged the development of long casting techniques. Indeed, with anglers wading out as far as possible, packing in as closely together as possible, it was essential to be able to cast far out to where the trout had retreated from the mass invasion of their element.

Of course, casting a fly in the general direction of rising trout was still a practice followed by some, although it was probable that the majority of anglers fished sinking lines no matter what was happening at the surface. Indeed, it was the view of one well-known reservoir expert that dry fly fishing was a total waste of time, since more trout could be caught by stripping a lure back on a sinking line. Thus the practice of fishing blind in stillwaters had an honourable ancestry, caught trout in sufficient quantities, and is therefore practised by a considerable majority of the one million plus trout anglers plying their skills today

After Grafham, more drinking-water reservoirs were stocked with trout up and down the country, and still these proved inadequate to meet the ever-increasing demand for water space. The situation was ripe for the development of smaller stillwater fisheries, privately owned as opposed to water authority controlled, needing to charge more for fishing in order to achieve an essential profit level, and thus needing to offer some extra inducements; either more trout to the acre, or a larger average size overall. It was size that proved the main attraction.

Opinions differ as to where the big trout craze originated, but in my view it was Packington that started the ball rolling – perhaps not too successfully, but successfully enough to make an impact on fishery management thinking. Alex Behrendt's Two Lakes fishery achieved publicity for catches of very big trout, and the delightful Damerham lakes seemed to be very well stocked with plenty of fine trout in the five

pounds plus bracket. Not huge by today's standards, but comparable with the first season or so at Grafham. Damerham apart, most of the fisheries that offered big trout seemed not to bother too much about quality, and no real big trout cult developed, mainly because the heavyweights that were caught were rather tatty broodstock that had outlived their usefulness on the trout farm and were nearing the end of their life cycle. All too often they were soft, floppy creatures, dark in coloration and fairly deficient in fins and tails. Still, some of them fought well enough, although generally failing to punch their weight, and many of them proved surprisingly palatable after they had paid a visit to the salmon smoker.

Then Dr Sam Holland took a hand in the game. Everyone knows the Avington story well enough, so rather than repeat in great detail the oft-told tale, leave it that a system of selective breeding of rainbow trout was set into operation which eventually resulted in fish attaining double figures in weight by their third year of life, and not by over-feeding, or force feeding, as ill-informed but very vocal opinion would have it. No one has ever satisfactorily explained how one force feeds a trout, or how one can overfeed it without causing early death, but bigots have never needed facts to reinforce their extravagantly denigratory denunciations.

Rejections from Sam Holland's breeding programme – trout which failed to grow fast enough to satisfy his exacting standards, or which lacked the perfection of shape and colour – began to be stocked into the three Avington lakes, and to attract the attention of both the angler and the angling press. In due course the size and quality of the stock improved to an extraordinary degree and no other fishery has ever produced so many large trout of such superb quality.

History tells us that Sam Holland produced the very exciting hybrid between the rainbow and the American brook trout successfully, something that no one else has ever achieved, at least in terms of producing specimens of more than eleven pounds in weight. He also managed to surpass previous growth rates achieved in the UK for the notoriously difficult American brook trout, but declared that he found it virtually impossible to improve growth rates for brown trout, although fishery records reveal that a good number over 10 lbs have been caught over the years.

Now, it is quite pointless to produce super-large, high quality rainbow trout, or indeed any sort of trout, unless they can be caught with sufficient regularity to gain publicity for the fishery, and logically for the farming operation also, because as Sam always said the fishery was the shop window for his trout farm. The trouble was that not enough of the big trout were being put on the bank. Some were hooked and lost, rather more than were actually put on the bank, and it seemed that most of these losses were due to anglers being taken totally by surprise when they connected with an unseen monster, and to their using tackle inadequate for the specific purpose. Problems existed to which answers needed to be found if big trout were to be caught on purpose, rather than by a set of fortuitous circumstances – luck, if you like. Being rather obsessive about catching such fish, I began to visit the fishery as often as possible, and in the early 1970s I began to fish there at least once each week of the season, sometimes twice, and occasionally three or more times. In the mid-1970s I actually entered the field of trout farming myself, basing my operation on Avington stock, and the joint facility of spending so much time watching trout either in their natural environment or in the rearing ponds gave me an unrivalled opportunity

to learn about the ways of rainbows and American brook trout; about their fads and general idiosyncracies. And, far from the least of my benefits was my long-standing friendship with the late, great Richard Walker – possibly the best fly fisherman I have ever known – and who was as interested in the great trout as myself.

Eventually I developed a tactical approach which permitted me to catch a very large number of double figure rainbows and brown trout, plus a dozen or more record-breaking American brook trout from clear stillwaters. Then by some not very complicated variations on the basic theme I was able to adapt to taking good trout from waters which were far from being as translucent as Avington. So, on the one hand there is the so-called Avington style for use in any clear stillwater, of which there are many, and on the other hand there is the adaptation of the Avington style for waters as coloured as, for example, Leominstead.

Clear Water Tactics

The best of the clear stillwater trout fisheries possess water which would make the average product from a household tap look turbid. In spite of this, ripples on the surface, reflected light or the sun's rays striking at an odd angle can make it very difficult to see beneath the surface with the naked eye. The use of polarised spectacles reduces these problems to a manageable level, and it is amazing how a decent pair of Polaroids can suddenly open the deep water of a lake to the eye. For the angler obliged to wear spectacles all the time, clip-on Polaroids are readily available and very effective. For people such as myself who need spectacles solely for reading – or for tying flies to the end of a leader – there are special polarised glasses available with small inset lenses, creating in effect a type

Alan Pearson landing a sizeable rainbow trout at Dever Springs, in Hampshire.

of bifocal lens. My favourites are the Cheetah glasses which are available in either amber or grey coloration and with inset lenses of either 1½x or 3x magnification. I believe, for those with more complex eyesight deficiencies, the insets can be to prescription, at extra cost naturally.

Assuming that one now has the facility to look beneath the water's surface, it ought to be a simple matter to locate trout, and indeed, it usually is, provided that there are trout to be seen. However, many people find it difficult to interpret what their eyes tell them, because their brain sometimes refuses to acknowledge the evidence of the eyes. This might sound peculiar, but how else does one explain the fact that although I have been able to show other people things like weed, or sticks on the bottom at depths in excess of ten feet, and they have described them to me in sufficient detail that I know they have good sub-surface vision, yet they have totally failed even to notice a big trout cruising along no more than two feet deep, no matter how many times I have pointed it out? If you can see a forked stick on the bottom in ten or more feet of water, then how can you not see a trout of about thirty inches in length, no more than two feet below the surface? I suspect that the sub-conscious brain says that trout are a foot long, therefore that big thing isn't a trout at all, it's just a shadow! Believe me, eyes are funny things, and they sometimes decide not to recognise objects that are clearly visible. How many times have you been doing DIY jobs, put a screwdriver down and then not been able to find it again, although it is there staring you in the face all the time?

Anyway, it sounds easy enough, doesn't it? All you have to do is put your Polaroids on, look into the water and spot your fish. Well, with practice you'll manage it easily enough, but then what do you do? It is not enough just to locate the trout, you also have to determine how deep it is in the water, and estimate the size. The deeper it is, the smaller it will look, and in real terms the trout you imagine is swimming six feet deep and weighing around four pounds might well be twelve feet deep and more like ten pounds in weight. This facility,

The finished product of rainbows and browns – superb fish.

Four double-figure fish up to 18lb caught from Avington.

determining size in relation to swimming depth has been termed 'depth perception' and is very important. Some anglers pick up the art immediately, but others require a great deal of practice. One very good angler, whose name I shall not reveal to spare his blushes, took three seasons to get it right and did not catch too many whoppers over that period. When he did get it right, he started catching very well indeed and has never looked back.

I am convinced that practice in viewing the sub-surface scene is essential, and the more practice you get, the better will be your proficiency. My recommendation is that you select a clearwater fishery known to hold big trout. Visit it as frequently as possible, but give up all ideas of casting at random or standing in just one place. Go kitted out as lightly as possible. One rod is enough, plus a landing net and maybe a

bass bag. You can get your priest, all the flies and leaders you need, plus other minor bits and pieces into your pockets without any difficulty. Tackle bags are an unnecessary hindrance and should be left in your car boot.

When you reach the water, move very slowly round the banks and be careful to give other anglers a wide berth. Keep peering into the water, and to familiarise your eyes with the underwater scene, study the lake bed to see what it consists of, and how deep you believe the water to be. Look at the submerged aquatic plants, look at anything that catches your eye, and every now and again, slip your spectacles off just so that you can check how much better you see with them on. If there's no difference, then either you have magic eyesight, or the specs are no good! What you are trying to do is learn something

John Pawson with a brace of triploid rainbows, 10¼lb and 8¾lb, from Aveley Lake, Essex.

about the water, about its varying depths and its weed beds and, in due course, about its trout population, their mix of sizes, their preferred lies, and their food pre-occupations, if any. Catching fish at this stage is relatively unimportant when compared with getting to know the underwater scene.

This is a learning process, and most people find that after some practice, they begin to learn quite quickly to the extent that they can avoid stops and starts, and just stroll casually along scanning the water as they go, and identifying the familiar landmarks of gravel areas, weed beds, sudden deep holes and shelves, the movement of shrimps and nymphs and minnows. They spot their trout too, especially the ones that are moving at mid-water or less, and they begin to realise that there are certain areas where trout are almost always to be found for some reason that may relate

to a current flow, or high density of life forms that provide the major part of their diet. They will also see trout swimming through areas at high speed, and this is often related either to it having just been spooked by another angler, or possibly that it is a newly stocked fish. New introductions often swim round a fishery at very high speed for anything up to two or three days, and I have tended to put this down to a need to explore, to define the boundaries of their new environment before settling to a specific territory. Nevertheless, it has to be said that not all fish do this. Some settle in very quickly without making the high-speed tour. What is important is that a trout which is covering good distances at high speed should be regarded as not worth bothering about, no matter how big it might be, because it is virtually uncatchable.

As experience is gained, situations will

arise when in an apparently fishless stretch of water some little oddity will jar the consciousness and make the angler look again. Something, not obviously a fish, has caused a mental alarm bell to ring and protracted, careful study may succeed in identifying just what that oddity was. It is, for example, perfectly possible to overlook a motionless trout where dappled light combined with a dappled lake bed creates a camouflage effect, yet the shadow of that trout may show clearly enough on the lake bed, giving the game away. An overhanging frond of weed may conceal the trout completely, except for a quivering pectoral fin, or a glimpse of a tail. A shadow, or just a glimpse of fin or tail is all that there will be to advise of the presence of a trout, and yet this is more than enough for the experienced eye.

So the most important tactical approach is visual. Use your eyes to find your fish, and the better you know your fishery, the easier it will become. Use the best Polaroids you can afford, and use a hat with a decently wide brim to exclude extraneous light. Dress drably so that you are not conspicuous on the bank and always move slowly and as quietly as possible.

The Killing Patterns

Having learned how to locate trout, and having practised your depth perception so that you are pretty certain when you see a trout that you know roughly how big it is, and how deep in the water it is, you then have to consider how best to induce it to take your fly. If it is only a foot or so beneath the surface, then your problems are slight, especially if it is taking a fly from the top. In theory, all you have to do is cast out a similar pattern of artificial ahead of the trout after drawing the necessary conclusions about probable route and cruising speed; wait for the fly to vanish into the

greedy jaws, and strike firmly. Alternatively, the preferred article of diet may be a nymph just sub-surface and here there is a wide variety of alternatives, the chironomid pupa, sedge pupa, damselfly nymph, mayfly nymph, one or other of the pond or lake olive nymphs, and so on. If you have been using your eyes correctly on your walk about you should have a pretty shrewd idea what it is that is proving attractive.

That is the easy option of your stalking procedures. Unfortunately, in nearly twenty years of stalking and catching really big trout, I have found that only a very small percentage feed in this way, and by far the majority have been feeding at depths from six feet down to about twenty-five feet. So how do you get your artificial down to those depths quickly enough so that the trout has not passed on long before it attains them?

Let me say that I do not like sinking lines or sinktip lines for this sort of work, not least because the line sinks a lot faster than the fly. I use floating lines always, and leaders from three to five yards in length. Obviously the weight has to be carried within the artificial, as part of the dressing. I have used many different techniques to weight flies – and perhaps it would be as well if I was specific about patterns. I am not convinced that lures are particularly effective for Avington-style fishing, and there is also a ban at Avington, and a good many other fisheries too, on the use of patterns of more than one inch in length including the tail.

The most generally successful patterns for big trout are nymphs and bugs, which may be tied as big as size 8 long shank without breaking the one inch ruling. Walker's Mayfly Nymph, Church's Westward Bug, Cronin's Rusty Nymph, and my own patterns of Green Beast and Wonderbug should all be tied to this standard, although it is quite feasible to reduce the Wonderbugs to size 10 without lessening their powers of attraction. In the early days we used the lead foil from wine bottles to weight these patterns. Seven strips attached to the back of the hook shank, one atop another, produced a very heavy fast-sinking pattern. We also tied them up with five strips and three strips, to give slower sinking speeds, and unweighted patterns were kept for the trout feeding near the surface. Applying the lead to the top of the shank meant that the nymph worked upside-down in the water; a useful attribute when working across the bottom.

Since those early days, my views have changed slightly, and I am now perfectly happy to weight some patterns with turns of lead wire under the thorax. It is quicker and simpler to tie flies in this way and besides, too many wine producers are now using plastic foil around the top of the bottle and it thus becomes increasingly difficult to obtain free supplies of lead foil.

When split shot was legal and freely available, a neat leaded nymph could be made by squeezing a suitably sized shot just behind the eye of the hook, having first smeared the split with strong waterproof adhesive, and then securing it in place with figure of eight turns of tying silk. The main body of the nymph was then tied behind the shot which then acted as the head and was painted with big bi-colour eyes. Two excellent basic patterns were Rose Jarmal's Flea Nibbler and another which I know as the Yellowhead which seemed to be a particular favourite at Damerham.

However, even these simple patterns seem complicated when compared with the Cucro and Cocro nymphs. The Cucro is made from fine copper wire wound into a cigar shape on size 10 or 12 standard shank hooks and finished with a single turn of signal green floss caught in by the wire as a thorax. The Cocro is tied to the same sizes,

and consists of a slim lead wire body with thorax and tail of signal green floss. It helps durability if the wire is well varnished after tying is completed. As an occasional colour variant, the Cucro may be tied with an arc chrome floss thorax, and can prove effective, but trout seem actively to dislike the Cocro with orange trimmings. I have no idea why this should be so.

The range of flies I am recommending does not seem large, but in my opinion if a trout will not take one of these patterns, then it is an untakeable fish – at that time. That is not to say that it will be untakeable in an hour or a day or so later. However, if I had to recommend other patterns, then on waters where there is no size discrimination against artificials, I would feel obliged to include Trevor Housby's Dog Nobbler and my own Capper. Everyone knows the Dog Nobbler by now, and I have found it quite lethal when cast to observed trout and worked slowly in sink and draw fashion to maximise the seductive tail wiggle.

The Capper is no longer available unfortunately, because it is a pattern not beloved by the commercial fly dressers. Frankly it is just too complex, long-winded and expensive to tie, which is a great pity, but I can see no way to simplify it. It is tied on a Partridge Draper nymph hook, which is a split shank pattern. Lead is applied to the shank as an underbody, over which is tied the floss silk body. Three pairs of marabou wings are tied in at the sides, projecting outwards, and a marabou plume tail finishes it off. Dry, it looks like a clumsy feather duster that has had an unfortunate encounter with a steamroller, but once submerged and fished in a series of short jerky twitches, it pulsates like some extraordinary life form from another planet. God knows what trout take it for, but take it they do! I encountered Brian Leadbetter at Church Hill Farm fishery one day in a state of some distress because he'd left most

The leaded nymph's passage through the water layers to the cruising depth of the observed trout.

of his flies at home. I gave him a couple of Cappers and advised that he start with a white one. He had to take it off after an hour because he was emptying the fishery of trout! In the afternoon, he tried the black one, and the slaughter was even greater.

Putting the Fly to the Fish

I would have to advise that there should always be a leaded pattern tied ready on your leader before you even start your walkabout in search of a big trout, and since it is obviously impossible to forecast how deep any trout you may see will be swimming, I strongly recommend that you use a heavily weighted pattern. After all, this does mean that you will be able to induce sinking to pretty well any depth you want at reasonable speed. If the fly sinks too deep, you merely twitch it back up again, or move it across in front of the trout fast enough to negate the force of

gravity. Should you start off with an un-weighted, or lightly weighted pattern you may have the frustration of watching the trout cruise off long before your nymph has got anywhere near deep enough.

Having spotted your trout and noted its depth and the direction in which it is moving, you now have to cast out far enough ahead of it so that nymph and trout arrive at approximately the same place at the same time. This is not quite as easy as it sounds because there are a number of factors involved, all of which must be given their full importance. Trout depth and swimming speed, nymph sinking rate, plus exact pinpoint accuracy in casting are all factors to be computed. If you have done your homework properly, you should have a very good idea of the sinking rate of your nymph, but the other factors will have to be guessed. It gets easier with practice I can assure you, but none of us gets it right all of the time. The main factor working to our advantage is the arrogant nature of the big rainbow, who frequently seems to believe that he is invulnerable, and takes not too much notice of something jigging about unless it is lying directly in his chosen path. This does mean that you can often enjoy more than one chance to induce a take, and this can be very useful, because if you get the positioning wrong the first time it is usually because you've got either depth or speed wrong, and you can correct these errors. Actually, if you cast too far ahead of the trout, this can sometimes be an advantage. You let the nymph sink deeper, and as the trout approaches, you lift the rod tip and cause the nymph to pop up in front of it, in the classic induced take manoeuvre. Indeed, it is surprising how often a trout will take a nymph worked in this way, when it has previously refused more traditionally-presented offerings.

Big brown trout are quite different in that you tend to get one chance and no more. Also, they are often willing to chase a nymph rather further than will a rainbow. American brook trout are different again. The positioning of their eyes suggests that they have excellent forward vision, rather like a pike, and they seem to prefer an offering presented a yard – even a couple of yards – ahead of them, and will rarely take the 'on the nose' presentation that rainbows require.

Handling the Hooked Trout

Playing the trout does very definitely depend upon the tackle that you are using. When I started playing the big trout game, none of us knew the correct flies, let alone the correct tackle for the job. Avington water is brilliantly clear, so a fine leader seemed essential. Fine leader plus big trout indicated a very soft-action rod and un-

qualified patience. So I used to set my stall out for the big trout using relatively small patterns, two- or three-pound breaking-strain leaders, and short, soft actioned glass-fibre rods with a rating of about AFTM 5 or 6. Having spent as long as an hour over trout of no more than thirteen pounds or so, I began to feel that I had got it wrong. I was not playing the fish, they were playing me. The longer the scrap went on, the more chance there was of hookhold failure or leader breakage, let alone angler fatigue-induced error.

With the larger patterns of nymphs that we were developing, it was clear that heavier leaders were essential, and it was soon discovered that since trout can see very easily even the finest of leaders, we could afford to step up the power. Six- or eight-pound breaking strain seemed appropriate and did not reduce catch rate, but grossly overpowered the soft rods. The development of carbon-fibre rods coincided with the first of a series of changes to tackle and stepping up to AFTM ratings of 7, 8 and even 9 certainly reduced the time spent in getting a big, powerful fish under control. On the other hand, short, poker-stiff rods are not very efficient for short accurate casting, so length became the next concern. Finally I became completely satisfied with the development of a 10ft 6in blue boron rod rated for AFTM 6–9 lines. This casts very accurately at close range, and has the length and power to effectively subdue a big trout very speedily, whilst still retaining sufficient subtlety of action to permit stepping down to three pound leaders in difficult conditions, or where tiny flies are required. I have to accept that there will always be a degree of personal preference in tackle selection, and what suits one angler may well not suit another, but I am greatly encouraged by the undoubted popularity of the long boron rod among the more accomplished seekers of big trout.

So, let's assume that the tackle is sound, correctly balanced, and adequate for the job in hand. As a test of adequacy, stick the point of your fly in a convenient tree stump, strip off about fifteen to twenty yards of line and walk backwards to tighten it. Lift the rod and apply pressure, as if you were playing a fish. Keep on piling on the pressure until the leader breaks. That means the leader is too light for you to apply maximum pressure. You may find that acceptable in view of specific conditions, but if possible you should step up leader strength by, say, two pounds, and repeat the process. You are seeking a balance of rod and leader that will enable you to exert maximum force on a hooked fish. It may sound brutal, but if you wish to avoid breakages in action, this is how you should gear your tackle up to the task. You are seeking the lowest breaking-strain leader that will enable such pressure to be applied to anything you catch.

Sometimes you can cast to an observed big trout and before it has a chance to express any interest, an impertinent and invariably smaller one of its brethren will nip in and seize the tantalising morsel for itself. Using your correctly balanced tackle you should be able to set the hook and haul the offending intruder out of the way in no time at all. I've been timed at fifteen seconds to land one of these pests which weighed some two and a half pounds, and I am surprised only that it took so long. Still, I seem to remember that the time quoted included the use of the priest and extraction of the fly as well. And the big trout was not at all disturbed, merely mildly curious at the eccentric behaviour of this wayward child, and perfectly willing to accept my offering at the very next cast. My diary states that it weighed 17¼ pounds and took ten minutes to land.

The secret of playing big trout is quite simply this. You have to gain mastery from the outset, show the iron hand in the iron glove. If the trout wants to make a run, apply all the pressure you dare, with judicial use of side-strain, and stop it in its tracks. Even better, use the length of the rod to turn it in the direction you want it to take. If it tries to dive deep, just hang on for dear life and let the rod overpower it. Whatever it wishes to do, oppose it, and never give an inch more line than absolutely necessary. Never relax the pressure, not even for an instant, and if your arm starts to give out, as mine has, on occasion, then clamp the line firm and change hands, or even use both hands.

Brutal and ugly if you like, but I will let you into a secret. Too many big trout are lost because the anglers who have hooked them are scared stiff to take the fight to the trout. They apply a little artistic and gentle pressure, give line at the slightest excuse and seem perfectly content to let the trout conduct the battle from its own territory, which may be fifty or sixty yards or more away. They wait patiently for the trout to tire, not even realising that it has been buried in a weed bed for ten minutes and is in the process of transferring the hook to a thick stem. The longer the fight, the greater the certainty of disaster. And what happens if from fifty yards away the trout heads back towards the angler at some thirty miles an hour? No one can possibly strip line at that rate, so touch is lost. Slack lines often mean lost fish, but just suppose the hook stays put and the trout heads away again at the same speed. You can do a nice little sum involving mass, inertia and all manner of mathematical complexities which will only tell you what any reasonable person already knows. Something has got to give! It may be the hook-hold, or the hook, or the leader, even the rod, but there is going to be a breakage of some sort, and the trout will not be landed. Unfortunately, in many cases it will not survive the encounter.

Rainbow trout possess an extraordinary characteristic. Put them under extreme pressure and stress and they will begin to bleed from the gills. This does happen with some frequency when they are being played, and is the cause of a tough scrap often coming to a rather abrupt end. Anglers are frequently unaware of the fact because blood is washed away in the water, and the first visible sign is the appearance of massive bleeding from the gills after the priest has been used. In fact, this is often blood that has been swallowed earlier, and is regurgitated in the death spasm.

So, needing to take every advantage open to me against a tough and wily opponent, I use the high pressure fight knowingly to induce this blowing of the gills. Surprisingly often, after a very tough scrap, the trout kicks for the last time as I lift it in the net, after which it does not need the use of a priest to kill it. It is already dead.

Brown trout do not possess this characteristic or at least, if they do, I have never encountered it either on the trout farm or any fishery. Nevertheless, I do try to keep the pressure on if I possibly can, but I am obliged to say that it is not always possible. Whereas a hooked rainbow will normally spend a second or two in apparent amazement that anyone has been impertinent enough to hook it, giving adequate time for the angler to get his act into gear, the brownie seems to react by making an instantaneous dash for the fire exit. Big brownies have done this to me on numerous occasions and although there is always the expectation that it is going to happen and therefore one should be prepared, unfortunately they get away with it far too often. By the time brakes have been gently applied, because sharp braking would cause breaking, the wily old brownie is usually a very long way off. There they usually cock a snook by jumping in the air,

shaking their heads, and snorting in derision as the hook falls out. On the other hand, on the few times that I have been fast enough to stop that initial instinctive run before it has truly got under way, I have not been over-excited by the rest of the fight. It is almost as if the trout sulks and refuses to play because of the thwarting of that initial ploy.

American brook trout are different yet again. I have caught some, and big ones too, that have put up as much fight as an old sock with a hole in it. Others have scrapped like demons, out-fighting rainbows or browns of more than twice their weight. Throw a fly anywhere near a small one and it will rush to its doom. Bigger ones can be as difficult and as picky as elderly spinster female relatives, unless you know how to get round them. Let me say that I am much better with brook trout than with female relatives!

First of all, you have to recognise the fact that brook trout seem to spend a large proportion of their lives in meditation. There they hang, perhaps no more than a foot below the surface, motionless and with their minds fixed upon some fishy nirvana. You could hit them with a stone and they would not notice. Then they return slowly to the real world. Their pectoral fins begin to quiver, their tails switch, and often they sink a foot or two deeper in the water. Then they are on the move, making short dashes, terrorising minnows, and generally behaving like the school bully.

I remember fishing at Avington one day with a group of friends. I wandered down to the bottom lake where I hoped to renew acquaintance with a big Cheetah trout that had bitten through my leader the week before. I found him, but he was disenchanted with my offerings, and by lunchtime I gave him up as a total waste of time. Hardly anybody would come to the pub for lunch, claiming to be too engrossed in the fishing, and I admit to being rather surprised that they had stayed firmly put on the first lake. They were still there busily flogging away when I returned from the pub, so I decided to try the middle lake where I found enough of interest to keep me engrossed until late afternoon, by which time the rest of the gang were straggling into sight looking rather disconsolate. One of them admitted that they'd been trying to catch what appeared to be a monster brook trout, but couldn't even induce it to take. I suspected that it had probably been snoozing for at least half the time they had been trying to catch it, and that the rest of the time they had probably been casting too close to it. My theory about forward vision of this fish, and needing to cast well ahead of it was something that I had been keeping to myself.

I checked my tackle, renewed my leader, put on a medium leaded nymph and wandered on to the first lake, accompanied by one of the gang. It took about five minutes to locate the brookie and he took my breath away. The others were right, he was big. He was also contemplating his navel, and took no notice when I made a couple of speculative casts to get the range right. Then I waited and watched. Only a few minutes passed before I saw the fins quivering, and the gradual sinking to a new position a couple of feet deeper. Then, as he moved slowly forward, I dropped my nymph a little more than two yards ahead of him and slightly beyond his apparent route. The fly sank a foot or so, and I gave it a long pull which was never completed because the brookie shot forward and engulfed the tempting morsel. It was a very good scrap, twelve minutes or so in duration, because I always find it more difficult to gain control when hooking a trout at long range. Still, there were no problems apart from my usual aches and pains, and

when first weighed in he scaled an exact six pounds. Unfortunately it was a very hot afternoon, and in spite of doing my best to keep it cool, it lost 2½ ounces before the weighing could be witnessed. However, it was very comfortably a new UK record topping my previous best by a fair margin. The others were not pleased with me at all!

There, in essence, you have it. The way to catch big trout consistently from clear water fisheries is first of all to get to know one particular fishery very well indeed, by walking the banks and studying the subsurface environment through Polaroid spectacles. Having taught yourself to locate trout and recognise their size and the depth at which they are feeding, learn to cast leaded nymphs so that as they sink, the fly and the trout's nose reach the same spot at the same time. Remember that this is true only for browns and rainbows; when stalking the American brook trout, the fly needs to be from one to two yards in front of it. Make sure your tackle is balanced adequately to stand up to considerable strain, and forget about gossamer leaders. Use six or eight pounds breaking-strain nylon. Take the fight to the trout, and try to keep on top at all times. Oh, and do take a large landing net, you cannot fold a big trout up to get it in a small net.

CATCHING BIG TROUT IN COLOURED STILLWATERS

There are two main differences in catching trout of large size from coloured stillwaters as opposed to the clearwater fisheries. Firstly, as is patently obvious, trout cannot be visually located in their holding areas where maximum visibility into the water is restricted to a matter of a few inches.

Secondly, the usage of drab flies cannot always be recommended, because of their lack of visibility in coloured water.

It could also be said that if water coloration is due to a suspension of mud or silt, it is pretty well a waste of time fishing for trout anyway, because they will not be in prime condition and the quality and flavour of their flesh is likely to be sadly impaired.

However, there are lakes possessed of water of excellent quality, where the coloration is due to peat stain from the surrounding environment. One of the most famous coloured stillwaters in the south is Leominstead, where a feeder stream brings in peat stain from the surrounding New Forest, and the problem is compounded by a dark bed to the lake and trees growing right down to the water's edge. You stand on one of the numerous casting platforms – the only way fishing is possible without undertaking a massive and unnecessary tree-felling programme – and nowhere can you see more than a few inches below the surface. On the other hand, take a glass and fill it with lake water and you will be amazed at its clarity. Nevertheless, it is clear that light penetration is restricted at best to no more than six feet. Aquatic plants will not grow at depths much in excess of three feet because of the lack of adequate light, and there is considerable evidence to show that the *Daphnia* with which the water is abundantly blessed is mainly restricted to the upper layers of water.

This indicates that it will almost certainly be a waste of time fishing deep with a sinking line, even though the depths fall away to close upon thirty feet. Trout certainly inhabit those depths, but will have become accustomed to the rich feeding of the upper layers of water. On this basis one can assume that floating lines, and slow or medium sinkers, will generally be most effective, and it will be necessary to re-

trieve fairly quickly if one selects a medium sinking line. Since it is usually impossible to stalk an observed trout because of the visibility problems, another approach needs to be developed. This should in part relate to the lessons learned on the small clear stillwaters in relation to preferred lies, where quite often big trout will be discovered holed up close to the banks. At fisheries such as Leominstead with myriad overhanging branches, footpaths not running close to the banks, and the concealment factor of the water colour, it would appear to be obvious that very many trout will take up bank-side residence, particularly when bearing in mind the 'larder factor' of the overhanging bushes, and the concentration of most of the food forms in the shallow water. Let us assume that the stock density per acre is the same for both Avington and Leominstead. At the former, the clarity of the water permits the development of life forms even in the deepest areas, around thirty feet in the old days, so the trout will be spread throughout the whole range of depths.

At Leominstead, the entire feeding stock is likely to be concentrated in the top six feet which puts a much greater demand on territorial space. Big rainbows are every bit as territorial as brown trout, so on the assumption that the biggest trout naturally occupy the best places it becomes advisable to watch for rises, or swirls in particularly promising spots. Sometimes a trout rising in leisurely fashion to a creepy-crawly that has fallen out of a tree, will reveal its size by showing big white lips as the succulent goody is quietly absorbed. At other times, a massive swirl will suggest that a big resident has taken steps to eject an unwelcome intruder. Having established a probable location, the art is then to extract that trout with the minimum fuss and bother. And, once the territory has fallen vacant, it is certain that another resident of good size

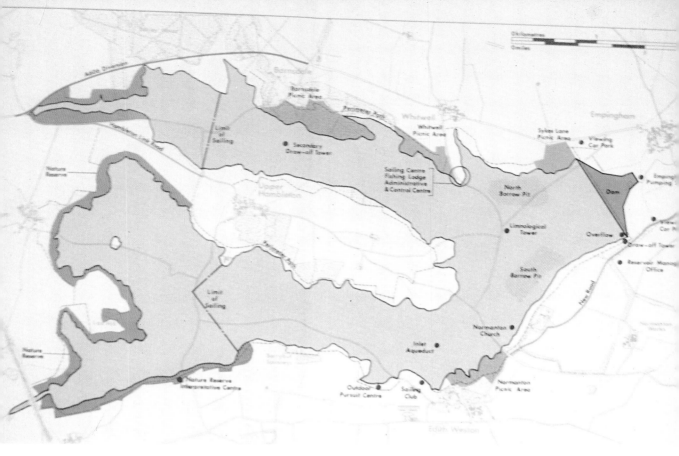

1 Map of Rutland Water, showing the two arms.

2 The reservoir in one of its foulest moods when safety needs to be observed.

3 The weigh-in at an international competition at Grafham Water.

4 Alan Pearson with his British record brook trout of 5lb 5½oz.

5 The wild brown trout of Lake Vyrnwy which are always returned alive on my visits.

6 Well-known angler John Snelson with a fine Loch Leven wild brown trout.

7 The Enid Blyton tower – the famous tower looking down Lake Vyrnwy near Oswestry in Central Wales.

8 England International John Pawson with his first ever double–figure rainbow; a triploid from Aveley Lake.

9 Two brace of cheetah trout totalling 20lb from Avington. These are a cross between rainbow and brook trout.

10 Bob with a 4¾lb tiger trout. These are a cross between brown and brook trout.

11 The wild Atlantic salmon and sea trout.

12 A 10lb stocked stillwater salmon caught at Ringstead Grange Fishery on a small lure.

13 Ordinary fluorescent materials under flash
light.

14 Ordinary fluorescent materials under green
light.

15 Phosphorescent materials in the dark,
showing their obvious advantages.

16 Tommy, the Bailiff at Rutland, shows what a wild rainbow should really look like with this beautiful 6lb specimen.

17 What a beautiful fish. A 5¼lb brown from Grafham.

18 A small part of Fred Wagstaffe's catch from Rutland, showing some fine brown trout.

19 David Wood's record-breaking 14½lb brown trout from the Queen Mother Reservoir. It felled to a trolled lure.

20 A catch of stocked salmon from Ross Fishery.

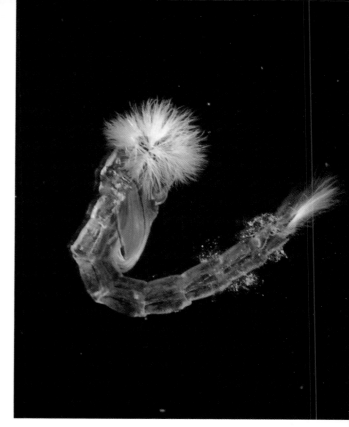

21 The mayfly nymph.

22 The chironomid or buzzer nymph on its way to the surface.

23 The damselfly nymph at the stage where it is taken by trout.

24 Lady Bower Reservoir on Snake Pass.

25 John Wilshaw playing a fish at mayfly time.

26 The ultimate prize – a large brown trout taken on a black chenille lure from
Draycote Water in a heat wave.

27 Fishing from a dam wall at Farmoor II, Oxford.

28 Brian Leadbetter with an 8lb 6oz Grafham super rainbow. It took a Zonker rabbit fur lure which imitates a small fish.

29 Bob with the runner up's medal in Spain in
1986. England finished in second place.

30 The popularity of the aeration tower with boats anchored all round it fishing
for the fry feeders at Grafham.

31 Mick Bewick with an 8lb Queen Mother Reservoir rainbow. The reservoir has the capability of growing a stock fish to these fine proportions.

32 The last view the angler gets before he reels in and packs up.

will move in before many hours have passed. In point of fact, I have extracted four big trout from one such holt in the space of a short morning.

In coloured water, catching big trout is every bit as much a matter of observation as it is on the clear waters, except that now one is looking for nods and winks rather than the actual form of the trout. Common sense enters into it as well, although sadly this is something that some anglers have never possessed. To them, catching big fish is always a matter of luck, but I prefer to think that the reasoning angler has the ability to manufacture his own luck – and if you can manufacture it to order, then luck no longer enters into it.

Take another example from Leominstead. A few years back I spent the morning at Avington and although it was a hot, heavy day the water there is always cool, and I was able to put three double-figure fish on the bank by lunch-time, the heaviest weighing in at about 11½ pounds. I spent the afternoon at a meeting in Southampton, and arrived at Leominstead around 5 p.m. The weather had got heavier and more unpleasant during the afternoon, and Leominstead looked as dead as any water can under these conditions. The few anglers who had persevered were putting their tackle away, and advised me that I was wasting my time, that not a fish had shown since mid-morning, and I could well believe them. However, I caught four trout before dusk, and the best of them was a new fishery record of 12 pounds 14 ounces. No, I did not use a trawl or a hand grenade, I used my head.

The fishery is fed by a cool stream that enters in the top left corner of the lake. Over the years it has carved itself a deep channel where it runs into the lake, and this is accessible from just one casting platform. The evidence of erosion indicates that this cooler water remains close to the bottom

for a fair distance, because the channel retains its shape, as one could see every time Leo Jarmal drained the lake down.

On a heavy day following a series of hot, heavy days, there would obviously be an element of staleness in the water, a degree of de-oxygenation in the shallows where most of the food supplies dwell. Therefore there would be a strong degree of probability that the entry point of the cool well-oxygenated feeder stream water, also food-rich, would be one of the few areas in which trout would continue to feed. The possibility was also strong that a particularly large and aggressive trout would occupy prime position. The effective technique was to cast out a heavily leaded White Wonderbug, allow it to sink to the bed of the channel close to the entry into the lake, and then after tightening the line, lift the rod tip sharply, causing the bug to dart high in the water, then drop back again. After about the fourth lift, there was a violent strike, and a prolonged battle with the big rainbow followed. Three other lesser rainbows fell to the same tactic, each hitting the bug very hard as I drew it towards the surface.

Thus, the difference between clearwater and the coloured water trout fishery is that in the case of the former, you can actually see the trout you hope to catch. In the latter, you can use knowledge gleaned from the former to define the most probable lies of the better trout and this allied with a judicious mixture of common sense leavened with an understanding of the habits and preferences of trout should assist you to take catches which are consistently of above-average size.

There should be no need for me to add that the tackle suitable for use on one fishery is exactly suited to the other fishery; there is absolutely no need to change any of the standard basics of rod, line and leader.

Flies

In coloured water, whilst it is perfectly true that imitative patterns can be excellent, I must confess to a personal preference for patterns containing plenty of marabou for visible bulk and movement and of highly visible colours such as black, white, yellow and orange. It rather depends upon the conditions of weather at any given time.

For instance, it would be rather pointless using a yellow marabou pattern when trout are obviously feeding greedily on a natural life form, be it damselfly nymph, chironomid pupa or black gnat. On the other hand, on one of those days when not much seems to be happening, a big buzzy and lightly leaded pattern in a high visibility colour can be quite devastating if cast at overhanging leaves and then allowed to plop enticingly into the water. A tweaky, jerky style of retrieve often works wonders.

Depending upon fishery rules, I would be very happy to use Capper or Dog Nobbler patterns for this approach, but if the rules restrict fly size, then patterns similar in nature but confined to a length of one inch maximum often prove satisfactory. Of course, if observation suggests that there is a plague of green caterpillars or some other creature in the bushes, then obviously it would be foolish to ignore the use of patterns of the approximate size, shape and colour of the beast that is most likely to be falling into the water. Why ignore natural ground-baiting?

Thinking about Leominstead has brought to mind the very unusual nature of the trout that could be caught there. Apart from stocked rainbows and browns, there were also wild browns, and sea trout that had made their way upstream and found themselves in the lake. Mainly these were fresh-run fish, but occasionally one might catch a very handsome specimen that could only be described as a land-locked sea trout. Having made its way into the lake and been obliged to remain there, it took on a very unusual coloration, tending towards greenish silver. I wonder how long a sea trout can remain land-locked and still rightfully be called a sea trout?

This raises quite another question about big rainbows. According to the American authorities who control world records, all our rainbows are classified as land-locked, as opposed to the migratory rainbows of the North American continent which are known as steelheads. The obvious subdivision is that the land-locked rainbows have never been to sea, whereas the steelhead spends its major growth period in the saline environment.

It has been known for many years that rainbow trout fry can be converted quite quickly from a freshwater environment to sea water. The advantages this offers are numerous, and include increased disease resistance and enhanced growth rates. So there are now a few farms converting their fry to salt water, and growing on in cages sited in sea lochs. It is proving quite easy to produce rainbows of very great weights, and although there are problems involved in transporting them and re-acclimatising them to freshwater, it is nonetheless true that specimens of weights well in excess of existing records are becoming available for capture.

The question is, which record? In my view, these rainbows cannot be described as land-locked because they have spent their high growth years in salt water. If our record administrators choose to ignore this fact, then they are flying in the face of the evidence and effectively contradicting the rulings of the world record administrators. What we need is a special rainbow record subdivision so that both land-locked and migratory varieties can be kept separate. I do not think it of the least importance that the migratory rainbow has not migrated of its own free will. The criterion is that it has spent the major growth period in sea water and so cannot possibly be described as land-locked.

DEEP TROLLING FOR IRISH AND SCOTTISH TROUT

Rather different in his approach to Alan Pearson, is another specialist fisherman friend of mine, Fred Wagstaffe. Fred loves the big waters. In fact, he is far more at home on a giant lough than on a four acre pool. Fred loves to hunt for big wild brown trout, fish that are very rarely caught on a fly. Here he tells you of that other kind of very exciting trout fishing.

Thirty feet below the rolling white-caps on the wind-swept surface of a rain-lashed lough in the remote west of Ireland, a yard of wild brown trout snapped its jaws shut on the lure and turned to dive for cover and safety beneath the rocky crags of the underwater reef from which it had emerged.

Topside, things started to go wrong almost from the beginning. The rod pulled round with irresistible force and I automatically tightened my thumb on the spool of the multiplying reel and lifted the rod sharply. The giant trout paused in its downward plunge, shook its head in violent rage and continued its headlong flight to the deep, dark sanctuary below the reef.

On contact with the fish, Bob, my boat partner, cut the outboard motor and started to reel in his line, leaving our thirteen and a half-foot boat helplessly drifting in the heavy swell, towards threatening black fingers of rock that seemingly beckoned us into a watery grave. A shouted

warning and, just in time, Bob noticed the danger and dropped the anchor overboard.

Within seconds the rope had tightened and the boat was safely held a short distance from the jagged tips of the nearby rocks. But down below the brownie, sensing the change of direction in line pressure, decided on a long, seering run alongside the reef before swinging out over deeper water and leaping high into the air.

While spray pounded over our frail little boat from the still-gathering wind and waves running before yet another fierce squall as it shrieked its way down the lough towards us, Bob, grim-faced, clutched the landing-net with white-knuckled hands as I desperately fought the great trout to a standstill and began, unceremoniously, to haul it towards us. A huge head broke surface and we immediately saw that the hook was connected to the fish's jaw by the merest sliver of skin. For the next five minutes I steered the fish very gently round in circles until it finally swam over the net and was heaved into the boat. On the scales it weighed thirteen pounds seven ounces. A truly wild brownie, but one which would not have been caught without a huge stroke of luck with any but the specialised method of deep-trolling which I will outline here.

On the majority of the big Irish and Scottish lakes it is natural reproduction in the feeder streams and rivers that does the restocking, not the tanker from the local fish-farm, as happens on lowland reservoirs. In Ireland's Lough Mask, as with many other such waters, there is a resident head of big trout that hardly get trapped. Indeed, some do fall to the artificial, or dapped natural mayfly or such, but they are only the tip of a very large iceberg. Such waters often allow methods other than fly fishing, simply because the size, depths and variations these waters present, allow other methods to be used without depleting stocks.

Using an echo-sounder on an Irish lough.

The basic reasoning behind my tactics for catching specimen wild trout from the Irish and Scottish lakes is not to wait for them to come to me, but for me to take my lures to them and to establish depths and types of underwater terrain where the bigger brownies live for most of the time. My colleague and I reasoned that we would not attempt to chase the odd fish at odd times when the occasional alternative might present itself. Far better to spend virtually all our time presenting the right lures in the right places and at the right depths and speeds.

Quite obviously, such big trout reach and maintain their weight and first-class fighting condition largely by predation on small trout and other fish species, so plugs and spoons, not the feathered creations of the reservoirs which seem to have such low appeal on these waters, is what we offered them.

In waters of such great depth and sudden variation in bottom feature, the most important piece of equipment is an echo-sounder. Without one it is like dabbling in the dark. There is no magic about an echo-sounder. It is no substitute for good fishing knowledge and technique. It just gives you the chance to have an instant picture of the depth and type of terrain below the boat, and it is that picture, plus good fishing knowledge and technique that gives you the edge over those wary giant brownies, skulking deep down at quite selective sites on what could seem like miles and miles of bleak and featureless water.

An example of such holding sites is where a ledge slopes away from shallow water and then drops suddenly at a depth of twenty-five to thirty-five feet. Other examples are a reef that drops away into deep water in a series of ledges and slopes rather than an almost sheer drop, a river-mouth where the in-shore, silted slopes give way to a sudden drop-off, and an island that gently tapers off into deeper water, then falls away steeply in craggy, boulder-strewn steps.

Some of these features can be spotted by studying the shore line closely, but the vast majority are hidden from detection except with the aid of an echo-sounder. Careful

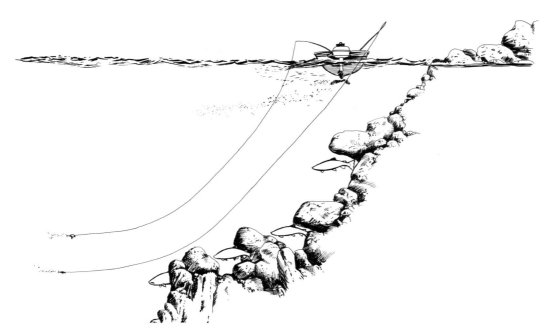

Trolling two lures on the 30ft contour line.

use of the echo-sounder will probably show many sites that may hold big trout, but which subsequently show not to do so. Then after carefully searching all those areas that seem to hold promise, one or two start to yield results and you notice subtle differences in those that do produce fish and those that do not.

The actual holding depth within such a site will vary considerably according to a number of factors. Generally the big trout will maintain a level close to their food source, but without risk to themselves. Light penetration, caused by time of day and weather conditions, will play an obvious part in this. The 25- to 35-foot depth-band seems to suit many of the big trout if other requirements, such as points of cover and nearby access to shallow water, are also present. I have caught big browns from between virtual nil depth to fifty feet, but it is that twenty-five to thirty-five foot level that has produced more for me than all the other depths put together.

The actual lures used varied a great deal. Plain copper or silver and copper spoons up to six inches long proved simple yet effective. Rather more elaborate have been a variety of plugs originating from countries such as America, Sweden, Finland and Japan. Some were single jointed; others double, treble or even multi-jointed. One thing all these lures had in common was that all possessed plenty of pulsating action when trolled through the water.

Lure colour is less important. In bright sunny weather and with a comparatively calm surface, it was the darker and more natural fish-finished lures that scored best. But in heavily overcast conditions, rough water and the poor light of dusk or dawn, it was the rather brighter finished, or lighter coloured lures that payed off.

Most important of all was to position the boat on the required depth contour, using the echo-sounder, and then follow that contour relentlessly. The man at the helm should have his eyes glued to the echo-sounder screen as it transmits and receives

A large, wooden, clinker-built boat is by far the safest for use on the enormous Irish loughs.

its electronic message, and steer as close to the right depth contour reading as is possible. Without doubt, it is the success or failure of the helmsman in carrying out this task which makes the biggest difference beween big trout and no trout.

You cannot compare the sudden and drastic depth changes in the rocky Irish and Scottish lakes with those of man-made, lowland waters over agricultural land. The echo-sounder might be reading thirty feet, yet a few yards away rocks could be showing through the surface.

The second most important aspect of this style of fishing is to be able to position the lures within two or three feet of the bottom and then keep them there for mile upon mile of trolling. There is only one type of lure that I know of which will dive and run at around thirty feet on monofil line and that is an American one called a spoon-plug. Designed for specialised deep trolling in the United States, it resembles a squashed frog in appearance! Made of metal, but with a plug-like diving-lip and various other angled vanes to add depth and stability, it has the most violent, rod-top-shaking action of any lure I have used. They are ideal for the job, but are not, to my knowledge, imported commercially

into Britain. To get hold of them one must have a contact in the States or know someone who is going to pay that country a visit.

It is a waste of time just adding lead weights and letting out more and more monofil line to take a lure down and keep it at the required depth at trolling speeds. Experiments showed that any given weight of lead and speed of boat would only allow the lure to sink so far. To let out more line after that optimum point had been reached simply caused the lure to rise in the water, not run deeper. This is because monofil weighted near one end causes an upwards arc through the water when trolled. The more line that is let out, the more surface-area of line in the upward arc is available for upward water pressure. Sounds complicated, but try it yourself and you'll soon see the result.

An alternative to adding more and more lead to the line is to use a line specially made for deep trolling. I have tried both wire line and lead-cored line and find the latter far more satisfactory.

I generally use one hundred yards of lead-cored trolling line of the type that changes colour every ten yards. Most reservoir trout anglers will have seen it in

A brace of specimen brown trout for Fred Wagstaffe caught while trolling on Lough Mask.

use as shooting-heads in eight- to twelve-yard lengths, or, perhaps on Rutland Water, in much longer lengths for deep, down-the-wind drift fishing.

In addition to the lead-cored line, I like to have at least another hundred yards of monofil backing. Travelling at, say, 3½ to 4 knots on the outboard motor, it could take up to eighty to ninety yards of lead-cored line to get a lure (depending whether it has any built-in diving features) to run at twenty-five to thirty feet. Hook into a big trout, especially in rough water, and the importance of that extra hundred yards of backing becomes immediately obvious.

Multiplying reels are best for this type of fishing and of course they must be of sufficient size to accommodate the bulky lead-line and backing. Something like a heavy, ten-foot salmon or pike spinning rod is ideal for this deep trolling. Anything too light or soft in action is just not up to the heavy stress of lead-cored line and lure being trolled through the water and then have anything left when a double-figure brownie slams into the lure.

In conjunction with the lead-cored line, I like to use a ten-to-fifteen foot monofil leader of twelve- to fifteen-pound breaking strain. If you think this is a trifle heavy, just consider that you are after ten- to twenty-pound wild brownies, in some of the harshest and most tackle-testing circumstances possible.

When the trout take these fast-moving, deep-trolled lures it might be assumed that they do so with difficulty; that they would find it hard to intercept at such speeds. In reality they seem to have no such problem. It is not unusual to feel a tap, tap, tapping at the lure (a feeling transmitted quite distinctly up the line and down the rod to the hands), for some distance. This, I believe, is caused by a trout that has homed in on its prey and is simply side-swiping it with its head to knock it off balance before sweep-ing in for the kill. Other predators like perch and pike do a similar thing.

Such deep-trolling tactics outlined here can start to produce results surprisingly quickly if the big trout's holding areas and depths can be discovered. My first week on Lough Mask (a water twenty-four miles long and three miles wide) yielded some good fish, but in a total of two weeks the score had gone up to four fish over ten pounds, including the thirteen pounder mentioned earlier. A friend made his first visit the following year and by sticking exclusively to the deep-trolling techniques, produced trout of sixteen and eleven pounds and another of almost ten pounds in a week's fishing.

A few years ago, I paid a week's visit to Loch Quoich, a nine-mile long, bleak, in-hospitable, storm-wracked water in the mountains of the west of Scotland. Camping and fishing there proved something of an endurance test, but as the loch had produced the British record brown trout of over nineteen pounds a few year's previously, my colleague on the trip, Ron, and I decided to stick it out.

Towards the end of the first day's deep trolling we had nothing to show for our efforts except a couple of tiny trout. Sunset came and we were wearily watching the echo-sounder as it tracked the full length of a large, rocky shelf stretching out into the loch. Suddenly the shelf ended abruptly, the bottom dropping away from thirty to over one hundred feet. Ron swung the boat round to regain the depth-contour and within seconds my fluttering, pulsating four-inch copper spoon jerked to a halt, held fast in the kyped jaws of an eight-pound four-ounce brownie.

Just twenty minutes later, after landing and despatching that fish, Ron was zig-zagging the boat through some under-water obstacles near a river-mouth when suddenly my lure jerked and I thought I

The ultimate brown trout from Lough Mask, caught on a 2½in copper spoon in the trolling style as explained by Fred Wagstaffe.

Fred Wagstaffe with a 7¼lb brown from Loch Awe, Scotland, caught on a trolled spoon.

was hooked-up on the rocks. But no, this turned out to be another big trout. When we finally hauled it in, we found it to be a nice clean hen fish of eleven pounds five ounces. Not bad, we thought, for our first day on the water! However, our luck was not to last. The weather was atrocious and made fishing very difficult most days. Ron hooked into a veritable monster of, I would guess, around fifteen pounds, but it broke free when he had to apply firm pressure because we were in imminent danger of being swept on to the rocks.

Such is deep trolling for big trout in the Irish and Scottish lakes – sometimes dangerous, often exciting, but never dull.

RED LETTER DAY AT RUTLAND

In this section, Fred Wagstaffe tells of his famous July fishing day at the mighty Rutland Water. Fred's catch is probably the best limit bag ever taken on fly (lure) from any water in the UK, Ireland or Europe.

That day early in July started off like many others on Rutland Water. Some of the bank anglers had been there since dawn. Most of the boat anglers had motored off into the distance. It was approaching mid-morning when my partner and I ambled down to the dock with our kit. After a little tackle-stowing and a chat with the wardens, we set off into the fine, summer day. What I didn't know then was that it was going to be a day when records were broken – when Rutland's big brown trout were going to be a good deal more co-operative than usual. It was to be a day when several years' fishing almost exclusively for big trout on this four mile long water was about to pay off. Half an hour later a brownie of nine pounds seven ounces was in the boat and the day had hardly begun!

Getting to grips with Rutland Water's legendary big brownies is a dream which many trout fishers hold dear, but faced with over 3,000 acres of often wild and wind-tossed water, with vast variations in depth and changeable moods, many end up disillusioned and disappointed. They then either revert to being satisfied with catching quantities of lesser trout, or go off to fish the easy, small waters filled with fat, tame 'stockies'.

It is not only Rutland that holds really big brown trout, however. Many of the lowland reservoirs which have been stocked with brownies for some years will have a resident head of large and almost totally wild fish. The Queen Mother Reservoir produced a fourteen pounder not long ago and even Northamptonshire's ill-thought-of Pitsford Reservoir comes up with a surprise eight or nine pounder on odd occasions to either the lucky or skilled and persistent fly fisher.

Persistence really is the key to the whole business of catching big, brown trout from Rutland or any other water. An intimate knowledge of the water is needed, along with a realisation that hunting these wily specimens on a regular basis takes commitment. It is so easy to be distracted by the shoal of two-pound rainbows that goes head-and-tailing upwind past your boat, especially on a lean day when not a single good-sized brownie seems to exist. One must realise, however, that to give way to such distractions reduces the chances of catching big browns.

I was out on Rutland one day in April, with a friend who asked me to show him how to catch big brownies. His assortment of floating lines, sink-tips and ultra-slow-sinkers were totally unnecessary given that specimen browns were the target. Fortunately, I had pointed this out to him in advance and he was equipped with a ten yard, lead-cored shooting head on one

Fred Wagstaffe about to embark on a day's lure fishing at Rutland. Note seven rods on show, one carrying a visibly monstrous lure.

rod and a full hundred yards of lead-cored line on another.

We pounded three stretches of Rutland's South Arm unmercifully, because I knew of several holding areas of good-sized brownies. They came from twenty to thirty feet down, hammering into large and flashy Waggy lures, tandems and tubes. They were not quite the monsters we were after, but respectable three and four pound-ers, with the best fish just topping five pounds. The only trouble was that it was me that was taking all the better fish, simply because my companion got bored with the deep-fishing routine every time some tiddler topped on the surface! Seconds later he would be flailing around, trying to cover anything that showed, with a team of tiny, traditional wet flies. That is fine, if you like that sort of thing, but I kept my head, my line and my lures well down, and our respective catches at the end of the day reflected the perseverance. His catch was two fish with a total weight of two pounds. Mine was an easy eight fish with a total of thirty pounds.

Probably the most important first step in any campaign to catch big, reservoir browns is to gain as complete a knowledge of the water as is possible, in the shortest time. A chart of the water, or Ordnance Survey maps of the area before it was flooded, can be of assistance for those reservoirs formed in natural farmland valleys. Used in conjunction with an echo-sounder, one can quickly build up a mental picture of whole areas of the reser-voir – not only the depth, but also sudden variations in depth, the position of sunken hedgerows and stream-beds, the silted, soft-bottomed areas and the stony areas preferred by brownies late in the season, where they accumulate for their ill-fated ritualistic spawning activities. I firmly believe that one can learn more in a single season about depth and other fish-holding features with an echo-sounder than one could hope to do in five seasons without one.

With the transducer (through which the signal is transmitted and received), G-clamped to the side of the boat, the echo-sounder can quickly be brought into use when setting out on the water, and just as easily dismantled at the end of the day. The power source can be either a twelve-volt car battery in the boat, or a six-volt battery fitted internally.

Once a comprehensive picture is built up of the reservoir's depths and features (both natural and man-made), it is important to gain as much information as possible about big brownie catches, and to store it away for future use. Bearing in mind time of year when such catches are made, weather conditions and any other scraps of knowledge you can gather together will come in useful. This is exactly what I did on Rutland. Indeed, this is my usual course of action whenever I determine to catch specimen fish of any species from any water.

Another most important factor when it comes to hunting big Rutland brownies is to be equipped to tackle them at whatever depth they are feeding, in whatever weather and water conditions they exist, every time you go out. You will have to carry a lot of gear around, but the alternative is to miss out on chances. Colleagues have laughed at me on many occasions when I have staggered the length of the pontoon towards the boat, with my arms full of rods. I generally start off with at last three or four rods set up, end the day with twice that number and still have some in reserve.

Take a blustery day early in May. The first rod to be set up was my heaviest, attached to which was a salmon reel holding a hundred yards of lead-cored line for deep, down-wind drift fishing. Another

Fred ensures a very good knot and tests it.

rod held a 550-grain weight and a lead-cored shooting head attached to lead-impregnated backing. The third was set up with a 450-grain, lead-cored shooting head attached to round monofil backing and the fourth rod could either have an Aquasink No 9 shooting head, or a Canadian lead-impregnated No 9 shooting head, both attached to flat 'Black Streak' nylon backing. Later in the day, I set up the Aquasink head, for the purpose of having two different lures for instant use, should the fish move up in the water. I also set up a sixth rod, holding a full-length, No 9 weight-forward Hi-speed Hi-D line, which will sink faster than the Aquasink or Canadian lead-impregnated shooting heads, but not as fast as the lead-cored shooting head. It will, however, describe a different arc through the water, which means it doesn't climb as steeply until the very final part of the retrieve. During the cold, early weeks of the season this can make a small, but often significant difference.

The day started with the wind still building in strength, so the 450-grain head was put to use and some reasonable browns of about four pounds came to our boat. As the wind increased, I switched to the 550-grain head and lead-impregnated backing, keeping my lures at the same feeding depth as before, despite the increased speed of the drift. I should add that I usually fish in the 'Northampton' style when using lures – drifting with bows pointing down the wind. The rudder and/or some special oar-clamps which fit under the rowlocks and hold the oar blades vertical in the water, assist in this. They act as stabilisers and steer the boat on a straight, down-the-wind drift. You can get the boat to swing and angle across the wind by turning one oar flat and leaving the other with blade vertical.

By side-casting across the boat's line of drift at a little less than right-angles, I was able (by flicking a great deal of lead-impregnated backing on the water after the cast), to get the heavy head and lure close to the bottom in twenty-five to thirty feet of water. Once the line had tightened, it caused the lure to rise and speed up as it swung round the bend. This speeding up and changing direction of the lure as it swings upwards in an arc is the hallmark of the classic sidecasting technique and is the downfall of many thousands of reservoir trout every year.

With the wind still rising, I lessened the angle at which I cast across the line of drift. This had the effect of reducing the swing, but maintained depth, which I considered to be more important at the time. Two more decent brownies came into the boat,

but then all went quiet except for a small fish or two, so I switched to full lead-cored line and moved over deeper water, thinking that the worsening conditions had driven the better fish down still deeper. An hour later, my lure stopped with a savage jerk some forty feet or more down and I knew instantly that this was one of Rutland's better brownies. Fifteen minutes later, with the boat awash, my partner netted a good fish of seven pounds fourteen ounces.

Later that day, as often happens at that time of year, the wind fell away, the sun came out and the whole mood of the reservoir changed. Suddenly fish were rising – both rainbows and small browns. I fished an Aquasink head and took odd brownies to four pounds, down to ten feet until the sun went down. These better fish were below the small ones on the surface, but the really deep water had gone completely quiet, so it was this or nothing. The prime aim on this day, and all my days when hunting specimen brownies, is to present the right lures at the depth where the bigger trout are thought to be feeding and keep them there for as long as possible.

Now take a mild, but windy, early September day. Such a day would see me with rods rigged differently. There may be one rod with a lead-cored shooting head to monofil backing in the boat, and even heavier rods and lines tucked away just in case they should be needed, but more rods would be set up for middle and upper-level lure fishing. Hi-speed Hi-D, Aquasink or Canadian lead-impregnated lines or heads would be on two or three other rods, plus a slow sink on another. In addition, I would probably have a rod holding a No 9 or 10 floating shooting head attached to very fine, floating backing for some quite specialised surface work close to and among the weed beds, using big white muddlers or my floating plastazote, drop-tailed fry imitation. These would be used to intercept the big marauders as they attacked the fry shoals hiding in the weed-bed fringes.

Surprisingly enough, I would have one rod rigged for loch style fishing. On the point of an eighteen-foot leader I would have a size 10 long-shanked Silver Invicta, tied long and light over an underbody of copper wire to give it the weight to act as anchor to the most important fly of all on the leader. This would be a hot orange palmer, heavily tied on a 10 or 8 long-shanked hook and fished on the top dropper so that it could bounce through the wave-tops.

Long, hot, dog-days can be murder, but all is not lost. If there is the slightest breeze or drift, I find it useful to make a long cast from the stern with a 350-grain lead-cored shooting head, then play out another twenty or thirty yards of monofil backing, perhaps fifty or sixty yards in all. The lure on the end of a fifteen-foot leader should be the biggest, flashiest in your box. I like to use a four-inch waggy lure, or a huge double-jointed muddler. Once the whole length of head and backing has sunk right to the bottom and the drift of the boat has started to tighten things up, I then start a fast, stop-start retrieve.

The effect on brownies skulking on the bottom can be electrifying. Sometimes they follow the lure almost right to the boat. At other times they take during the retrieve, but invariably it is just as the lure shoots forward after a pause. Occasionally, you can feel the brownies tapping at the lures with the side of their heads and if a double-hook is used they sometimes get foul-hooked at the side of the face. I always ignore the taps, but get ready for a savage take after the next pause. If you can find a concentration of brownies, this is one way to provoke a response from at least a few of them before they tire.

A Leicester friend of mine and I were out one hot August day and we were doing no good whatsoever. I suggested we do a few slow drifts across the deep water, out from Barnsdale Creek in the almost flat-calm North Arm. I lay a long line out with the aid of the dying breeze and started an erratic retrieve. Within seconds, I felt a tapping and a few minutes later netted a 2½-pound brownie. The next retrieve produced a 3½-pound brownie, and was followed by another, even bigger. By this time, my partner was rapidly trying to set up his lead-cored shooting-head outfit. Barely had he rigged up when I hooked into something really solid which shook its head then rocketed skywards. It took just a second or two to travel from about forty feet down to three feet above the surface and I could see that it was a brownie of perhaps eight pounds with my waggy lure stuck in the side of its face. Another quick shake of its head and the lure went in one direction, the trout in another. After that all went quiet again, apart from an odd follow by a bored-looking brownie.

Hunting big brownies towards the season's end depends largely on pin-pointing tight-knit groups as they gather prior to their spawning attempts. Again, I set up a number of rods with varying lines, but mainly those for deep fishing. Unlike early season fish, these back-end brownies will often travel some distance to rise up through the water levels to attack a lure. Because of their aggressive instincts, I find it often pays to offer them large, heavily dressed lures, fished in a fast and erratic manner. The takes can be shattering, in more ways than one.

I was well and truly caught on the hop out on the South Arm of Rutland Water on the last day of the season. We had drifted the boat towards the mouth of sailing club bay on a moderate westerly wind, when we discovered a 'nest' of brownies in an

Fred playing a big fish in Rutland's South Arm shallows.

aggressive feeding mood. Two or three medium-sized fish came into the boat after taking my partner's lure and I was beginning to get a trifle impatient for some action. Then, as I was retrieving a four-inch waggy lure up to the side of the boat with my shooting head just starting to lift off for the next cast, an enormous brownie shot upwards, engulfing the waggy and shot back out of sight in less time than it takes to blink an eye. It happened so fast that I didn't even react. Ping went the leader, and I sulked for an hour! A little later, though, another one tried the same trick. I was ready for it this time and in came a near six pounder.

A week or so before, Rod Lee and I were running lures deep on lead-cored lines through two noted late-season, big brownie areas on either side of the trolling area of the reservoir (along the Normanton bank and the Sykes Lane bank), drifting towards the dam at high speed in a near gale and

rolling white-caps. At one point, we were drifting rapidly towards the Three Trees land mark on the Normanton bank when something very large slammed into my lure and decided to head for the other side of the reservoir. We were travelling at such speed that I thought that we would be washed up on to the shore long before I could boat the fish. I bullied it to a stop and hauled it upwards. Glancing fearfully over my shoulder at the rapidly approaching stones, I asked Rod if he could see the fish, and if so, how big did it appear. Rod is apt to over-dramatise, but the brownie did turn out to be seven pounds nine ounces and was landed just in time for us to start up the engine and steer away from danger.

Later, when we were drifting towards the dam on the Sykes Lane side, we were getting takes about eighty to a hundred yards off the dam, but such was the wind strength and the high speed of drift, that

Fred's famed waggy lure showing the wiggle action of the tail. It resembles a swimming fish when retrieved.

the boat was in danger of being washed on to the dam rocks. Disaster was only averted on several occasions when, within a few yards of the dam, the one of us not playing a fish started up the motor and surged in a wide arc.

Each time, it was at the same spot that one or both of us hooked into good brownies and we nearly ended up on the dam at the same spot. By coincidence, a bank angler had picked exactly this spot to cast into the teeth of the wind and although we apologised profusely every time he had to pull his line out of the way of our wildly drifting boat, I am sure he was less than pleased with our actions!

So far, I have mentioned very little about lures. I use virtually all the popular and well-known trout lures at some time or other – in single, double, tandem and tube form. But I also rely heavily on some special creations of my own, particularly that infamous trout killer, the waggy lure. The waggy is based on a plastic sandeel. The wiggle-tail on these sea-fishing lures adds extra action on the retrieve in addition to any movement put in by rod and water manipulation. It is this waggy-tailed action and the multiplicity of variations on its

basic design that makes it such a deadly lure in many, although by no means all, situations.

I use Delta sandeels in two and three-and-a-half-inch sizes, although many of them appear longer once I have tied them. The small ones are usually tied on long-shanked single hooks, either size 6 or 4. I start off the head by tying in a pair of eyes, cut from a length of metal bead chain, most often used for sink and bath plug attachments. These are tied underneath the shank of the hook, otherwise the lure will turn upside-down on the retrieve. The bulk of the head is then tied in using chenille in a figure-of-eight movement over and around the eyes until a suitable head is formed. The back or 'wing' dressing varies. It could be marabou, strips of shredded mylar or a combination of these and other materials. The throat hackle could be tied half or full turn, usually in orange.

The large waggy lures are infinitely more varied. Some of these are tied on two large single hooks in tandem. Others may have a single hook in front and a double at the rear. These are usually low-water salmon hooks. Occasionally, I use doubles fore and aft, going up to full salmon hooks

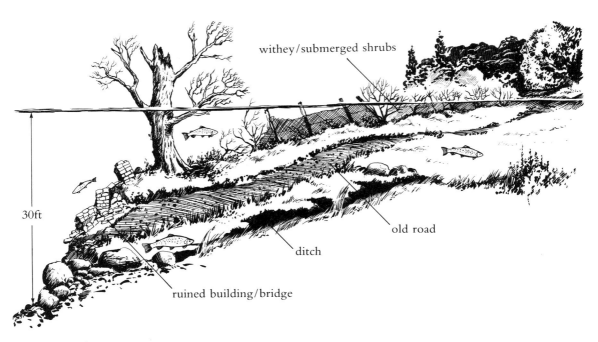

withey/submerged shrubs

30ft

old road

ditch

ruined building/bridge

Cross-section of a reservoir.

for high-speed drifting in rough water. Most large waggy lures have the same metal eyes as the small ones, but I use a wider range of back-dressing materials.

I generally only use the white sandeels, but sometimes I add black stripes down the body and tail using a permanent marker-pen. This, coupled with a black chenille head and a dark dressing plus, perhaps, a few strands of shredded silver or gold mylar is then known as the Tiger Waggy and is an absolute killer in the right cir-cumstances. Sometimes I stick to a mara-bou back dressing, or one made of two or three shades of shredded mylar. At other times I might do more elaborate over-back dressings of buck-tail and shredded mylar, goat hair or squirrel.

I also tie up some highly buoyant waggy lures for deep-down fishing, using just the tail section of a 3½-inch Delta sandeel, attached to a size 4 or 2 low-water salmon double. The head and part of the body is shaped from plastazote, which makes the whole thing highly buoyant. With a simple

'wing' or over-back dressing of marabou or shredded mylar, those early season brownies that travel far to intercept a lure just love them.

So, back to that day in early July. My partner and I had motored out and decided, almost by chance, to anchor and fish the hot spot area at the mouth of Whitwell Creek. There are many occasions through-out the season when anchoring will beat drift fishing for results. These are usually times when the fish are gathered in com-paratively small areas. I like to anchor the boat from the stern so that it swings less in the wind. The man in the front of the boat casts across wind and the other casts down, or down and across wind on the other side of the boat.

The wind was easterly, blowing into the mouth of the creek, so we anchored about fifty yards up-wind of the floating cages holding young stock fish. The first fish to come into the boat was a nice 3½-pound brownie and fell to a waggy on my part-ner's rod. The next fish weighed in at nine

The gun starts a big competition at Rutland.

pounds seven ounces and was quickly followed by one of nine pounds one ounce and another of seven pounds. All fell to variations of the waggy lure and all to my rod! My partner took browns and rainbows to four and a half pounds but the really big fish stubbornly avoided his lures and took mine instead.

We rested the water from time to time when things went quiet, then switched to another variation on the waggy theme. Sometimes we were using Canadian lead-impregnated lines with a smaller waggy lure, at other times we were using 350-grain, lead-cored shooting heads and big buoyant waggy lures. The fish came to the lures in short bursts, with quiet spells in between – a four pounder to Ron, then a five pounder to me. That's how it went on until mid-afternoon, when a buzz of activity around the fishing lodge caught our attention and we were asked to go in so that

some photographs of the catch so far could be taken.

At around 4 p.m. we set off to anchor over the hot spot again and were told when we left the dock that we needed about ten pounds more for the single and double limit-bag weight records for any catch of trout from an English reservoir. We intended going in again at 6 p.m. so it didn't seem likely that we were going to succeed, especially as we had only three more fish to catch for our limits!

The first fish was a little rainbow of about a pound and our spirits dropped. The next fish was a brownie of three and a half pounds. Then, at about 5.50 p.m. I hooked into another big one, which steamed around in great circles until my wrists ached from playing it. Finally, at dead on 6 p.m. Ron dipped his big landing net into the water and heaved a nine-pound six-and-a-half-ounce brownie into the boat! What a day! Three nine pounders, a seven pounder and a five pounder were the best of my eight-fish limit for a total weight of forty-eight pounds – a record. With Ron's not inconsiderable catch added, it took the total double-limit weight to over seventy pounds – another record.

I would just say in conclusion that on the following day we went out again, to the same spot. This time it was Ron that scored with the big fish. Not only did he catch a brownie of seven and a half pounds he also pulled in a big, eight-pound rainbow for good measure. I caught nothing!

MY WAY WITH THE BIG RAINBOWS

My guest writer for this section is Mick Bewick, a most dedicated big trout hunter who specialises in fishing his home water, the Queen Mother Reservoir at Datchet. I asked Mick to reveal some of the secrets of his success and he unselfishly agreed to tell all. I personally rate this reservoir as having the ability to grow on a one pound stock fish to weights larger than have been landed so far. These fish, both rainbows and browns, are true wild fish and catching one is a notable achievement. Catching them regularly, as Mick does, needs dedication, determination and a lot of skill. Here is how he goes about it covering a typical season.

I have fished the Queen Mother Reservoir at Datchet since the year following its opening in 1976. In that time I have caught, or seen taken, some very large fish indeed. Although a concrete bowl, and a rather large one at that, the Reservoir holds so much food and has such a vast depth that the trout have everything they could possibly need to keep packing on the weight. They even manage to become full-tailed specimens, unrivalled anywhere through the winter. The fishery rainbow record which weighs twelve pounds two ounces and which grew from a pound stock fish will, I believe, soon be bettered. Dave Woods' 14½-pound brown trout taken in 1985 grew to that weight from a fingerling. Does that give you an inkling of what is to come?

Scale readings of the three eight-pound rainbows I caught in the winter of 1987 proved that they had not even reached their third year. That is what I call a growth rate. But how to catch these huge fish? At the start of the season, the better, over-wintered fish tend to gather on the line of moored yachts in around forty-two feet of water. If the winter has been a fairly harsh one, some spectacular catches of rainbows will be taken here for sure. A milder winter will see them more spread out.

I use a powerful ten-foot rod capable of handling a size 10, high density shooting head. Long casting is vital and you will have to achieve forty yards or more to be in with a chance. Lure choice presents few difficulties – use a Datchet-style Booby, a variant of Gordon Fraser's original Booby Nymph, the only difference between the two being that instead of the little polystyrene balls being fixed to the hook-shank in a bit of nylon stocking, the Datchet version uses an oblong of the same material, lashed on to the hook with a figure-of-eight whipping trimmed to size. I tend to prefer a short-shanked hook as I feel that this combats the tap-tap takes you get when fishing the Booby, the fish going straight for the head.

The best early-season colours are white, fluorescent green, black and green and hot orange tied to a ten- or twelve-foot, eight-pound leader. I never use a light leader as this is just asking for trouble at Datchet. The colour of the leader is important, possibly more so than the actual strength

Mick Bewick with one of his typical limit bags, caught whilst fishing a Booby on a sunk line off the aeration tower.

and I would not thank you for any colour other than green. I usually anchor out in the yacht moorings and cast as far as I possibly can, letting everything settle for a couple of minutes before commencing the slow figure-of-eight retrieve. Even with the twelve-foot leader, the Booby rides downwards hovering along, just above the bottom. The takes can come at any time but are most likely to occur just before the shooting head leaves the bottom. If nothing happens within half an hour I move along fifty yards and repeat the performance. At this time of the year, it is a much better plan to move to the fish rather than hope that the fish will move to you.

When the weather warms a little and the wind blows into the clubhouse bank fish move in to feed on snails, sticklebacks and buzzers. Now I would anchor just thirty-five yards out from the bank using the same tackle as before but shortening the leader by a couple of feet. The cast is made straight at the bank, the lure landing within a yard of the shore. Takes can very often come on the drop as the line pulls the lure under. I took nine good rainbows fishing like this. The best of them scaled over nine and a half pounds. It is better to retrieve after the line has been allowed to sink for about twenty seconds or so. The Booby just creeps down the concrete slope and they cannot resist it.

Should the trout not be feeding on stickle-backs, an alternative lure can be a sparsely dressed Waggy, tied to a fifteen-foot leader, stripped back as soon as it lands on the water. This tactic really can sort out the bigger fish and seems to work best when the waves are crashing up on to the bank. The pier to the left of the clubhouse is a great big fish holding spot. The best way to fish this area is to anchor near enough so that you can cast the lure under the first arch. The killing patterns are an all-white Razzler variant, waggy lures and the Booby.

I have also made up some good bags of above average sized fish, on bright sunny days, by casting under the fifth arch with a lead-cored shooting head and a tandem White Muddler, although I don't really think that tandems work as well at Datchet as they used to. Until the end of June the outlet tower can be well worth a few visits. This is Mike Peters' domain and it is a spot which has yielded his remarkable catches of big brown trout.

The lures to use here are large tandems and triple-hooked lures, up to seven inches long, worked slowly up the side of the tower from a depth of nearly a hundred feet. Because of the vast depth, the best tackle to use is a ten-yard shooting head made from trolling line and a rod man enough to put this over the horizon. The takes can happen at any time but more usually as the shooting head is just entering the rod. Mike has taken brown trout to nine pounds plus here and has lost even bigger ones.

I have caught rainbows over seven pounds and have taken nothing under five when fishing here. I did hook a large brown on a six-inch long white tube but apart from that, the big browns have eluded me. When I used to fish the tower mark regularly, I estimated that a fish came along every forty hours. Needless to say, not that many anglers have the patience to stick it out. Those who do, could well be rewarded with the fish of a lifetime or just go insane with boredom!

From the end of May, if you see Kevin Hart dashing around the bank like a whippet, then you know that it is worth changing to a floating line. Around this time of the year, the trout can become preoccupied with caddis. Kevin's method is to fish two leaded stick-fly variants on a very long leader and a long loch-style rod. This set up doesn't make for good casting, as you can imagine, but you don't have to fish the

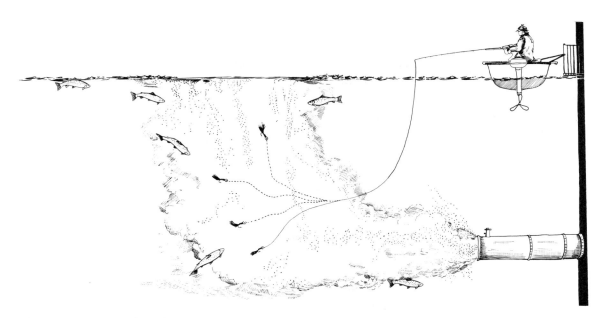

The aeration pump, similar to the one at the Queen Mother Reservoir, not only provides more oxygen but also an irresistible current which trout find very much to their liking. The way in which the angler is anchored means he can use this current to work his weighted lure in sink-and-draw fashion.

flies that far out – ten yards or a bit more is plenty. Make the cast and allow the leader to sink, letting the wind work the line around in an arc. Retrieve only when the tip of the fly line begins to sink. The takes, when they come, will be difficult to miss.

Short-line loch-style fishing from the bank sounds a most unusual way to fish a concrete bowl fishery, but Kevin has perfected a method of taking rainbows over eight pounds. He prefers an eleven-foot rod, light double tapered line and a twenty-two-foot long leader holding three small, traditional wet flies such as the Invicta, Silver Invicta and Soldier Palmer. Kevin and I kept the most effective bob fly – a Soldier Palmer tied with a light pink, fluorescent wool body – secret for a few seasons. It should be fished by casting slightly down the wind, allowing it to drift around to within a couple of yards of the bank and then retrieved with a slow figure-of-eight just before dibbling it over the last few yards. Unless the takes come to

the bob fly they may not be easily spotted. Any unusual movement around the flies is well worth a lift of the rod. This method produces some superb rainbows in the two- to four-pound range and it is not that unusual to hook two on the same cast. Landing them both is another matter.

It is better not to stay rooted to the same spot but to cast and then move a yard or so on. This way you can cover a long stretch of bank just as if you were sitting in a drifting boat. This odd-ball tactic can work well from June through to October and if the weather is mild, right up to the end of the season.

Those hot, flat calms in July and August, which normally confine fishing to early and late in the day, can provide some of the best fishing of the whole season at Datchet. It is during this doldrum time that the aerated water at the inlet tower, on the end of the pier, attracts good numbers of three-pound-plus rainbows which home in on the hoards of sticklebacks which gather

The Queen Mother Reservoir produces wild rainbow trout over 10lb, such as this one caught in winter.

in a massive column from the surface right down into the depths.

I tie my boat to the south side of the tower and using a high-density line, fifteen-foot leader and either a white or black green-backed Baby Doll, I cast out no more than eighty feet. The line will reach the bottom as the flow from the aerated water will stream out at a slight angle. Most of the takes come when not even moving the fly, the water turbulence having taken care of that part in the proceedings. I tend to hold the rod about a foot off the surface and about the same distance from the tower. It is not unusual, by any means, to have the rod wrenched into the water before you can strike.

Like all fry feeders they go mad for ten minutes and then everything goes dead for a few hours. I once took thirty fish weighing more than a hundred pounds from this spot in a month. My best limit was getting on for a third of that. Five and six pounders are not uncommon either and because of their size, and the underwater snags, I tend to play the fish as hard as I can. It is best to get them out of the depths whenever you can and to play them on the surface.

Late September through to November sees the larger trout, in the margins, feeding on the sticklebacks. Again, boat fishing and casting into the bank from about thirty yards out is the best method to adopt. Don't be too surprised to see large shoals of heavyweight rainbows cruising around the far side of the reservoir around this time. They don't seem to feed when gathered together like this, for some reason, but it is possible to winkle a few out with a bit of stealth.

First, I find the shoal. I don't make a single cast, but creep away from them in the direction they are moving, hiding behind the wave wall and being careful not to cast a shadow on to the water. I flick out a team of lightly-dressed nymphs from about ten yards away. A little peach one tied with the same wool as Brian Leadbetter uses for his Peach Baby Doll is a firm favourite. Then, when the shoal is just about to pass over the lightly leaded flies, I raise the rod top, pulling the flies past their noses. I hooked a fish weighing eight pounds doing this one day and it was by far the smallest of the shoal. It looked half that size in the water, so how heavy were the biggest?

It was while fishing for these giants that Mike Peters told me he had seen a rainbow of over twenty-five pounds. I smiled, thinking he had spent too long at the pub. A few days later an angler stopped me to say that he too had seen a fish bigger than the twenty-seven pounder at Avington. I argued, telling him that although the reservoir was known for its big fish and it may well be as long as the Hampshire monster, it could not be as fat because we didn't have cages for them to scrounge under anymore. After chatting for about five minutes I saw the huge rainbow just doddling along. I walked behind the fish for a good two hundred yards. It was the biggest rainbow I had ever seen. A conservative estimate would put it in the twenty pounds plus bracket. Don't believe me? I didn't believe Mike either. I can tell you that the next time I saw Mike I apologised and I promise you I hadn't been anywhere near the pub that day!

4 A Journey through the Seasons

Some interesting facts from Bob Church's diary.

MARCH

Keep it Simple for Success

Before that never-to-be-forgotten day when he catches his first trout, the newcomer to fly fishing faces what must seem a host of difficulties. Eager to learn any possible short cuts to success, it is quite easy to understand the frustration when he reads that even the so-called experts cannot agree about the best methods and where and when to use them. Lures, wet flies, dry flies or nymphs – which is it to be? Slow sinker, fast sinker, lead core, floating line or sink-tip line? Small fishery, large fishery or gravel pit? Just where does the beginner start? There is also the very real danger that the novice will befriend an experienced trout fisherman and try to copy everything he has seen, ending up with an enormous handicap. For the newcomer even to attempt to imitate the old hand is a sure path to failure.

The first requirement, if he is to be steered along the road to success, lies in the catching of those first couple of trout. These early trophies will provide all the confidence a beginner needs. But how to catch them? It is difficult for someone on his first outing to fish next to an experienced angler, only to watch trout after trout being hauled out before his eyes. There is simply no substitute for experience and this must be understood right from the word go. It helps if he can mix with others on the bank and he must begin to keep a diary which will be invaluable in the years to come. Trout behave in exactly the same way under the same sort of conditions which helps narrow the field of possibilities a great deal.

So now it is mid-March and the majority of fisheries are open. I know it is frowned on in some circles, but I would advise the newcomer to do a bit of touring around the reservoirs in those early weeks as they open their doors. The fishing is usually pretty easy and so a degree of confidence is quickly built up.

Even on opening days there are a few things to look out for, however. The first is to avoid a shallow area with a wind blowing from behind. Even if it does hold fish, they will soon move away with the slightest disturbance. With very little weed about, a slow-sinking line can be used with confidence during the early weeks. My own records prove that the lure must be a black one such as the Black Chenille, Sweeney Todd, Viva, Black Zonker, Ace of Spades, Christmas Tree, Black Muddler, or my old favourite, the Black and Peacock Spider.

Whichever one you choose, don't go too big – a size 10 is about right. The correct line will be either a Wet Cel I or Wet Cel II which goes down just that little faster. For the longest casts they should be in shooting-head form but forward-tapered lines are a must if you cannot get on with one. I must stress the need for extra distance, as it really can make all the difference, especially at hard-fished waters.

The first trout will, in all probability, be a stock rainbow of about a pound. If nice and silver, it is worth taking home. Spooning its stomach will reveal a few tiny green and brown chironomid larvae telling us that the fish were grubbing about on the bottom for what they could pick up. At this time of the season, food is pretty hard to find. The very reason that they took the fly in the first place was because it represented the first decent mouthful in weeks. More important is the fact that the small lure was accepted – a large one would have frightened them away or invoked that frustrating, tap-tap sort of take which comes to nothing.

By midday or perhaps a little sooner, the fish will have become pretty bored with seeing lures, so the time is right for something totally different. Even the newly introduced stockies wise up a little by the middle of opening day. Now switch to a floating line. At the risk of getting tangles, put a dropper half-way down a nine-foot cast using a Water Knot. I always use six turns for added strength when using five- or six-pound nylon. Tie on something buggy like a Corixa, Shrimp or a Stick Fly or perhaps a Green and Brown Nymph on the point. The dropper can hold a size 12 or even a size 14 Black Buzzer or standard Pheasant Tail nymph.

Straight away, the fish are seeing something different. Instead of the lures being retrieved in a straight line they are deceived by the rise and fall of the nymphs and if there are any willing fish about they should take without problem. Later on in the afternoon it is often a good idea to take off the dropper nymph and to substitute a Blae and Black, Mallard and Claret, Zulu, Greenwell or even a very much out of season Invicta. If through fishing pressure, the angler has been forced to remain in one spot, it does pay to leave the water for a spell to rest the swim a little. If your neighbour does the same, then the chances are that any fish hovering about at extreme casting range will move in closer now that the disturbance has gone.

For the evening session go back to the lure and slow-sinker for a while, but this time use a white-based pattern, again sticking to the size 10 rule. An old Grafham early season standby is an albino Black and Peacock Spider. Other patterns worth a try are Cat's Whisker, Light Bulb, White Chenille, Missionary or a white Frog Nobbler. Come dusk and packing up time I should be most surprised if the newcomer has not completed his first limit. I suppose I shouldn't have mentioned the word limit as I gather such talk is bad for our sport, but perhaps like me, our beginner doesn't see the point of leaving trout to die of old age. I always thought that we went fishing

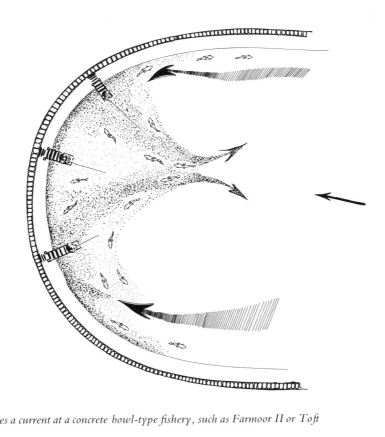

How the wind creates a current at a concrete bowl-type fishery, such as Farmoor II or Toft Newton.

to catch fish, but perhaps I am getting a bit old fashioned.

There are a few pointers I have left until now in the hope that the novice will take them to heart. The first is that if a pitch has been fished for a reasonable time without so much as a tweak, then for Heaven's sake move. The chances are that the fish are just not there to be caught. It is no good whatever staying rooted to a spot unless you know that it is a well known holding place like a deep gulley or perhaps a deep-ish place with the wind blowing on to it.

With the season seeming to open earlier each year and the banks lined with anglers when you arrive, where do you go? Do you just muscle-in between two others, hardly daring to look them in the eye hoping that they will not complain? If you do get away without an argument, the chances are that your cheek will be re-warded with a pound stock fish but cer-tainly not one of the over-wintered fish, which will be swimming around in much quieter places. At such times, take courage and head for the wind-lashed shores. Two places on a reservoir that receive the least attention are where the wind blows straight into the face or where it blows across from the right. Casting is awkward and you will need to punch a line under the wind or bring the rod around to keep the line and hook away from your head, but the rewards will often be worth it. If you are left-handed, of course, you have got it made.

The turbulent water attracts the trout to venture close into the bank as it washes hibernating food items out of the silt. Mind you, I am not talking about trying to fish

A double-limit catch at Aveley Lake, with Con Wilson, in extremely cold conditions.

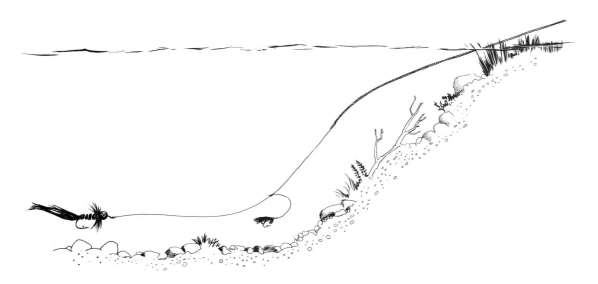

The lead-headed lure and Viva combination at the point of lift.

into the teeth of a gale or when the water has become coloured. Trout do not like muddy water, and in any case, they cannot see the fly too well either. What they do, though, is congregate in numbers just on the edge of the coloured water backwash. A concrete bowl reservoir like the well managed Toft Newton in Lincolnshire opens its doors in March. Even when you have a saucer shape the wind-blown currents need to end somewhere. I suggest that you discover where this happens as this is where most of the trout will be.

Trying to use an extra dropper or lure becomes far too much of a hazard when casting into the wind which is difficult enough as it is. Even using one on a standard twelve-foot leader presentation leaves a lot to be desired because of the blow-back effect. You should shorten the leader to a maximum of ten feet and tie on a size 10 Black Tadpole. This can be a variation on the theme but it must be weighted. Get the line moving really well by double hauling and then make the final delivery low so that it cuts under the wind.

As the flat nylon backing shoots out through your left hand, apply the brakes by stopping the shoot, pinching the nylon in your left hand, forcing the lure to flip over ahead of the line and leader. At this time of the year there should be little bottom debris so let the lure sink right down to the bottom. The retrieve should be slow, in longish pulls or a series of twitching hops.

For twenty years my early and late season trips saw me quite happy to fish a standard lure with a small lead shot pinched on the cast next to the hook eye. This was in pre-Trevor Housby Dog Nobbler days. Now everyone has tried out Trevor's marabou-tailed invention. There are many reasons for using weighted lures. This can be the knowledge of the effectiveness of a sink and draw lure fishing on a floating line (although Trevor often uses a sinker to effect), or it could just be blind faith following a tide of publicity. Whatever the motivation, early season catches with such a lure can be successful to say the very least.

The start of the winter boat fishing competition at Patshull Park Fishery, near Wolverhampton.

At both ends of the season, the trout move into the deeper areas of the smaller waters. Most methods will catch fish now, but do give the deadly two-lure system a trial. I use a medium sinking line, twelve-foot leader and dropper fixed half-way along and a good selection of size 8 marabou-tailed, lead-headed lures in fluorescent orange, lime green, yellow, blue, white and perhaps, olive, red and pink. You will soon see the need for all these colours. You fish one colour for an hour, with success, and then the trout suddenly decide they hate it. The colour switched, back come the fish. All these colour changes only apply to the point lure, the dropper being permanently filled with a size 10 Viva which stays there whatever happens.

If you are bank or boat fishing, then make for the deepest part of the lake and if in a boat, drop in the anchor as quietly as you possibly can. There are two such places in the far left-hand corner of Ring-stead Grange and another quite close to the entrance at Horseshoe Lake near Cirences-ter. A good place for boat anglers is close to the dam on Packington's Great Pool, Hall Pool and at Patshull Park. Start the session with a fluorescent orange lead head on the point and make a long cast. As the line begins to sink, feel it down through the depths. With time, you will feel it actually touch the bottom. If you start the retrieve then, the lure will stay deep, bouncing along the bottom with the small Viva a couple of feet higher up.

I used this tactic at Patshull Park in a competition fished by about eighty anglers. I headed for the dam and the fish were there in numbers, but so were the others. At one stage, half a dozen people were casting to the same spot. The orange lure worked well for the first hour, until everyone realised what I was using and followed suit. The catch rate plunged so I began to fish first a yellow, then a blue and

The controller fly method used in conjunction with a fast-sinking line, where a team of two conventional midge pupae dressings are used with an ultra-buoyant tail fly.

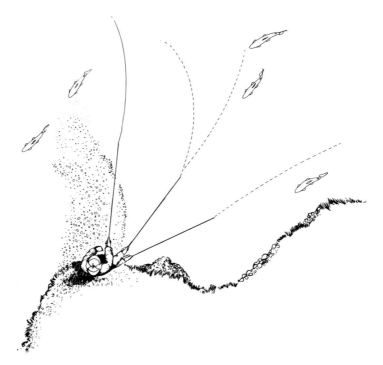

The headland point of a bay gives the angler a great vantage point from which to intercept cruising fish.

A nice catch caught on the Buzzer, at Tittesworth Reservoir, Staffordshire.

so on. In short, four hours fishing brought twenty trout – two-thirds of them to the ever-changing point lure. Apart from being an attractive lure in its own right the other, and equally as important, function of the leaded lure was that I knew exactly where I was fishing. It is a method you cannot use very often in the summer because of the bottom weed, but when the bottom is clear then do give it a try.

Fluorescent materials have provided the best results and experiments using lures incorporating luminous flashabou strands in the tail are encouraging. Do not be tempted to use a marabou-tailed lure holding too much weight. It will make it dive far too quickly for this method. I tend to use the foil off wine bottles and aim to create a lure that will sink about twice as fast as the line itself.

APRIL

Things Start to Buzz!

After the easier early season fishing when he who works harder and casts further catches the most trout, comes the more difficult period when the shell-shocked survivors begin to feed naturally. April on the reservoirs heralds the first small, black midges with the most activity being concentrated in mid-afternoon, extending through into early evening if it is not too cold. The chironomid pupa is better known, I suppose, as the buzzer. Irish anglers call the same creature the duck fly. On waters like Lough Corrib, the first hatches really do stir the brown trout into action.

There are, however, times when adult, small black buzzers will be seen in pro-

Angler Barry Capener caught this almost salmon-looking brown trout of 12lb 5oz fishing from the dam wall at Grafham. It took a Buzzer nymph.

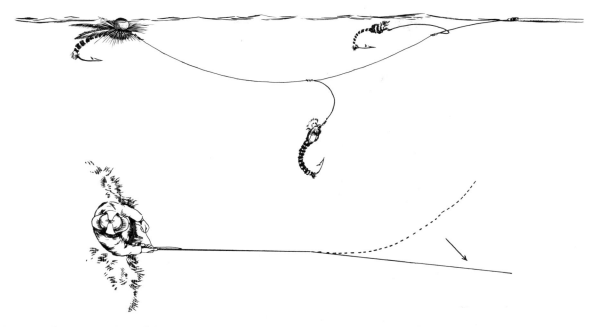

Peter Pike's Para-midge is fished on the point together with two common Buzzer dressings.

fusion and not a trout will rise. This is an indication that the water is still too cold. However, they will still be feeding on the larvae and newly-hatched pupae as they struggle for life in and around the decayed bottom weed. Warmth, then, is the key factor in selecting your fishing spot. A good place to head for is where the water is sheltered from strong wind, yet where there is still enough movement to create a small ripple. The point of a bay where the water is around eight to ten feet deep would be my first choice, providing as it does, the opportunity of covering a wide arc of fishable water. Boat fishers must seek out the same sort of conditions.

Anyone contemplating fishing a team of nymphs from a boat must make it as stable a platform as possible. Anchors fixed at bow and stern are a must. One anchor will allow the boat to swing about all over the place. To be really effective, early season nymph fishing must be done very slowly indeed. The less you move the flies, the

more you will catch. On mild days, the emerging fly is taken well and only occasionally will the adult, winged creature take their fancy, but a prolific hatch of millions of buzzers of the same colour and size can present problems.

For now, of course, your trio of offerings have just become part of a very large crowd. So how do we turn the odds in our favour? Quite simply by stepping up the size. So when the hatch is in full swing, I would use a size 10 or even a size 8 long-shanked Cove Pheasant Tail. If, however, the hatch has peaked, then a smart switch back to the size 12 and size 14 patterns is in order.

It is worth noting that the pupal stage of the buzzer can last up to three days. It will spend much of this time on the bottom, where the wings take shape. Then the moment arrives for the journey to the surface and freedom. Up they go, in their thousands, only to be met by a 'sticky' surface film which they cannot penetrate.

Two brace of Buzzer-caught rainbows from Bewl Water, caught in the quiet water on the upwind side of the reservoir during the evening.

John Goddard's Suspender Buzzer, which has been improved by Peter Pike.

Masses of them twist and wriggle about, a few inches underneath the invisible barrier, only to be scooped up by the trout.

This buzzer behaviour allows us to fish our imitations anywhere between the bottom and the surface. As a general rule of thumb, I would advise fishing the pupae well sunk during the day and then, as the evening rise begins, to grease up and fish the imitations just beneath the surface. If there is a light breeze blowing this last method can be lethal.

Some years ago, I perfected a method while fishing at Pitsford which is nothing more than a size 10 normal-shanked Black Muddler, on the point as a controller, with two buzzers on the droppers. The cast is made across the wind, allowing the team to drift around just taking in the slack. The beauty of the Muddler is that it achieves perfect presentation without any need for greasing the leader (something I am never very happy about doing). I go further, and rub the nylon down with mud before even starting.

A useful pattern which made an entrance on to the stillwater scene a few years ago was John Goddard's Suspender Buzzer. Its buoyancy comes from a polystyrene ball encased in a piece of nylon stocking and then lashed on to the hook near the head. I use them quite a lot, tied as an emerging pattern and to imitate the larger pale olive and ginger buzzer. These larger flies do not hatch in anything like the same numbers as their smaller black relations but their sheer size does bring the better fish to the surface. The first definite signs of a hatch are the swooping terns who dip down to pick the insects off one at a time.

My favourite pattern was sent to me by that brilliant fly dresser Peter Pike. It really is life-like and does deceive the better trout. I am not proud of the fact that I have been smashed up several times by super-fit fish in the four to six pound class while using this floating buzzer. Mind you, I have landed my share as well. I often fish this fly static, casting up-wind of a rise, when I can, and leaving it there for the feeding trout to stumble across. The strike should not be too hasty and as with all large dry flies, you must allow the fish to turn down before lifting the rod.

The easier, early outings are most often followed by much harder times. One good reason for this is that the general standard of fly fishing is so good when compared to only a few years ago. Constant full houses and good catches certainly deplete the initial stocking more than some managers dare to admit. However, all the waters that enjoy a weekly stocking should now come into their own and these fisheries are the ones to head for now. Buzzer fishing will

be the order of the day. Some useful patterns to try include Carnill's Poly Ribbed Buzzer, Peter Gathercole's True to Life pattern, the Suspender Buzzer, Blae and Black, Zulu, Pheasant Tail and Mallard and Claret.

After my discovery of using a buoyant lure as a controller, I got around to thinking how I could imitate the rising pupae. Life-like presentation is at its most important when nymph fishing, either from the bank or from an anchored boat. The problem is, of course, that the retrieve is confined to only a few choices and the question was how to add to this limited repertoire. Early one April, I was fishing with my son, who had devised a small lure after chatting with *Trout Fisherman*'s Steve Windsor. This weird creation, the mother and father of all suspender patterns, was being eaten by stockies wherever it was offered. The killing retrieve, Steve told me, was to fish it on a sinking line and, after pulling in a foot or two of line, to pause and watch the bow in the line between rod tip and water – just like a coarse fishing swing tip. The takes were more like eel runs, the thing was being taken with such confidence.

Before you even think of it, I realise that the stockies were taking the big ball of plastazote for a jumbo-sized pellet. If at this point, the sporting aspect worries you, cut the hook off at the bend, for it is not its undoubted fascination for stockies that interests us, but its use as a controller. Using my version of it in April, I wondered what would happen if I coupled it with buzzer nymphs while sticking to the same fast-sinking line. The long pull made the controller plunge. The following pause allowed it to rise up again bringing the buzzers with it, just like the natural insects.

The stark, white ball worried me as it stood out so much, so I coloured it dark brown with a waterproof pen. After playing around with leader lengths, I came to

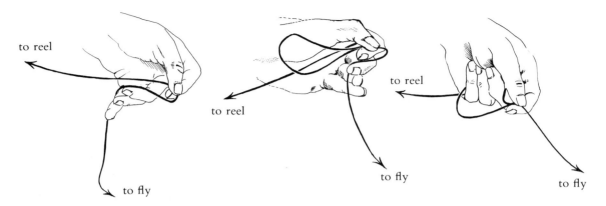

The figure-of-eight constant retrieve is something that must be learned if you are to become a successful nymph fisherman.

the conclusion that a yard-long piece of five-pound nylon, with a dropper positioned half-way between the permanent two-foot long butt piece and the point was about right. The takes are so confident that I often leave things until the line goes solid in my hand. I think that the trout see the pupa rising and just swim off with it in search of another, hooking themselves in the process.

While many anglers tend to fish close to the top, we know from our spoonings that trout take buzzers in vast amounts without ever coming near the surface. Couple that fact with the way nymphs behave on this unusual tackle set-up and you will clearly see why it is so deadly. Patterns fashioned with marabou bodies like the Spring Favourite are the ones to use, but the best of all is a pattern which has little white marabou tufts at head and tail and a body formed of medium brown marabou, ribbed with gold wire. The thorax is made up of the same material covered with a shell back of grey feather fibres. The method has tremendous potential for later in the season when corixa and sedge pupae are on the menu. The controller, by the way, has the plastazote encased in a piece of brown stocking and then lashed to the centre of a size 8 hook. For appearances sake, I form a

body of brown chenille and give it a Coch-y-Bonddu hackle.

Don't be a Booby!

I suppose it was a sign of the stillwater scene in which we live. I was spending a day at Packington on the popular, day ticket water at Broadwater Lake. As usual I arrived mid-morning to find all the best spots already taken. I caught a couple of rainbows by long casting with a slow-sinking shooting head and a little Viva Tadpole, but I soon realised that one angler was really showing how it should be done. As he was fishing on the opposite side of the bay, I could watch what he was doing quite clearly. A long cast out with what looked like a fast-sinking line was followed by a couple of sharp pulls with no further movement for a couple of minutes or perhaps more. Then he started a figure-of-eight retrieve before another long pause. In all, his time between casts was a good five minutes. Two casts later another fish was on the bank.

Gradually, the news spread that the successful angler had been using what were later to become known as Booby Nymphs. The angler who invented this pattern, of course, was Eyebrook specialist Gordon

An 8lb 12oz triploid rainbow caught by casting into the wind with sinking line and Booby Nymph tactics.

The tantalising sink-and-draw action of the Booby Nymph fished on a sinking fly line and short nylon leader.

Fraser. It was written up in the angling press and the few who tried the new pattern were amazed by its success. Most never even bothered, believing the Booby to be yet another nine-day wonder. How wrong can you be!

In April 1987, the Booby was back in the news again. This time it was Brian Leadbetter who was in the limelight, following his exploits in the European Open Championships at Bewl Water. The day was divided so each angler spent half the day in the boat and the other on the bank. Unusually for Brian, he blanked in the morning boat session, but he wasn't finished yet! Bewl was gin clear under a bright sky. With everyone nymph fishing away, Brian fished a pink Booby from the word go and landed eight fish, winning that session easily.

It would have been safe to assume that close imitation, buzzer fishing would be the best tactic. After all, in such clear water the trout could clearly inspect anything long before they decided to take or reject. But on the day, the top bank catch to nymph tactics was just three. Brian's re-

trieve that day was a slow figure-of-eight and his leader was just a couple of feet long, attached to fast-sinking line. As far as I can see, the Booby scares a lot fewer fish, as the angler is not constantly casting and retrieving. The rise of the Booby on the pause is obviously a green for go signal while the static Booby hovering just above the bottom gives the impression of a safe meal. This has to be the case, as I have been forced to use forceps to retrieve my fly at times.

On one occasion, I had taken three good fish and decided to switch to what was a new method to make up the rest of my limit. I fastened a white Booby to a leader just eighteen inches long and cast out. Thinking I was in for a long wait on what was proving to be a difficult day, I put the rod down and walked around a little bay to chat to another angler. I hadn't moved more than a few paces when the reel started screaming. That fish weighed five pounds and had swallowed the Booby. The tying of the Booby is similar to that of a typical tadpole except that it has a pair of polystyrene balls trapped in a bit of nylon

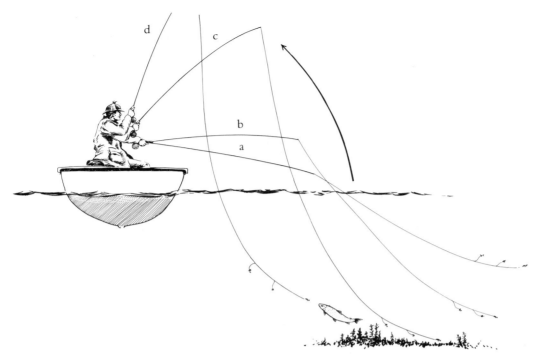

The drop-back technique as used in conjunction with a moving boat either with or without drogue, when the angler is casting to the front with a sinking line (drifting in the traditional manner) – (a) indicates the initial long cast, (b) the flies' descent, (c) the initial movement from the lake bed in conjunction with the rod moving upwards, (d) the sweep of flies and where trout may often take, (e) a fish following the flies when near the surface, and (f) the effective suddden downward movement of the rod making the flies fall naturally through the water layers where trout may again often take. The shaded arm shows the downward movement that will drop the rod tip to effect (f).

Occasionally, a good brown will be caught with the drop-back tactic, like this fine Rutland fish.

stocking and tied in at the head of a size 10 hook. A carrot-shaped body is formed from dubbing on seal fur or Antron. This can be any colour you choose. The body is ribbed with oval gold thread. The tail is a spray of marabou of the same colour as the body. Try pink, brown, yellow, olive, orange, white with the attractive green fluorescent butt as well as a black version.

MAY

The Deadly Drop Back

Any fly fisherman who thinks that he can be successful in the competition context without a sinking line should think again. During April and May a sinking line will be the correct choice ninety-nine times out of a hundred. Don't even begin to think

what may happen in a few weeks time. That's another story and more of that time later. When I began competition fishing seriously, about five years ago, I did so purely as a challenge and to see whether I was good enough to make the grade, but before taking part in my first match, I already had the knowledge accumulated over twenty years of fishing other styles to draw on and that has stood me in good stead. Basically, the change required only a few adjustments – the biggest being forced to fish in front of a drifting boat in what were often unfavourable conditions for that style.

I enjoyed some success from the word go, probably because I had that long apprenticeship with an all-important feel for sinking line work. Couple this knowledge with complete confidence and you will catch fish if they are there to be caught

– believe me. So what are the factors which must be considered when taking up competitive fishing?

Firstly, one must always know exactly where the flies are in the water and how they are behaving. The long cast has been made and the flies are falling down through the water but the inevitable is happening. The boat is drifting forward towards them quite quickly, despite the action of the drogue. You are now in the unhappy and certainly unwanted position of having an ever increasing amount of slack line between your retrieving hand and the flies. You counteract this by slowly retrieving the line as the boat progresses forward. In reality, a thirty-yard cast will be halved, but not to worry. You have kept in touch with the flies and that is vital as during the next fifteen yards they will be travelling just where you want them to be – along the bottom and among the trout. The takes can come at any time during the long, slow and even pulls, but a time to really expect that pull back is when the flies change direction for their swim towards the surface. This all-important change of direction can be exaggerated by lifting the rod slowly and in one long swoop. Now comes the most important moment of all and knowing just what to do next has given me my success in many of the early season competitions.

As you bring the flies to the surface, in the long sweep, watch for the top dropper to appear. Very often a trout will be following close behind, but is not quite convinced whether to take the fly or not. Remember that the water will still be cold and that the trout are not yet in the 'up and at 'em' mood. These reluctant trout can be converted into takers by pausing very briefly at this point and then lowering the rod top quite sharply, so that the fly sinks back into the water. Now is the critical moment. Keep a weather eye on the leader and nine times out of ten you will suddenly see the

leader form a different angle. It may move to the left, the right or even plunge downwards. Whichever happens, lift the rod and the fish will be on.

This wrinkle can make all the difference between success and failure in a competition. Far too often, competitive anglers rush the last part of the retrieve and never even see the fish that may well be just inches behind their flies. Casting competitions do not impress anyone, least of all the trout. Experience is the key to success. Unlike most other sports, fly fishing actually allows you to improve as you get older. Frank Cutler is coming up for seventy years of age and is a prime example. He has always got that ace tucked away up his sleeve, just waiting for the right moment. Frank fished for England in the Spring and Autumn Internationals in 1987 and his team, Herts Federation, came third in the big Benson and Hedges match, with him taking top rod.

Having confidence in your tackle is something else to consider. When using the sinking-line method, make sure that you use the right rod and not the long one you will employ later on in the season for floating-line and bob-fly work. For the heavy work, I prefer a ten- or 10½-foot boron to give me that extra power and stiffness on the strike. The longer, softer rods tend to 'nod' like a soft spring while retrieving a sunken line and are clearly unsuitable for the task in hand. Too many fish will be pricked and lost if you persist in using one.

The knowledge that your fly is going down very fast is a great help. After all, you want to fish the bottom not the mid-water. The High-speed Hi D and the Canadian lead-impregnated lines are firm favourites, but the Canadian has been replaced by something even better and now sinks faster than ever. Early season stocked trout tend to move to well-known holding spots year after year. These honey pots are usually on the down-wind end of the reservoir and have provided some of my best catches. A good wind with waves a foot or so high makes the trout less cautious and, provided you manage the boat properly, catching them should present few problems.

However, just because you have threaded a fast sinker through the rings does not mean that you have to head straight for the deepest water. In fact, you should do exactly the opposite. The whole object of the exercise is to get flies fishing where the trout are, and that is on the bottom. That is something we can do in relatively shallow water. Over deep water it would be impossible in the style we are fishing and the fish will not be there anyway.

It is as well to know when to leave a hot spot too. When an armada of boats is giving such a place a real thrashing, the fish will gradually stop taking, even if they are still there in numbers. The knack is knowing when to leave and to head for pastures new, where the fish may be fewer but more willing. But which patterns to use in early season? Some wonderfully creative patterns have been knocked together over the past few years and I go along with the idea of using something different to everyone else.

A well-known standard pattern for the opening weeks is the mini Viva, but the problem is that everyone uses it. After a week or two of being continuously hurled out by thousands of anglers, country-wide, even this one will have lost its charms, so I suggest that you switch back to patterns of your own. Fish them with confidence and you will be more than half way there. You can, of course, fish a nymph on a sunken line. Indeed, I often hedge my bets and fish one of each until a clear pattern emerges. A tip worth remembering is to fish two and not three flies. That way they will fish

cleanly on an even keel increasing their attractiveness a great deal.

Hunting the Stillwater Salmon

By the middle of May 1988 the Ringstead Grange fishery in Northamptonshire had already seen a hundred salmon brought to the bank. Regular angler Andy Brown, from nearby Corby had even managed the feat of taking a limit bag of half a dozen salmon. Impressive figures for a 35-acre, landscaped gravel pit fishery, you will agree. But let's go back to the beginning. Stillwater salmon stocking was the brainchild of Tony Chattaway back in 1984. The experiment has proved controversial, to say the least. Some have condemned it out of hand while others have praised Tony and those pioneer fishery owners who stocked with salmon.

The first stillwater salmon were slipped into the Ross Salmon Fishery in Gloucestershire. The four- to six-pound fish reared in a sea loch on Scotland's west coast had migrated down the motorways in a tanker and were put straight into the freshwater. But would they survive the rigours of the journey and the sudden change from salt- to fresh-water and would they take a fly? I went to see for myself, and soon discovered that the salmon took up stations just as they would in a river. But now, instead of using rocks and so on to escape the force of the current, they liked to sit in holes in the weed beds just like pike.

The five fish which fell to myself, Steve Windsor and my son, Steve, proved that they certainly would take a fly and that they fought like tigers on reservoir gear. I found that if you cast a Stoat's Tail on a floating line and strong leader across one of the gaps, you were in with a really good chance of a take. Just like on a river, the first cast was likely to produce the goods.

A 12lb salmon is the size of fish that will give you a fight to remember for the rest of your life, if caught on a fly.

Unfortunately for the fishery, the following month brought heavy rains and both lakes turned a thick chocolate, reducing visibility to zero.

When the water eventually cleared, salmon began to take again, but these were not the push-overs of a few weeks earlier. However, a few forward-thinking trout fisheries took an interest in the idea and began to stock with salmon, really as an added bonus for their trout anglers. Other fisheries, which soon joined the bandwagon, were Cleatham Lake near Scunthorpe, Rainbow Lake at South Cerney in Gloucestershire and of course Ringstead Grange.

Cleatham's owner, Gerald Denton, told me that all the salmon he stocked were eventually caught. Harold Foster at Ringstead Grange gave his lakes a couple of early stockings and was more than pleased with the venture. No more were stocked after May, but in September, one was caught and two others lost. That fish, which had spent four months in freshwater, was in superb condition. Both owners were by now totally convinced that the salmon experiment was a success but only when they shared the lake along with the browns and rainbows.

With a few fish being caught through the summer, interest was roused, making the expensive venture a worthwhile proposition. Rearing salmon in sea cages is big business, producing over three million a year for the table. The fish we catch come from these same cages and they do seem to be perfectly suited to our purposes too. But how to tempt one with a fly? Most certainly it pays to be the first angler on the water. If the fishery opens at dawn that is when you must be there and you must be mobile.

Have a cast or two in each of the weed gaps and then move a couple of paces just as a river fisher would. Standing rooted in the same spot for hours, casting into the wide blue yonder may bring a few rainbows but not many salmon will take an interest. At Ringstead Grange, one of the most productive spots lies in the far left-hand corner looking out from the lodge, with the actual taking place where the shallow waters slope off into the deep hole. As for flies, I have great faith in anything black like the Stoat's Tail and its variations. Other favourites are the Blue Charm, Munro, Hairy Mary and General Practitioner, all tied on Partridge or Esmond Drury short-shanked trebles. Saying that, most salmon are taken on ordinary trout flies, nymphs and lures.

Remember that when you do get a take from a salmon, allow the fish to turn away with the fly and to take a little line before you strike. If you react as you would to a trout, then most of the offers from salmon will be wasted. Gerald Denton had taken over from the Anglian Water Authority at Toft Newton in Lincolnshire and was quick to turn the fishery into a first-rate trout water. He also wasted no time in stocking salmon. His thinking, like that of Harold Foster at Ringstead, being that if the fishery was performing well from good trout fishing returns, then anglers should be given some salmon to play with. I shall long remember Gerald's face as he struck into a four-pound salmon which had been swimming free in the reservoir for the previous five months. He realised then just how much enjoyment stocking with salmon had given his anglers.

Both owners consider that stocking in March, April and May with more in September is the best policy, cutting out some of the risks of transporting fish such a distance in hot weather. Records prove that almost all the fish stocked are in fact caught, so there is little or no wastage. But do salmon feed in freshwater? The answer has to be a most definite yes. One ten pounder had thirty sticklebacks in its

Olives will hatch on the calmer, upwind side of the lake.

stomach. Buzzers, roach fry, shrimps, larvae of all sorts, even an apple core and things you don't mention in polite company have all been found in salmon taken at Toft and Ringstead Grange. The heaviest stillwater salmon so far are the twenty pounder from Toft by John Eaton of Horncastle and Owen Squire's near eighteen pounder from Ringstead.

So what began as an experiment has proved, beyond any doubt, to be a sound sporting proposition which could grow in popularity. I hope so.

Enter the Pond Olive

If like me you keep a diary, a flick back through the pages will provide a reasonably clear picture of what to expect. For example, in the third week of May, I fully expect to be boat fishing at Pitsford, and if the conditions are right, the pond olives will be hatching in numbers.

On one such day it was overcast and quite windy, just as it had been for a few days before. All the signs were that we were in for a good day's sport. Usually the better fish, which have managed to keep clear of the early season barrage make a cautious reappearance about this time. Pitsford's stocking policy ensures that trout will be distributed pretty well all over the reservoir.

Setting up an eleven-foot boron and weight forward floating line, I headed for the shallower and weedy areas which have always been favourite for an olive hatch, motoring along slowly keeping a weather eye open for the little up-winged flies. A whole fleet of olives came across the point of a bay.

The odd fish began to rise in competition with the swooping swallows. A breeze had built up, trapping the olive flotilla in a foam lane and the trout had seen them. No matter how often I fish, I still tremble when tying on flies at times like these. A wet fly I invented for just such a time at

Pitsford, some years ago, is called the June Fly, and on went a size 14 to the point. The centre position was taken by a size 12 Olive Quill and a fully palmered dark rust coloured Grenadier went on the bob.

Two brownies took an immediate liking to the bob fly and I boated these with my first few casts. Along with the regulars at Pitsford and hopefully other fisheries too, I returned these without taking them out of the net. Browns can live a long time, are costly to stock and to be honest don't eat anywhere nearly as well as rainbows. My first rainbow was a two pounder, so fighting fit that it stripped a full line off the reel in a flash. The tell-tale spoon showed more olives than anything else. There were buzzers too, and a few specks of *Daphnia*.

As the morning drew on, fish came steadily with four browns returned and three rainbows kept. Then two boats motored through my drift and that was that. Of course, they were not to know of the localised olive hatch. In the early afternoon, I had the hot spot to myself once again and even though there were not too many fish to be seen, they were still there – a couple of feet down and quite easy to rise. The June Fly was scoring well as was the Olive Quill, if to a lesser extent, with a surprisingly speedy retrieve.

Taking care not to motor anywhere near the active fish, I noticed quite a lot of boats just sitting at anchor. This, in my opinion, is a cardinal sin when fish are moving. But each to his own. My partner was catching well too, which pleased me and although I had taken some very nice fish already that season, to over eight pounds, this modestly sized catch had thrilled me.

Many reservoirs and gravel pits support good olive hatches. Although this fly is around from the third week of May to the end of June, they reappear in late August and early September. The best hatches occur in the shallows around the weed beds which have been home to the nymph colonies. Rutland's South Arm shallows are a superb area to drift over at olive time. Just ask Tom Saville what happened in 1987!

Some other useful patterns to try at olive time are a standard length Pheasant Tail with an olive thorax, a Hare's Ear tied with dyed olive fur, the Spring Favourite, Greenwells' (both wet and dry), olive Soldier Palmer, Apricot Spinner and a dry pond olive. Tie them all on size 12 hooks.

The Wet Fly in Another Role

It was early May when Nick Nicholson was fishing at Pitsford. The trout had taken a month's hammering and were hard to come by. Boat fishing at anchor was the order of the day for most, and he did well to boat six over-wintered fish when others either blanked or managed only the odd fish. The method he used was unorthodox but was no fluke. He has repeated the performance many times since. His method was simply to fish a team of three, well spaced and bushy bob flies on a fast-sinking line. Now who would consider doing that?

Going right back to my early days at Eyebrook and Ravensthorpe, the usual style was to fish with three wet flies on a greased silk line. As the day wore on, instead of re-greasing the line to keep it floating, very often I would neglect the chore meaning that I was fishing with a waterlogged and sinking fly line with old standards like the Greenwell's Glory Invicta. We all know that these patterns are tied to imitate a winged adult, but my laziness had allowed me to fish in a style very much like Nick's. My catches were good too. My diary shows an afternoon catch at Ravensthorpe of twenty-two fish which all took a bottom-fished Greenwell. The same method worked at Pitsford when it opened, in

The bridge at Pontoon where the salmon run from Lough Cullin into Lough Conn on the Moy system.

1963. The new plastic-coated lines came shortly after that and the old method died a death. Like most other old silk line men, I took to the new lines and became sinking line and lure mad for quite some time.

A couple of years ago, I turned the clock back and tried out the old favourite wet flies with a modern sinking line. The results at Grafham, Pitsford and Rutland proved that it had not lost any of its winning ways, on many occasions beating all modern nymph and lure tactics. But why should a wised-up trout be fooled by an adult winged fly moving along the bottom? This cannot happen naturally, of course, so just what is the reason for the success of the method?

My first thoughts were that it worked simply because no one else was using the style. I strongly believe that quality trout become bored and wary of the same old lures. If they see and refuse it once, then twice, they will never take that particular lure. At least that's my view. The spider-type patterns such as the Black and Peacock, Zulu and Red Tag could imitate a bottom dwelling creepy-crawly nicely but a Blae and Black must surely look like an adult chironomid and a Greenwell's Glory, an adult olive or possibly a chironomid too. To eat the adult winged fly, the trout has to find it on the surface and investigations of stomach contents prove, surprisingly, that very few winged flies are eaten at all.

Are trout really stupid enough that they mistake an Invicta for a sedge flying around underwater? Of course they aren't, but they do take this particular pattern in April long before any sedges hatch at all. We must admit that about 80 per cent of all our imitations resemble very little of what a stillwater trout actually eats. We are back to the point which Arthur Cove has stressed

The hawthorn fly.

so many times – that presentation is the single most important thing in all that we do. The fly itself is of secondary importance. But back to the sunken style. I now think that flies fished this way work because they are being offered where the trout swim for the biggest part of the day. It possibly helps too that the flies are much smaller than the majority of offerings hurled at them for weeks on end and are accepted as snacks rather than a larger meal.

Variations on a Mayfly Theme

The mayfly is becoming more abundant with each season and that has to be good news. On the quality Irish loughs the mayfly festival is never in doubt. Hatches continue throughout the summer and sometimes well into September. On the other hand, many lovely English streams have been ruined by abstraction and pollution over the past forty years, killing off their once thriving mayfly populations.

As always, nature has a way of fighting back and now there are more trout waters boasting a hatch than ever before. Many of the gravel pit fisheries and small waters boast good hatches and some of the larger reservoirs, like Ladybower in Derbyshire and Tittesworth in Staffordshire, are well known for their annual mayfly bonanza.

The Irish mayfly usually begins to hatch in numbers during the last week of May and by the first week of June the hatch is well underway. The fishing on our own English waters would then be over. The best mayfly hatch I ever saw was on Lough Conn. Paul Harris and I were lucky enough to have Kieran Connolly as our boatman for the day. Kieran, who now lives in England, goes back home for a six-week holiday every year and guess where he spends every day of it? Encouraged by the sight of an odd mayfly fluttering about, we rounded the bay into the lake proper and motored straight into a hatch of mayfly that would defy description. By the time we packed up for an early tea we had

Mayfly time in Ireland and a fine brown trout is landed off Lough Conn.

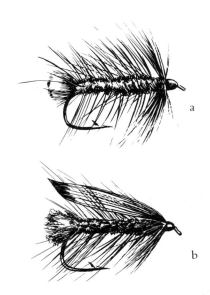

(a) Soldier Palmer and (b) the winged version.

caught twenty-three fish to two and a half pounds, returning all but ten, as requested by the hotel owner, Brendan Geary.

The successful team that day was a size 14 Black Spider on the point, a similarly sized Green Peter in the middle and a size 10 mixed yellow and olive mayfly on the top dropper. The fish did not come too easily at first and it was not until I sprayed up the mayfly that the action really began. We were casting no more than a few yards and retrieving slowly through the waves before holding the mayfly quite stationary for a moment or two. Our drift was no more than a few yards away from the shore. It is a great mistake to allow the boat to drift out more than say ten yards, as this puts the flies over deeper water. We rose about a hundred fish that day to make our catch. Needless to say, it was the mayfly that took the bulk of the fish with many of the takes coming while the artificial was either static or just barely moving.

The secret of fishing Conn and the other

wild loughs is not to cover the same water twice. Apart from the fish being put down (a line of thought which some boatmen do not follow), there is so much water to fish, so why waste it? Fishing in the traditional loch style, with a good boatman, beats all the other more elaborate styles more in keeping with rainbows. Remember, you are trying to catch wild brown trout and possibly a salmon too and the angler who has served his apprenticeship with rainbows at the small fisheries must have a re-think.

An added bonus is the superb scenery which you can see nowhere else in the British Isles. At the Pontoon Bridge Hotel, where I often stay, the dining room overlooks the lough and I know of no better way to end the day than to discuss the day's happenings as the sun sinks behind the hills. This is the best medicine I know for unwinding from the everyday pressures of life.

The deceptively simple Irish style works

A simple piece of mud is a good nylon de-greaser.

Brian Geraghty of the Irish Tourist Board found the rainbow trout at Rutland Water very much to his liking. He used the traditional method of short lining.

well on our own reservoirs where mayfly exist. But how do we take on the ever-growing number of much smaller fisheries which also enjoy a hatch, like the chain of gravel pit fisheries which stretch all the way from Leamington Spa right across the Cotswolds? Then, of course, there are the superb Hampshire waters to look at too. One such gem is Dever Springs at Barton Stacey near Andover. Owner, Nigel Jackson has transformed what was little more than a swamp into an excellent fishery stocked with larger than average fish. Both his lakes lie close to the little River Dever, a tributary of the hallowed Test.

I first visited the fishery in 1987, with Conn Wilson. I had wondered why he made the long drive to the water when he had some really good fishing on his door-step. Spring Lake, the smaller of the pair, is reserved for dry fly or nymph fishing while any methods are allowed on the larger and deeper Willow Lake. Armed with the knowledge that a few mayflies had been seen, I worked on the theory that the nymphs would be active deep down. I set up with a nine-and-a-half-foot carbon rod, weight forward floater, six-pound leader and a lightly leaded Dick Walker Mayfly Nymph. I could hardly believe the response with a trio of rainbows, all over three pounds, coming quickly to the bank.

Oddly enough, although the fish were quite happy to take the nymph, a few had begun to rise, not to the adult mayfly but

A specimen 7lb 2oz rainbow caught on the mayfly from a small fishery.

to hawthorns being blown on to the water from nearby blossom hedges. Despite this surface activity, I stuck with the nymph and cast towards a clump of rushes where I thought a better trout may be lurking. Lurking he was, and hungry too. Within seconds the fly line had been ripped off the reel. I had to follow the fish, passing the rod over the head of another angler. That trout fought like a salmon and at seven pounds was something to smile about.

After lunch I was pursuaded to try the Hawthorns. I found just one in my box which I sprayed and cast across the wind. The fly line bowed slightly with the drift, straightening out as a trout snapped up the dry fly. Keeping a gentle arc in the line is a good idea, as it shows when the trout really does have the fly in its mouth and is not simply trying to drown the fly with big noisy rises. I went on to take double my limit which included three more four pounders.

To say I was impressed with the fishing would be an understatement. The fish were so good and obviously thriving in the crystal waters. The trout are carefully graded before stocking. Any with eroded tails are rejected and go for the table. There is little more off-putting than to catch a big trout only to find it has horrid fins and tail. I have fished the water half a dozen times since and was lucky enough to hit the mayflies on two occasions. As on all small waters, trout do become nervous during the main part of the day and head for the middle of the lake and sanctuary. I had spotted a few mayflies being blown across into the deeper water being taken a long way out. My outfit not man enough for the job, I tackled up a No 9 floating shooting head, tied up a five-pound leader and sprayed up a special mayfly pattern. The leader was cleaned with mud.

Double haul casting with a following light wind gave the essential additional

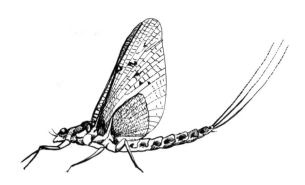

Mayfly adult (sub-imago).

range and my fly was fishing fifty yards or so away. A few just wanted to splash the fly, but not the four rainbows which scaled a score of pounds. That may have been an unorthodox way of fishing a dry fly, but I was satisfied that my end tackle was as sensitive as if I had been using much lighter gear and I shall never be afraid to try the dry fly at long range again.

On some of the smaller fisheries, trout have a liking for the spent mayfly and this need not happen in the evening as you might expect. I remember well arriving at a Cotswold fishery to be greeted by a yellow hammer sitting on a post with a mayfly in its beak. What a welcome! It was a perfect summer day and even if conditions were not great for fishing, I was more than happy as there were just a few anglers at the waterside. I don't think I have ever seen so many different kinds of fly before or since. Mayflies, alders, damsels and sedges – you name it, they were there. I never expect catching trout to be easy during the sunny days of mid-summer, especially on crystal-clear water where the fish can inspect everything in detail. What I do expect is a session when you have to dig deep into experience to outwit the cautious trout.

I had made up my mind to fish the dry mayfly for the whole day. If I caught fish

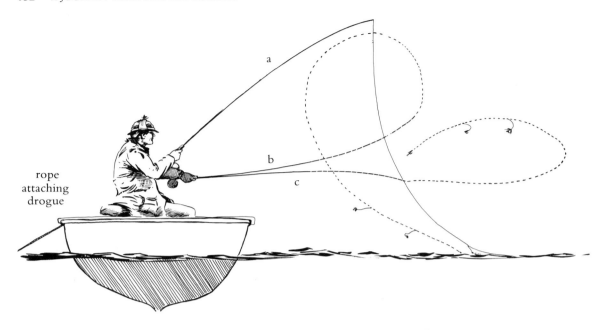

A traditional roll-casting sequence depicting the retrieve of the three wet flies. Rod (a) shows the beginning of the movement when the top dropper or 'bob' fly is dibbled across the surface. Rod (b) shows the movement forward as the tail fly reaches the surface close to the boat. Rod (c) shows the completion of the cast, the shaded arm denoting the power movement coming downward to effect a clean roll cast.

or not it would impose a set of rules for me to stick to. In the past, I had weakened, switching to the nymph if the dry fly approach proved unsuccessful. On that day, I would remain a purist.

It certainly wasn't a day for rushing about. With so few anglers you could pick your spot. The first angler I spoke to was Tom Westworth who had travelled down for the day from Morecambe. Tom was fishless but had risen a few and had been broken by a strong rainbow in the six pound class which had taken his mayfly. I spotted· a few rises in an awkward reed-fringed corner of the lake, crept into position and watched. I saw a trout take two spent flies from a surface littered with the dead and dying flies. On went a green, spent pattern and the second cast produced a perfect rise. The fish fought well and as I drew it closer, I saw that it would scale

about three pounds. But as I slipped the net under it, the fish dived and broke the fine hook at the bend. Back I went to the rush bed and ten minutes later I had a couple of good fish on the bank. Tom was in action too on a spent pattern when the dun imitations had failed.

JUNE

Lessons on Loch Style

As soon as summer arrives, there are sighs of relief all around, for now we can think about fishing on or near the surface at the big reservoirs. One aspect of the style which has captured my imagination is how the top dropper can have such an effect. Fish it well and the fish rise from nowhere but do it badly and you may feel that the

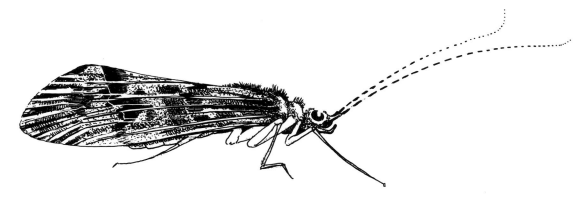

The adult sedge.

fishery needs re-stocking. Fishing the surface from a boat has gained rapidly in popularity thanks mainly to the upsurge in competition fishing. The majority of clubs now organise friendly events and eliminators for the English team. Even when not actually taking part in matches, anglers are fascinated by the traditional style of fishing from a broadside drifting boat.

Before you even consider what flies and methods to use, to do consistently well, you will require the utmost in concentration. The eyes of a master at the style are never still as he scans the water for signs of fish. The trout's direction and speed computed, the flies will be cast into the projected path and a take fully expected. Ideally, I would prefer a wave off of about six inches or so, but anything up to a foot or a little more is good too. Provided the air temperature is about average, and the sky not too bright, it is a certainty that fish will be well up in the water. If they are not showing do not worry. What they will be doing is moving up the wind about a foot down, on the look-out for food, which can range from minute *Daphnia* particles to buzzer pupae.

If the conditions are good they will rise, fly or no fly. This is where we are really tested as fly fishers. As the wind freshens and the waves get higher, I step up the leader strength and fly size. It is now a good time to try some gaudy patterns to tempt the fish up from deeper down. For the lighter wind, however, my leader is put together with two yards of six-pound nylon joined by one of five-pound stuff using a six turn Water Knot. A similar knot joins the further yard of nylon, a pound lighter still. My bob fly choices for a light wind are a size 14 or perhaps a size 12 Black Pennell, Red Tag or wingless Wickham all of which match a fly skittering along the surface. While the trout may not actually take the bob fly itself, it will often entice it to take the others on the cast.

It is a good idea to try a nymph on the point and sometimes something like a Mallard and Claret or Greenwell's Glory on the centre dropper. When drifting slowly in light winds you will be fishing the deceiver method at its very best. A stronger wind will not necessarily mean a faster drift if you use a good drogue. What you must do is change your leader to something a full pound heavier all the way through to cope with the larger waves and the bigger flies. I always cast a little further in these conditions as it gives the fish a better chance of seeing the fly.

Years ago, I fished quite frequently with Cyril Inwood and he really was a master at this style of fishing. One of his favourite leaders was a size 10 Butcher on the point, a Mallard and Claret or Invicta in the middle and a size 8 red-bodied Soldier Palmer for the bob. I have seen him get the fish almost leaping into the boat after the Soldier Palmer and takes at six feet away were not uncommon on a good day.

Nick Nicholson and Peter Gathercole have fished Rutland Water a great deal from a boat. Nick once asked Peter to tie him some hot orange and gold palmered flies as he had the feeling that they might work. He was right and both he and Peter enjoyed some super fishing with the pattern which seemed to beat others hands down when the temperature was rising. Naturally enough, Peter christened the pattern Old Nick and the fly has been a firm favourite for the past ten years.

As summer progresses, I try some of my Irish lough flies when the sedges are flying. It is now more than obvious that these Irish patterns work well on our own fisheries. The Green Peter and the brown or claret Murragh are well worth an outing. Talking of sedges, I do tend to take a lot of fish on the Invicta used as bob fly. A new one which I use in mid season, I call the Thicket, which is a sort of larger than life olive imitation. It works well both in a flat calm and high waves. Another winning bob fly came as the result of a lucky mistake.

One day, when changing flies, I tied on a Claret Pennell instead of the ordinary black version. After quickly taking a good brownie, before I noticed my mistake, I decided to keep it on. It was a good decision for it produced seven out of the eight fish I caught that day.

A Dry Fly with a Difference

For thirty years, fishing a dry fly on the big reservoirs was always considered to be some sort of a joke – a tactic for the eccentrics. Many would now admit to using dry flies when the suitable occasion arose. But what has happened over the past few seasons has certainly made all reservoir fishers think twice before they call the style an old codgers game. I say dry flies because they were greased to float on the surface, but in many cases they were little more than some kind of emerging buzzer and not a dry fly in the normally accepted sense of the dressing.

The story really began at Grafham with club members such as Dave Barker, Bob Worts, John Moore, Mike Ball and Andy Linwood spending a lot of their time on the water experimenting with various dry flies, and slowly the dry fly nymph was developed. Soon, their catches were beginning to look better than those of their friends', using conventional wet fly, nymph and lure tactics. Not only were there good bags of average fish caught but some very big ones too. The whole thing climaxed with Bob Wort's Grafham record ten-pound three-ounce fish which took him over two hours to bring to the net.

All this happened at a time when fishing was difficult, with less stock in the water than had been enjoyed for some years. A number of important competitions were to be fished later that month and some anglers were giving the new method a try. Dave Shipman from the Rutland club was using the style to great effect. While others were struggling, he averaged nine fish a visit. Then he won three big events in a row – the Pro-Am, the Benson and Hedges English National and the Midland Final eliminator for the English National. Dave's tactics were straightforward enough, or so it would seem. He was fishing three well spaced buzzer nymphs on a five-pound leader. The flies were different from the accepted buzzer dressings being very rough looking creations of seal fur of ginger brown, dark olive, red and orange.

It was important to grease up all three

A Viva lure with its distinctive green tail was used to catch these two fine specimens.

The ultimate prize – the World Championship winning trophy for the sport's father figure, Tony Pawson.

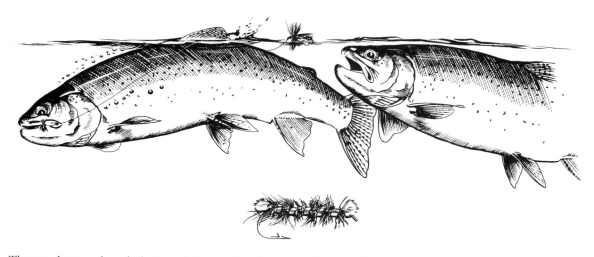

The new dry nymph method. Trout (a) approaches the floating fly; trout (b), on turning down, shows the correct point at which the strike should be made. The inset depicts the Shipman Floating Buzzer.

nymphs with generous blobs of Gink then religiously to de-grease the rest of the leader. He then cast down the wind from a broadside drifting boat. The secret was then to leave the nymphs static as the boat drifted towards them. The retrieve needed to be just enough to remove the excess slack line. The strike must not be too hasty as some trout try to drown the fly before taking it in their mouths.

It was obvious that those who were doing well at Grafham had come to terms with the 'new' method. Some very good surface fishers who judged it to be a flash in the pan failed miserably. To tie up some of the Shipman nymphs, you need seal fur which floats well and is translucent when wet. A piece of white, nylon wool is tied in on top of the hook to leave short breather tufts at head and tail. Then dub on the selected seal fur forming a carrot shape, ribbing through it with gold wire. Some of Dave's friends gave their nymphs the addition of two turns of ginger hackle but this did little to improve the performance.

Green is Best

Each year, from the beginning of June until the end of July, green is the major colour in the natural food choice and it follows that it is a shade which must be included in our artificials. When using wet flies, the old favourites such as the Olive Quill, Greenwells' and Golden Olive are good, but I have a pattern of my own which beats them all. Results with this pattern, known as the June Fly, have been excellent. If fish are showing in near flat calms during the evening and are being difficult, do try a size 14 on a four pound leader. You won't be disappointed. Cast close to a rise and then retrieve with a slow figure-of-eight. It is a fairly simple pattern to tie. I use sizes 12 and 14 and sometimes a size 10. A gold, lurex tag slopes around the bend. The body is pale green wool left rough but slim, and the hackle, just one turn of dark brown cock. The wing is grey starling. My second green pattern has also proved its worth. It is a nymph called the Spring Favourite.

The Juniors. The Welsh Youth Captain receiving the winners' trophy in an international event held at Llan Degfed Reservoir. Welsh Secretary, Moc Morgan, joins the celebration.

This one has a body of dubbed marabou to give the impression of life. Again, this one works when fish are showing but ignoring all your offerings. Tie it on the same sized hooks. The tail is a fine spray of white cock hackle fibres, and the body, olive marabou ribbed with fine gold wire or tinsel. The thorax is built up of the same material and then covered by a grey feather shell-back. The throat hackle is a spray of primrose yellow, cock hackle fibres. Tie a suspender-style version for static fishing.

It is not just the small imitative flies that succeed in this mid-summer period, and one lure which often produces the goods is the Leprechaun. This pattern was invented by Peter Woods about fifteen years ago. Because of its fluorescent green, chenille body it was really only tried as an experiment one June day at Grafham when it was very hot and the water thick with suspended green algae. It had been a difficult day when everything else had failed. Peter set up a slow-sinking line and put on his new creation. What was to happen during the next hour caused a stir, for he was to put eight good rainbows in the boat while his amazed partner remained blank.

The fluorescent green was the attractor and since that day, many lures, nymphs and even dry flies have incorporated small sections of lime green in their make-up, like the Viva, Christmas Tree and so on. Then there is the Fluorescent Green Nymph which really is a great rainbow killer. Tie this one on sizes from 14 to 10. It

The winning professionals team of a major competition at Rutland Water.

has no tail but tie silver lurex right around the bend and two-thirds of the way up the shank where you build up a small ball of fluorescent green chenille. The hackle is three full turns of long Iron Blue Dun fibres.

I must mention a dry fly used by Hector Woolnough at Pitsford. Basically it is a sedge imitation with that all important green butt. Time and time again, other patterns have proved to be less effective so do tie some of your own green or olive versions and fish them with confidence.

Joining the Competition

I have been involved with competitive fly fishing for several years and, despite what the critics may say, I have yet to see any bad feeling creeping in, as it has in some other competitive sports. Of course, it

helps when you live in a fishing-mad town like Northampton and have top waters right on your doorstep. I can be at Pitsford and Ravensthorpe in less than fifteen minutes, at Grafham, Draycote or Eyebrook in twice that time and at Rutland in just a little longer.

Back in 1963, I became a founder member of the Northampton Specimen Group, a small band of around thirty all-rounders. That roll-call included people like Cyril Inwood, Dick Shrive, Brian Leadbetter, Bob Draper, John Snelson, Ron Kyte, Frank Cutler, Bob Morey, John Ieldon, Jim Collins, Bev Perkins and Brian Furzer.

The Benson and Hedges International Team Championship has grown so much, with nearly 800 teams taking part in 1987. In my own club we choose a team of six by mutual agreement when everyone's current form is considered. A preliminary match with another local club is followed by the area final. Below is what happened to our team last year when we met up with a very strong Midlands field at Grafham in June.

Grafham had been fishing really well. Three days earlier, I had taken fifteen trout in a competition fishing the top with Grenadiers and Soldier Palmers. But now we were greeted with a very strong north wind for the second day running which had really stirred up the water. There is no question that this did not bode at all well when having to fish to strict competition rules. It was going to be a hard slog for everyone, but perhaps our knowledge of the water and all of its moods would see us through. We did well to gather eighteen trout in the difficult conditions and easily won the low-weight round. John Ielden took the heaviest fish of the day — a rainbow of four pounds six ounces.

The tactics were to make short drifts in the very rough water along the south shore by the fishing lodge. Although virtually all of the fish fell to floating lines, I did get two of my rainbows on a medium sinker. John's big rainbow came in the big waves very close to the shore indeed, at a spot where most boats would have turned and motored out again long before reaching that part of the drift.

In low visibility conditions like these, black-based patterns on the biggest hooks allowed are my first choice. Some will have a dash of fluorescent material at head or tail. Old rivals Grafham Fly Fishers were second, followed by Cambridge Invicta. All three teams qualified for the English final to be fished in a couple of months time.

We were drawn to fish on the second day of the event, which gave us a chance to see what happened on the first day. The Grafham club came first, with the Rutland boys close behind and Bristol Grenadiers third. From what I could gather from top man John Moore, who had taken fifteen fish for Grafham, the South Arm was producing the goods. I drew a cheerful partner in Geordie Davison from Newcastle and we agreed to head down the South Arm, but to fish a few spots on the way. We stopped off first half-way between Normanton church and the yachting club.

I had a flier with a brown of about a pound or so on the first cast, and so the fun continued until we had put five fish into the boat. I fished the floater while Geordie stuck to his chosen Intermediate line. We were quickly joined by a dozen or more boats and the heavy pressure soon killed off the sport. By the end of the third drift, Geordie had taken a five to four lead before we left for new and less congested pastures.

Our next port of call was the top side of a wood where a moderate wind was blowing on to the shore. Starting the drift two hundred yards out, I again took a fish first cast and Geordie picked one up as we reached the shore. But as we motored back out again, in came the boats again. The next problem was how to get rid of them. I motored well out and pulled up my hood so that no one would recognise me. By now we were travelling down the centre of the Arm and putting down a lot of fish. It seemed pointless to go any further as there were so many trout there so we turned round to put our flies to the rainbows working their way up a wind lane.

The engine cut and we began a really long drift, the wind taking us right along the left-hand side of the reservoir. During the next hour I went well ahead of Geordie who I felt had stuck it out with his Intermediate line for too long. The fish were smack on top and that is where they were taking our Grenadiers and Soldier Palmers. When I had put the seventh rainbow in the

An angler fishing to a rising trout, at the edge of the ripple where the fish take with more confidence.

boat, Geordie saw the sense and changed to a floater. In no sense at all was this just stockie bashing. My best fish had gone to a good three pounds and we felt pretty pleased with ourselves as we motored back in driving rain. A great day had been made even better by making a new friend.

In the event Geordie took a dozen fish for sixteen pounds and my sixteen scaled twenty-five. The very powerful Bristol Reservoirs team had done well too, totalling eighty-three pounds to take first place. Dark horses Herts Federation followed just a couple of pounds short and my own team slipped into third. All three had leapt the all important hurdle into the International final at Grafham and it was smiles all round. For the individual prize I was pipped by a pound by my good friend Terry Oliver who had gathered eighteen fish in the South Arm. All the fish came off the top to the same flies which really are unbeatable in such perfect conditions.

The Irish pattern, the Green Peter, is very good at sedge time fished in Ireland or in the British Isles.

Anticipation was running high as the big day approached. It was to be staged as a two session event. In practice and on a good fishing wave all of our team performed well, with double limits. Again the tactics were floating line, small flies and a slow retrieve. Taking part were six clubs from England, four from Scotland and two each from Wales and Northern Ireland.

In the first session I had drawn to fish with Bristol's John Braithwaite which meant that a friendly tussle was on the cards. It was overcast and I had set up with a Cove Pheasant Tail on the point, another favourite buzzer imitation called the Tiger Nymph in the middle and the usual Soldier Palmer on the top dropper. All three were dressed on size 12 hooks.

John and I matched each other fish for fish until we hit a quiet spell with John leading six to four. I fined down the leader to four pounds and lengthened it to twenty feet. I also stepped down the fly size. During the early spell, the breeze had switched directions three or four times and there were periods of flat calms. I then hit a purple patch hooking nine fish in an hour and a half, but landed only six. The session ended with ten to John's seven.

Once again, the Bristol team had done well with Steve Pope weighing in twenty pounds. The Bristol clubs were lying in first and second places with the Grenadiers just slightly ahead. In fifth place, our faces were a little long until we realised that only a pound or so separated the third placed Welsh side Llanilar, fourth placed Dromore from Northern Ireland and ourselves. The next day dawned bright and with that dreaded flat calm. Again I had been drawn with a Bristol man – Geoff Marshall from the high flying Grenadiers. He really showed me the way home with half a dozen fish taken off the top with what else but a Grenadier fished three at a time. I would never have believed that this tactic could

possibly work in a flat calm had I not seen it for myself. I had to make do with a brace. Thankfully my team mates, John Snelson and Brian Leadbetter, had made up for my shortcomings.

The rest is history. Bristol ruled supreme with the Reservoirs side taking first place with a hundred and ten pounds. Grenadiers were second, just five pounds behind. Then came a big cheer for Dromore who had picked up a thoroughly well earned third place with over ninety-two pounds. Llanilar were fourth and we were fifth. A word of advice for when fishing this sort of event. Don't ever think of them as being stockie bashing outings – be prepared to go and search for the better fish.

JULY

Into the Twilight Zone

What is it about sedge time on the bigger fisheries that makes July and August the most consistent fly fishing time of the whole season? There are a number of factors which make this so. Firstly, the weedy areas close to the bank, where the sedges hatch at their thickest during the evening, bringing the fish into easy range on areas which will have been virtually barren of trout. Rising fish are a common sight at this time too, the trout being drawn to the surface from their feeding close to the bottom by the insect activity.

It is a time for fishing imitative patterns

including the dry fly. There are a couple of exceptions to this rule, but more about those later. It is more than possible, on such sunny days, to slog away for little or no reward. Daytime fishing at this time of the season is best done from a drifting boat but bank fishing can be devastatingly effective during that magical hour before darkness falls. It is now that the crafty regulars appear – just as the anglers who have spent their day thrashing the water are heading for the car-park.

Ninety-nine times out of a hundred, the fishing can be guaranteed to get better as dusk approaches. Even flat calms can be fished with confidence once the sedges begin to appear. The only thing which can kill it stone-dead is a hatch of the dreaded *Caenis*. This has happened to me a few times at Pitsford and the trout switch on to the little horrors every time. Why, I know not.

Whenever you can, it pays to put your adult and pupal imitations into the edge of the ripple. We often see lots of Grousewing Sedges about but I am not convinced that trout really take to them as we think they might. Stomach contents show plenty of buff sedges and medium brown ones too, but you won't find many Grousewings. Frank Cutler has a theory that they taste bitter and he's probably right. He usually is about such things.

Sedges seem to hatch best in the calmer, sheltered bays and this is one time that flat calms don't bother me. This applies to both bank and boat fishing in the evenings. Now the simplest of all methods will put fish in the net. Go straight for a twelve-foot leader holding a size 12 dry, Bi-visible sedge pattern, making sure that the leader has been thoroughly de-greased.

You will see what seem like dozens of trout rising but it is a big mistake to keep lifting off in an attempt to put the fly into the path of a rising fish, odd though that may seem. Although there are plenty of rises, the odds are that the disturbances will be made by only a few, highly mobile trout. With that in mind, it is important not to frighten them away. Far better to be patient and to put your fly out twenty yards or so and then wait for the fish to find it. The fly must be treated so that it floats proudly. The trout are just mooching about sipping in the sedges and will soon come across yours. Remember, no retrieving. Just cast out and leave everything else to the trout.

Pitsford is only a few miles from my home and its sedge hatches are as good as you will find anywhere. I had been enjoying some superb evening fishing before inviting photographer Peter Gathercole to join me, in the hope of catching the thrill of a sedge rise on film. Apart from handling the camera, Peter fished too and his successful tactics may surprise you. He used an Intermediate line coupled with a bushy sedge-like pattern as a dropper and a size 12 Goldie on the point. In short, this little lure took six out of his eight fish and in less than a couple of hours' fishing time. His trout had all been busy gorging sedge pupae and I suppose those little tangled bundles of wings and legs could easily be mistaken for the little Goldie. This is one of the exceptions to the rule I mentioned earlier. There are others too.

Meanwhile, I fished more traditionally with my buff Silverhorn pattern, a small Brown Sedge imitation and another imitative wet pattern just sub-surface, casting into the edge of a light ripple and retrieving at a slow to medium pace. A brown and yellow seal fur pattern is also a great favourite of mine. It's not unlike Dr Bell's famed Amber Nymph which is a great pattern at this time, as is a Stick Fly tied on a long-shanked, size 10 hook. I usually reserve this last pattern for deeper fishing.

Sometimes, as darkness approaches, a

The ghillie lands a fine sea trout for Paul Harris on Lough Feeagh.

strong wind will pick up and even though the sedges will seem to have vanished, the trout will still be up and looking and will jump quite merrily on anything skittering about on the surface. A favourite tactic now is to tie a size 10 standard-shanked Muddler Minnow on the dropper with a Cinnamon and Gold on the point. Cast well down the wind, retrieve very fast and be prepared for some heavy takes.

Finally, for the final ten minutes before darkness brings the fishing day to an end, the time is right for yet another exception to the rule. It is nothing more than a size 8 long-shanked Black Chenille fished fast through the top. This often produces the best fish of the day and indeed rarely fails when the fish have been mopping up the sedges earlier on.

AUGUST

Sea Trout and Salmon on the Drift

The beauty of a trip to the west of Ireland is that not only do you have all that superb wild brown trout fishing but there are the migratory fish to enjoy too. Although I prefer Ireland to Scotland, in recent years, some of my friends have had some terrific sport there and on the islands off the west coast. Some of their sea trout have reached double figures and that is pretty good going for wet fly fishing from a drifting boat. This then is the ultimate challenge.

Many anglers enjoy a change of style for their annual holiday, and all the migratory fish waters I know are ideal, having both good family hotels and superb scenery. The challenge is made even more exciting

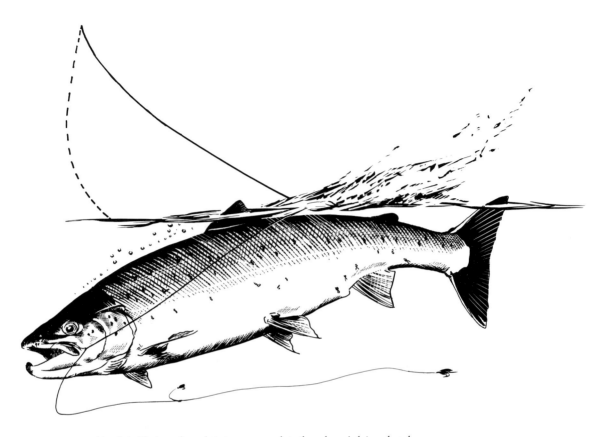

To ensure a good hook hold, drop the rod tip to accommodate the salmon's leisurely take,
giving enough slack line to take the fly well into its mouth.

when you realise that you are attempting to catch a truly wild fish. This thought alone is enough to excite one into feeling that the whole idea is something very special indeed. Irish loughs I have fished in recent years include Innagh, Ballinahinch and for the first time in 1987, the Burrishoole fishery in County Mayo made up of two waters, the lower Lough Furnace and Lough Feeagh.

As we drove through the wild countryside, the hedgerows were heavy with fuschias, honeysuckle and foxgloves and the heavy scent of summer filled the air. Chris Mills looks after the fishery. His knowledge of things sea trout and salmon is immense and but for these fish, just

itching to be introduced to our flies, we could have talked to him all day. He had arranged for us to fish with top local boatman Pat Hughes who, like his father before him, is a ghillie at the famous fishery.

The tackle set-up is just the same as for drift fishing our own trout, the only difference being that the leader strength should be stepped up to cope with the heavier fish. We were advised that our top dropper should be a well-oiled Daddy-Long-Legs but to use whatever we fancied for the other positions. I showed Pat a black hair-wing which had a few strands of pearl flashabou. It brought a nod and that was good enough for me.

Incredibly, we were both into sea trout

Two brace of sea trout taken on imitation daddy-long-legs, on Lough Feeagh in the west of Ireland.

from the off and within ten minutes, I was into a salmon which had taken the Daddy but which came off in a flurry of spray. Paul too was into action, his Stoat's Tail being much to the sea trout's liking. He also rose a couple of salmon which veered away at the last moment.

When fishing short line tactics it is worth remembering that while a fast retrieve will take sea trout, it does nothing for salmon. On the other hand, a very slow retrieve and dropping the rod on the take will take the salmon and you will miss out on the sea trout. We lost five salmon that day, all of which took on the fast retrieve but which were, of course, not hooked properly. All were summer grilse of about six pounds. Losing salmon like this is a common experience among trout anglers who react too quickly to the take. You must allow the salmon to turn down on the fly, pausing long enough for it to take line before you lift the rod. Sorting out when to strike quickly and when to drop the rod top really does take some experience.

We had become so involved with sea trout that day, it was only at the end of the session that we fully realised how things could have been very different. Instead of our fast-stripping, single-hooked flies for sea trout, we could have used little double or hair-wing trebles, fished slowly and caught salmon instead. Not that it mattered anyway, as we had experienced a day to remember.

The following day, we decided to try the lower Lough Furnace for salmon even though we were advised by Chris that few fresh fish were there. During the morning, a number of salmon splashed about but ignored our offerings. It is difficult to tempt them with a fly rod when they are not taking. I managed to rise one in the end but it refused at the last moment. Stillwater salmon fishing is no different from river fishing in as much as you need all the

conditions to be just right. You also need an element of luck. The sheer anticipation alone is quite enough to keep you going cast after cast, as you feel that every retrieve will put you in contact with the king of fishes. Indeed, I think that it needs a few blank days to make you really appreciate how much it means to catch a salmon on the fly. Just wait until it happens to you. Then you will know exactly what I mean.

Trolling on the Oars

It is a fact that the bigger trout seem to be taken in by a lure running at a smooth, even speed. Trolling on the oars gives this movement and there are a few specialists around who have used the technique to put trout into double figures in the boat. About ten years ago, Brian Bates and Tony Dixon would be out every single weekend at Grafham. Criticised by many they stuck to their chosen task. They were after big trout and not their smaller brethren, which the rest were attempting to catch. Their best fish was a fine brown trout which weighed eleven pounds, five and a half ounces.

Some of the bigger reservoirs allow trolling on the oars in designated zones. The areas cover quite an expanse and so there is a lot of bottom searching to be done. Many anglers would not dream of trolling, seeing the method as un-sporting and needing little skill. Of course, there is trolling and trolling. Done well, it can take fish which normal styles would rarely succeed in catching.

There is far more to trolling than simply hanging a sinking line, complete with big lure, out of the back of a boat. The gear must be purpose-made for the job. A very powerful, ten- or eleven-foot rod is essential. For reels, the old Ariel takes some beating, as does the more modern Line-shooter. Both are free-running and take a lot of backing. The lines range from a full

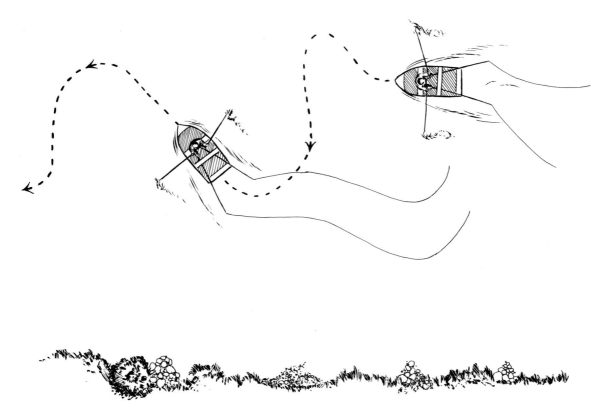

Route taken by an angler when trolling the lure under oar, giving the artificial wide arcing movements at about 150yds from the lake shore.

hundred yards of lead core to a ten-yard length of shooting head made from the same line. Fast and medium sinkers are used too. Usually, the leader is a minimum of eight pounds. The lures themselves range from a size 6 long shank to tandems and tubes.

Before setting out on the water you need to make sure that the oars will stay put if, for any reason, you have to let go of them. A thick, rubber collar about five inches across fits snugly over the in-board side making them quite safe. Even in the hottest weather, trout don't always sink into the deepest water and for much of the time, running a lure along the twenty- to 25-foot contour is about the right place to be.

You need to experiment a little to dis-

cover just how much lead core to let out, and the time for doing this can be shortened if the anglers work as a close team. Trolling only works when this happens anyway. It is a wise move to keep the hook points razor sharp, as brown trout in particular have jaws like a vice and a hook-hold is not always that easy. The angler not rowing should hold one rod all the time but he must, at all costs, resist the tap-tap takes and wait until the following fish really does take a firm hold.

It is best to cover the chosen fishing zone in a zig-zag, so combing the area thoroughly. The constant change of direction also gives the lure added life as it accelerates around the curves when the boat changes direction. An accurate map of the reservoir is

Fruits of the labours. Brian Bates caught this 11lb 5½oz brown trout on his specialised trolling tactic at Grafham Water.

invaluable as it will give you a fair idea where the old roads were, where trees once stood, the location of the ditches and so on – all great places for a trout to live.

Following the *Daphnia* Shoals

Strong winds and high waves wake up the sulking trout but it is a fact that too many boat anglers waste far too much time trying to get their craft to drift in the desired direction or even to anchor up in the right places. The water movement also ensures that the *Daphnia* billions will be packed into a small area. In Rutland's case this often means that both *Daphnia* and rainbows will be concentrated about three hundred yards from the dam wall.

The correct choice of fly line is critical. The lure must be presented at exactly the right depth and this will most often be within three to four feet of the surface. That is where the fish will be shoaled so that is where our lures must be too. For broadside drifting, I use a very slow-sinking fly line rather than something quicker which will bring the lure back underneath the fish. A floating line will catch a few fish but will be nothing like as effective as the slow sinker.

It is important to slow down the boat with a good drogue and I use one that is five feet square for this job. While the large waves go roaring by, my boat drifts along nicely giving me all the time in the world for good tackle control. A fast-drifting boat with too small a drogue or none at all, leaves you in a state of perpetual motion, casting and retrieving, casting and retrieving. A hopeless situation you will agree. Even though the waves are rough, you may feel like anchoring up some seventy yards from the windy shore having discovered this to be the main fish-holding spot. To do this safely, you need a weighty anchor attached to a long rope with ten yards of meaty chain. When it is rough, always put the anchor out from the bows. That way you won't ship a drop of water, but try anchoring out from the side and you are certain to be in for a wet and uncomfortable time.

Hot orange patterns work wonders at this time and Old Nick, in particular, is really deadly. To dress it, use a size 10 hook and tie in a bunch of hot orange hackle fibres for the tail. The body can be either gold or silver tinsel palmered with a hot orange cock hackle. A further three turns of another hackle is added at the head. I tend to use two and not three flies in this situation and Old Nick has a permanent place on the dropper.

The point fly is another orange one but this time it is one of my own fluorescent Ugly Duckling series. Dress it on a size 10 hook. Tie in a bunch of hot orange cock hackle fibres for the tail, followed by a body built up from gold Candlelite. The wing is fluorescent marabou and the head a ball of hot orange fluorescent chenille. But just what is happening on the up-wind side of the reservoir, away from the wind and the crashing? There won't be much *Daphnia* so forget the orange patterns. It is likely too that the water will be much clearer and the trout that much harder to tempt. There won't be that many flies hatching either, until much later on in the day. Nevertheless, a sedge pattern of some sort must always be on your cast. A Mallard and Claret can be pretty good as can a Fiery Brown on the point position and for the dropper, nothing beats the old Soldier Palmer.

Follow that Muddler!

Muddler fishing from a broadside drifting boat is deadly in July and August. Rainbows are predators and when the water temperatures are high and spawning problems have long been forgotten, they develop this killing instinct to a fine degree. A Muddler Minnow stripped fast across the surface will draw them like a magnet.

If you are to do the job properly your tackle must be more specialised than for normal surface wet fly fishing. The set-up I favour is a powerful ten footer, in carbon or boron, capable of casting a No 9 or 10 floating shooting head with ease. The backing will be thirty-pound, flat, black nylon which gives that easy added distance, especially if you give it a good stretch before you begin. Storing it on a wide-drummed reel is essential, otherwise you will end up with those nasty tight coils which make tangling a sure thing. For leaders, I use six- or seven-pound stuff for the smaller muddlers and step up only a pound when using bigger versions. The impact of the take is often so fierce that it is all too easy to get smashed so don't risk light leaders. That would be asking for trouble. We now have an outfit which will put the lures long distances without too much false casting. I have a reel which will cut out the tangles and a rod strong enough to hook and handle good fish at long range.

To be successful, both partners need to fish in exactly the same way. The boat is set to drift broadside on to the wind. If the breeze is only moderate, there is no need to slow down the drift, but if the wind is really blowing and the waves are big, a drogue fixed to the central rowlock will slow things up. Both anglers fish as far as they can downwind, then pause for a second or two. Then the muddlers are stripped back in long fast pulls. In a big wind you will need a size 6 lure with a large

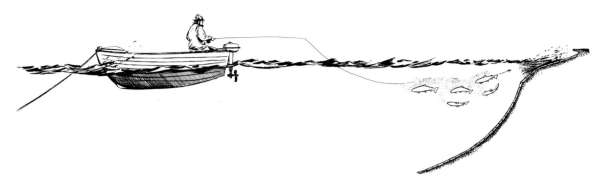

An angler fishing at anchor, casting towards the wind-trapped blooms of concentrated Daphnia *where, of course, shoals of rainbows are feeding. The inset shows the detail of* Daphnia.

un-clipped head. A useful rule of thumb is that the bigger the wave, the bigger the Muddler which we should use. I often use a dropper when fishing the Muddler this way. Something bright like a size 10 Peach Baby Doll is useful, a couple of feet in from the lure as are Old Nick, Goldie, Zulu and Mickey Finn. In the lighter winds I use a size 10 or even a size 12 Muddler. Either way you will be certain to get any amount of bow wave follows which fail to come to anything but the action makes the style exciting to say the least.

I like the standard Muddler but it does pay to be versatile. Try the white, black, orange and red versions as well as the more exotic Minstrel, Badger or Texas Rose. As well as the hair-winged patterns I also use them winged with marabou and some using quite a lot of flashabou. Popping bugs can be used in exactly the same way as the Muddler. They cast well and the pull produces a noise which can be heard quite clearly as the popper skitters and jumps its way back to the boat.

If at the end of the day, you are still a couple of fish light and you have any energy left, there is still a chance to make up the bag. A few sedges will be hatching in the quieter upwind bays and so now you can switch to the size 12 Muddler to imitate

a skating sedge. Aim for a much slower retrieve, even as slow as a figure-of-eight.

SEPTEMBER AND OCTOBER

Time to Dap the Daddy

The Irish loughs abound with inlets and bays where the professional boatmen moor their boats. The first lesson visiting anglers learn, just as I did, is that when fishing, life over there is lived in bottom gear. You will never believe just how much fun you have been missing until you have spent a day afloat on a lough with a local ghillie. When your sides are not aching with laughter at the never ending tales, he may well be singing a song. A stop for lunch is a must, no matter how good or bad the sport has been. Everything stops for lunch in Ireland and when afloat, this means a trip to the nearest island and a brew from an old black kettle on a driftwood fire. I can smell it now, just thinking about it.

Perhaps the most important lesson I have learned from these men of the lakes is just how incredibly effective dapping the natural insect can be. On every occasion when a suitable wind springs up, the dappers will

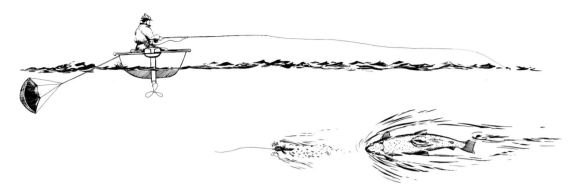

An angler fishing from the boat casting as far downwind as practicable, and stripping back as fast as possible. The inset shows the clearly-defined 'V'-wake made by the quickly-moving muddler and the pursuing trout.

double the catches made with normal wet fly fishing methods. This has long been considered a fact of life by the ghillies who maintain that a catch of six fish to the wet fly is good but that one of double that to the dap is hardly worth a mention.

The presentation, of course, is so natural that if a trout is up in the water anywhere close to where the dapped fly settles then he will take it with confidence. Most of our reservoirs allow dapping with both natural and artificial flies. That being the case, it amazes me why we have been so slow to adopt the method. Perhaps we are just too lazy to spend time collecting the naturals. The tackle presents little or no problems. You can quite easily manage with a long trout rod or better still a light salmon rod, six yards of floss line joined to a hundred yards of ten- or twelve-pound nylon backing, a short leader and a size 10 or 12 fine wire hook. You can, if you wish, buy some of the hooks specially made for dapping live insects which have a clip to hold the creature without damage.

It is possible to dap on any water if the wind is strong enough. I have seen it done from the bank but it is really a boat fishing method. To get the insect on to the water, simply hold the rod vertically and pay out the dapping line until it clears the tip ring.

Now you lower the rod and you are in business. Leave it there for a second or two then just lift the rod again and repeat the process. Jiggling the rod can help too, as it makes the fly skitter across the top in a series of little hops and jumps. Try doing that with normal wet fly gear.

Although, over in Ireland, natural mayflies, sedges, grasshoppers and daddys are used, the latter are by far the easiest to collect from deep grass and outbuildings close to the water. Fish over six pounds have been caught dapping at Grafham over the past few years by those wise enough to

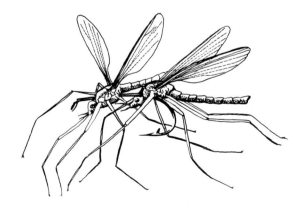

Two live daddy-long-legs (craneflies) ready for presentation on the special dapping technique.

Afloat with dapping rods on an Irish lough.

use the old method. The heaviest fish I have ever heard of being caught on a dapped natural was one of over thirteen pounds from just outside Cushlough Bay on Lough Mask.

Begin the dapping day right at the top of the wind. After all this is where the natural flies first land on the water before drifting further out on to the lake. Takes can come out of the blue and will either be a confident sipping in of the big fly or else a great splash at the moving fly. When they try to drown the fly like this just wait awhile and the trout is certain to make another and more determined move. Whatever happens next, take your time. The line will straighten out and then it is merely a matter of lifting into the very surprised fish. Playing a good trout without the drag of a fly line is something else, believe me.

Fishing the Artificial Daddy

If you run out of naturals don't worry, just tie on a big and bushy artificial pattern instead. If the naturals are about in numbers, then an artificial fished on a normal floating line works well too. There are dozens of dressings for the big creature, one of the best being the one devised by the late Cyril Inwood, which is virtually unsinkable thanks to its cork body.

It has four pheasant-tail fibres tied in at the tail to stick out an inch. The body is thin cork protected with a ribbing of fine gold wire. At each side of the shoulder there are two more legs of pheasant-tail fibres and four or five turns of a stiff ginger cock hackle. The wings are two pairs of ginger cock hackles tied in the spent manner. The hook can be a size 10 or 8 long shank.

A wild 3lb 1oz brown trout caught on an artificial Daddy.

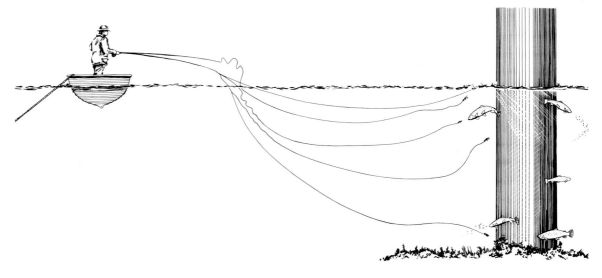

Cross-section showing angler in anchored boat casting towards a valve tower, or similar construction. Rod (a) shows the long cast, often necessary. As the lure touches down at level 1, rod (b) shakes slack line, enabling the fly line at level 2 to drop unhindered and on a constant plane through levels 3, 4, and 5. The reason for fishing close to the tower is because it harbours great shoals of small fry on which the trout move in to feed. Takes can come at any point from levels 2 through to 5, with level 5 being the most usual.

There are two schools of thought on how to fish the artificial Daddy patterns. One suggests keeping them high on the surface like the pattern I have just described. The fishing tactic is to cast well out but not to retrieve the flies – just to keep in contact, taking up any excess slack line as the boat drifts forward. This method does require a great deal of concentration but I have faith in it, simply because it works. The alternative way is to cast two or even three artificials and then to retrieve them slowly back against the waves. This method seems to work best in a light ripple.

Time for the Fry Feeders

The survival rate of coarse fish in bigger reservoirs has been very high indeed over the past few years. And what do trout just love to feed on at this time of the year? You've guessed it – fry. What usually happens at the big fisheries is this. There comes a time when because of falling water temperatures both fly hatches and *Daphnia* dwindle down to nothing. Catches from drifted boats begin to drop, but now is the time when the ever-patient bank fisher comes into his own. Vast shoals of fry now

A Missionary lure which imitates a small fish.

A unique picture, this 7lb rainbow first took a Black Frog Nobbler and after a few minutes' fight broke the line when diving into a weed bed. Five minutes later the same fish took another fry pattern and this time it was landed. Note both lures are left for the camera to record.

begin to show right in the margins. Their size can vary from a couple of inches to more than twice that as they seek the protection of the weed beds, jetties, moored boats and anything which will give them shade.

I have taken many good rainbows stuffed to the gills with two-inch roach during the last couple of weeks at Rutland Water. These fish have the tendency to feed very close to the bank in the first couple of hours of daylight and again in the last hour before darkness falls. Boat fishers are rarely able to get out on to the water at these killing times but, because they can anchor-up in the deeper water hot spots, they are still in with an excellent chance during the main daylight hours, especially if the day is clouded over.

September is the time of year when the very cautious brown trout of July and August suddenly go a touch silly as they show signs of shoaling together in preparation for their abortive spawning ritual. When this mood is upon them, they are far easier to catch than at any other time of the year. Many will become preoccupied with the fry, nature probably telling them to eat as much as they possibly can before the onset of winter.

Incredible catches of brown trout from Rutland Water and the other large reservoirs have focused a great deal of interest in the stillwater fishers' biggest prize. As we all know, brown trout become harder and harder to fool when they top the three pound mark and this fact, along with their relative rarity, makes them all the more valued.

By this stage of the season, the rainbows

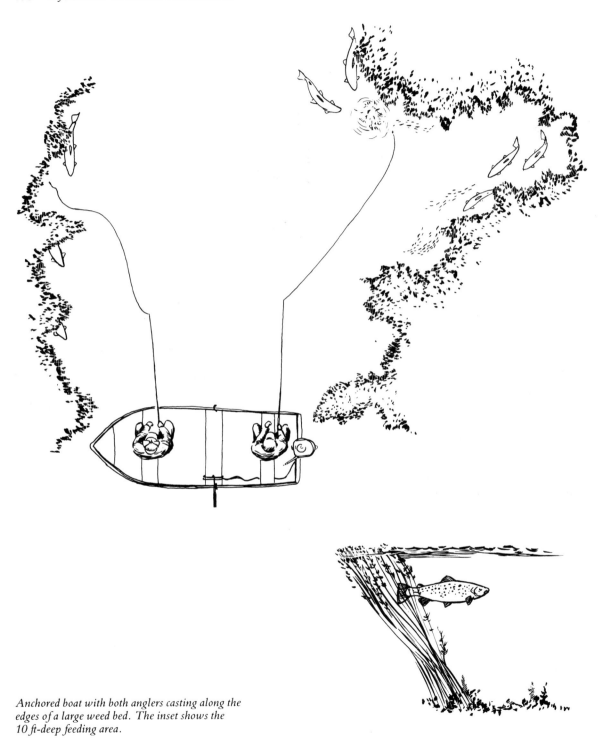

Anchored boat with both anglers casting along the edges of a large weed bed. The inset shows the 10 ft-deep feeding area.

A 10lb 2oz brown trout landed off the bank at Rutland Water.

are in the peak of condition following a summer of heavy feeding. To be quite honest, the fight of a big rainbow which has been loose in a big water for a year or more leaves any brown trout standing for sheer power and speed. These superb rainbows join in the fry-feeding bonanza just as the browns do and it is quite possible to catch a rainbow of just a pound or so, crammed with fry.

There is another type of fry feeding which I must mention. I refer, of course, to the sticklebacks which provide great sport at Draycote and the Queen Mother Reservoir near London. I enjoyed some fishing of the very best order when fishing a competition one October day at the Queen Mother. I had managed to find an area where good-sized fish were hammering into the stickleback shoals, scattering them a couple of feet out of the water on to the concrete wall. Inch by inch these doomed little fish would flip their way back towards the water but few escaped the jaws of the waiting rainbows. Nice work if you're a rainbow but not if you're a humble stickleback!

By casting an Appetiser on to the concrete with a sinking shooting head, I was able to imitate this journey towards doom and finished up with ten good fish topped by a real beauty of six pounds fourteen ounces, to win the competition easily. The secret, of course, is to find the fry. That

Double-figure browns are always a possibility from Rutland.

done, you can be certain that trout will not be too far away. Don't be impatient if you see fry topping without signs of feeding trout. In my experience, trout fry feed in short bursts of about half an hour or less before retiring to digest. They cannot possibly keep on eating such large food items for hours on end, although I did once find no less than eighty fry in one rainbow.

By mid-September it is all beginning to happen. At Rutland, early morning bank men will be having a whale of a time. Rainbows to four pounds and browns, even heavier, really get the old ticker pumping I can tell you. What really sets the adrenalin racing is the sight of a massive brown trout leaping clear of the water no more than ten yards from the boat. Brown trout, in particular, will leave the security of summer homes and it is not unusual to see them playing about in the waves. Lures like the hot orange creations, which have worked their charms, should now be forgotten in favour of the fish imitators. Although the old favourites, Appetiser, Jack Frost, White Muddler, Baby Doll and Badger Matuka are well worth a try, do give some of the newer patterns a chance. These are such as the waggy lures, floating deer-hair fry and of course the lead-headed, marabou-tailed lures, big and small.

Make sure you use your most powerful rod which must be strong enough to set the hook in the mouths of those big old brownies. Forget the light leaders of a month or two ago and certainly never use anything less than six-pound nylon with seven or eight pounds being even more sensible. A good surface method is to scrape the waves through with a white or natural coloured Muddler Minnow alongside the weed beds. The retrieve speed should be varied to suit the conditions and the mood of the trout. Sometimes only a very slow movement will induce a take, at others you must move the lure very sharply indeed.

Home-made sink-tip shooting heads can be very useful at the back end as they allow you to fish quite deep without fouling the bottom weed. I rate them highly and they are a must for fishing from the bank. The fry feeding situation will continue right through until the end of the season in late October. There is, however, one point to watch for. The later it gets, the more the browns will be seen shoaling together. If you find one in a taking mood, do be generous and return any that may be slightly out of condition. Just think how good that fish will look next season, a couple of pounds heavier.

A Floating Fry Pattern

I tied my first ever buoyant lures twenty years ago from cork or rubber foam and fished them a foot or so off the bottom with some degree of success. Ten years on, Mick Nichols and I fished Grafham regularly for big fish and again used foam rubber bodied patterns fashioned on the Jersey Herd principle, fishing them across the surface in the shallower places where trout were attacking fry. At this stage of the game, the idea of fishing a static or wind-drifted lure had not dawned on us. Some years later, and again at Grafham, I came upon a bank angler who had six very large fish on the bank. He volunteered the information that all had taken a white Baby Doll dressed really fat and smothered with Mucilin to keep it right on the top. The lures had just been cast out across the wind. What could be more simple than that?

The penny dropped and the floating fry idea began to make inroads into Grafham's stocks of bigger fish. Dave Barker from Cambridge began fashioning his deep-hair shaped patterns which he coloured with various colour-fast pens to imitate the ailing perch which were dying in thousands. I began to use a plastazote bodied Baby Doll

This lucky angler caught this 10lb-plus wild rainbow from Rutland Water with his first cast at first light. His excitement was such that it finished his day's fishing.

complete with painted-on eyes and these produced several nice trout, but it wasn't until I had caught a four-pound rainbow from Blagdon that I began to have faith in the method.

A successful wrinkle, developed by Peterborough's Bob Forbear and his friends, was to cast out a buoyant lure on a floating line and long leader from the dam wall at Rutland Water. If you have faith and patience then along will come a trout and suck in the lure just like it would a tiny dry fly.

There are plenty of materials to choose from and some of the finished articles look more like floating dead fry than the real thing. I tend to use flat ethafoam for my own imitations and the new pearl mylar and Candlelite for the bodies. As well as the buoyant lures tied on ordinary long-shanked hooks, imitations work well tied on fine tubing. Buy a box of cotton buds, snip off the ends and you have just the tube you require. If you have never tied up a tube before, stick a darning needle up the tube and then fix it in a vice. From then on, continue as you would with a normal hook, the only difference being the need to tie off and secure the materials at both ends.

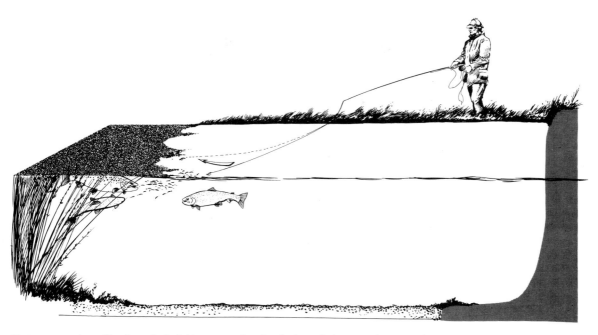

Cut-away section of bank angler's fishing area, showing both angler's approximate casting area and the trout population's distribution amongst the fry-rich weed beds.

Armed with all the right patterns, where can we look for some specimen fish? Most of the big waters will produce their fair share of big fish but three in particular quickly spring to mind. Of all the big trout holding fisheries the Queen Mother Reservoir must head the list. It has given up ten, ten-pound plus rainbows and a brown trout of fourteen and a half. However, because there are no weed beds at Datchet, a back-end approach with conventional lures would be the best plan of attack. It is quite possible that this brown trout record will be broken, the other places where it could perhaps be equalled being Grafham or Rutland. At the moment, I would put my money on Grafham because once again the bigger fish are coming out in good numbers.

It is not long ago that Haydn Jones captured a brown trout, over thirteen pounds, in Lymage Bay while netting coarse fish. This is the same spot where Bob Morey took the biggest brown trout ever caught in a Benson and Hedges contest. That fish weighed nearly eight pounds and came in a gale. It is the same place too, where my son Steve hooked a fish that stripped off a full fly line and all his backing. The fish slipped the hook after slack line was accidentally given while trying to follow it on the motor.

Some quite big browns have been taken on the pike fishing days held at the season's end. The best I have heard of being Mike Brady's fourteen pounder which snapped up a large spoon. I mention these examples to inspire you to attack Grafham just as we did all those years ago. Certainly, the big weed beds are back again so it is just a case of watching for the concentrations of fry. That, of course, and a great deal of patience.

From the bank, I would bet on an early start and concentrate on the Savages Creek area. It is here that many of the bigger fish congregate prior to the abortive spawning efforts. The other main area would be the dam, around the valve tower and around to the north shore. When Rutland produced its glut of big browns about eight years ago, the influence of the stock fish cages played a major role. The large fish found easy pickings under and around these fish-filled cages in Whitwell Creek and off the point of the Hambleton Peninsula. That situation no longer exists and these better fish can turn up anywhere.

The Three Trees gravel patch half-way between the church and the dam would be my choice for a back-end effort. Browns just cannot resist the pull of such a hard-bottomed area as October nears its end and the spawning urge comes upon them.

SOME USEFUL FLOATING PATTERNS

Dead Roach Lure

Hook: 6 or 4 long-shank.
Tying silk: White.
Body: Pearl mylar.
Back and tail: White ethafoam trimmed to shape.
Head: White varnish.

Tube Dead Fish Lure

Tube: Various lengths. Three inches is effective.
Body: Pearl or silver mylar.
Hackle: Crimson cock hackle fibres.
Back and tail: White ethafoam cut to shape.

Add a length of red silicone tubing to take the size 10 or 8 treble.

Almost Dead Fish Lure

Hook: Size 4 extra long-shank nickle.
Silk: Black.
Underbody: Strip of ethafoam.
Overbody: Pearl Bobbydazzle or Candlelite.
Back: Bronze peacock herl.
Tail: Spray crimson marabou.
Hackle: Crimson cock hackle fibres.

Injured Fish Lure

Hook: As above.
Silk: Black.
Tail: Bronze peacock points.
Underbody: Ethafoam strip.
Overbody: Pearl Bobbydazzle or Candlelite.
Hackle: Orange cock hackle fibres.
Underwing: White marabou.
Overwing: Grey squirrel.
Eyes: Imitation Jungle Cock.
Head: Black varnish.

Fish this one with a stop-start retrieve which should be speeded up if trout take an interest but do not take.

5 Odds and Ends

A CRASH COURSE IN COMPETITIVE FISHING

How does a competition fly fisher tick? Just what does make him keep on going despite failure? Probably the best possible way of getting underneath the skin of this relatively new animal is to set myself up as the budding competitor and to answer my own questions as they spring to mind.

Question: How can I find out about trout matches?
Answer: First, join your local fly fishing club. You would be most unlucky not to have a club near you as they are now so widespread. Indeed, some 760 teams entered the Benson and Hedges Championship in 1987 and obviously not every club in the country was represented. Your local fishing tackle dealer will be able to put you in touch with a club and he will probably know of matches in your area.

Clubs may be independent or part of national organisations. Ireland, Wales, Scotland and England all have their own governing bodies. To get on to the English fly fishing team for the Home Internationals you would have to qualify by first doing well in one of the regional eliminators, but you don't have to belong to a club to enter an eliminator in your area. Qualifying matches are regularly held at Bewl Bridge, Grafham Water, Draycote Water, Kielder and Chew Valley.

Question: What standard of fishing am I likely to find in these qualifiers?
Answer: Three or four years ago most of the competitors were comparatively inexperienced and a few anglers used to win consistently. Today the competition is much tougher and I would say that 90 per cent of the field go out with the serious intention of winning and are capable of doing so if things go well for them.

It is now much harder to finish among the qualifiers or prize-winners but the higher standard is, in itself, an incentive to do well. If you win, you know that you have fished really well. If you lose, it is no disgrace and you should not be disappointed – you have been fishing against some of the best trout anglers in the country.

Match fishing is not only about winning. I firmly believe that the greatest attraction is the social side. Often you are paired with a complete stranger, but after sharing the experience of a day's boat fishing you find you have made a close friend. After contests at Grafham Water and Rutland Water the anglers meet in the bar and re-live the day's fishing, swopping experiences.

Question: Is special tackle needed for this kind of boat fishing?

Answer: In the early season – up to May – you can get away with a standard length rod because a lot of the fishing will be with a fast-sinking line. The man who enjoys his lure fishing will adapt straight away, though in matches fished to international rules the use of flies bigger than a standard length size 10 is not allowed.

From June onwards, the nature of the fishing favours the use of a longer rod as you will be fishing the surface and working the bob fly becomes important. In a light ripple you want to be able to dibble your flies as far away from the boat as possible. That is why regular match fishers favour soft-actioned rods of up to eleven feet.

Question: How long a leader do you need and how many flies do you fish?

Answer: Normally, I use a twelve-foot leader with the bob fly six feet away from the end of the fly line. The centre dropper is three feet from the point fly. In windy conditions, when I am surface fishing I may shorten the distance between the fly line and bob fly. This gives greater control. I stick to three, well-spaced flies with a floating line although international rules permit four. Four flies may be all right when you are just laying the flies on the water and then lifting them off again – the traditional form of loch fishing – but the trouble with four flies is that they are comparatively close together. One fly can

therefore affect the way another swims so that neither looks right in the water. With a sinking line, I often use a cast of only two flies for the same reason. I do not want to spoil the swimming actions of the patterns I am using.

Question: What type of leader do you use and how fine do you go?

Answer: Most nylon needs treating before being used as leader material. The nylon picks up grease from your fingers, so no matter how you want the leader to behave, it will float high in the water. The late Cyril Inwood, one of the finest trout anglers this country has produced, taught me to put a blob of mud on the boat seat before setting out. Then you can rub your leader with mud to ensure that it sinks. Real clay mud is slightly abrasive so it also removes that unwelcome shine that most nylon has in varying degrees.

A proprietary mix of Fuller's earth and washing-up detergent will do the same job. For joining nylon and making droppers I use five turn Water Knots. If there are two-pound plus fish about, I tend to use six-pound nylon. Occasionally I go down three pounds if the fishing is slow and the water clear, but I then have to fish with great care to avoid being broken, especially on the strike. Some anglers incorporate a short length of power gum in the leader to act as a shock absorber when fishing fine, but I prefer to rely on my own judgement entirely. Sensitive hands and a feel for tackle come only with experience and practice.

Question: With such fine tackle it would be dangerous to hustle trout towards the landing net. Is there a danger of spending too long playing fish?

Answer: It is only in difficult conditions such as no ripple and clear water, that I fish really fine. I know that the fishing is going to be hard and my target catch is therefore lower. Sometimes after heavy rain, all suspended matter in the water falls to the bottom and the trout can see everything that is going on at the surface. If the day is bright, some anglers will be defeated by the conditions before they start. The trick is to be positive. Tell yourself that four or five fish could well win the match. So fish fine, cast a long line and let the flies stay out a long time.

Question: How many fly lines are needed?
Answer: You certainly need a floater and a fast sinker, but I would be dead without my slow sink line. I use it in place of an Intermediate line and it sinks just a bit quicker. Another line that does a job for me is the Wet Cel II. It is described as a fast sinker but it goes down at medium pace rather than fast. Certainly it does well for me at times. I see no call for a sink-tip line – that is more for the bank angler. Braided leaders of various weights affect the depth at which you fish your flies but such leaders are not allowed in some competitions – don't ask me why.

Question: How about hooks? Can you fish doubles and trebles?
Answer: 'Wee doubles' are favoured by Scottish anglers to fish deep but I fish only with flies tied on single hooks and I have no complaints about their holding power. Certainly, you get days when you hook and lose fish. The next day, fishing in just the same way, you will hook eight fish and boat every one. That's fishing.

Usually, you can tell as soon as you feel a fish whether it is going to stay on. Confidence certainly has something to do with it. It is no coincidence that an angler who gets a fish in the boat early often goes on to finish with a useful bag. The trick is to establish a catching rhythm. Once this is achieved you can almost will trout to take.

Question: Is it worth practising before a match?
Answer: Practice can work both ways. A few years ago, the day before a National at Rutland, I fished with Brian Furzer. We took sixteen trout each and were off the water by early afternoon. The next day, using the same flies in the same areas, Brian took eight fish and I took five. Generally, it is helpful to visit a water to get an idea of where the fish are and what they are taking, but there is no value in knowing the best area in a fishery. Other anglers will certainly have this knowledge too, so you need to have another plan to fall back on.

Nothing puts trout off more quickly than boats continuously motoring over them. If a lot of boats hammer a small bay for an hour or so, the fish go down and takes cease. You may be tempted to fish on, hoping to add to the two or three fish you have already caught, but the odds will be against you. It is much better to try somewhere else, where the fish are still feeding confidently. If you keep picking up a trout every half hour or so, you will finish well ahead of the herd who have persisted in the hot spot.

Question: Are extra boat seats allowed in matches?
Answer: Local clubs may have their own rules, but normally seats of the plank type are allowed provided they are no higher than the boats' gunwhales. Sitting high gives you a better view of approaching fish. Fishing from the bow boat seat is not too bad, but if you are low in the stern you can be at a disadvantage.

Question: Can you take a spare rod out with you?
Answer: Yes, but under international rules you are not allowed to have a second rod assembled. It must stay in the bag. The spare, in my case, is just in case of break-

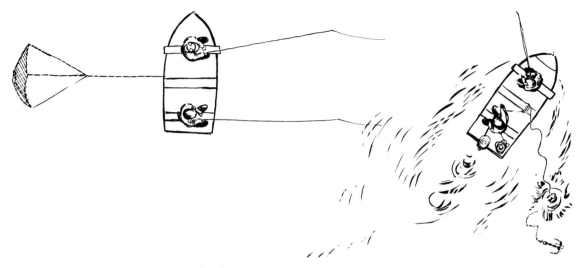

Never drop the anchor in the path of a drifting boat.

age. I can change lines in about ten seconds. There is no need to change your cast when you swop lines. I nail knot about two feet of eighteen-pound nylon to the end of all my fly lines and then form a neat two-inch loop. The leader is tied to the loop on the two-foot butt section. When I want to change lines, I wind in until the top dropper reaches the top ring, change reels and re-tie the leader. There is no fiddling about re-threading the line through the rod rings. Most anglers change reels rather than carry spare spools, I find.

Question: Is false casting poor form when you are fishing loch style?
Answer: Modern loch-style fishing is far removed from that lay-it-down-and-lift-it-off method of yesteryear. The old way is still fine when trout are rising to natural insects, but these days we are fishing mainly for rainbows – fish which respond to a retrieve that triggers their aggressive instincts. The modern loch fisher, therefore, tends to cast a little bit farther than the traditionalist, fish small attractors like a Dunkeld, pull them through the water a

little bit faster and then work the dropper flies near the boat. He is getting the best of both worlds.

Obviously, you cannot put out a line a reasonable way in one go, but you should aim to keep false casting to a minimum. It helps to use a weight forward line, usually a size 7 but possibly a weight forward 8 in a big wave. There is nothing worse than sharing a boat with an angler who is constantly false casting because he can't get his line out. Usually the angler is struggling because his tackle is not balanced.

Question: Are you allowed to stand to cast?
Answer: Not usually, although there are proposals to change international rules to permit an angler to cast to a fish rising to the side of the boat or behind. I do not like the change myself and the English Federation will not adopt it. Standing to cast, apart from being risky, scares any trout near the boat and makes tangles more likely. One of the delights of loch-style fishing is that a pair of anglers can fish in perfect harmony, each confining his cast-

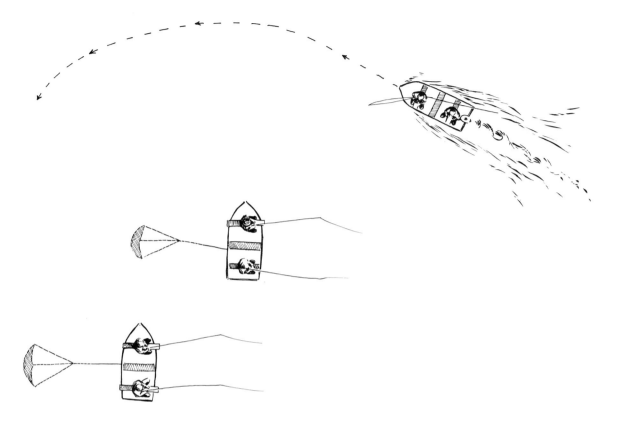

Always motor back upwind in a big semi-circle before rejoining the drift. In this way, the surface feeding trout will not be frightened.

ing to the water in front of him, unless, of course, his partner is out of action.

Question: What has accounted for the growing popularity of competitive trout fishing?

Answer: The success of the English team in the 1987 World Championship was certainly a boost. I know we were 'at home' but you still have to win, and the pressure is on the home side to do well. The match commanded plenty of publicity as the best fly fishermen from twenty-three countries around the world were taking part. England's success was good for the sport. In the end, it comes down to the fact that this

is an enjoyable way of fishing, which brings lots of anglers together. A few years ago there were many critics of trout matches. The element of competition was considered distasteful. But fears have proved unjustified. Loch-style fishing is sometimes described as 'the gentleman's handicap' but, even when a competitive element is introduced, anglers have shown that they can still uphold the best traditions of boat fishing for trout.

Mike Green of Corwen proves that you can wade out too far sometimes.

BOAT ETIQUETTE

Boat etiquette, or rather the lack of it, can make or break a day. Some boat anglers seem to have little or no knowledge of those unwritten rules of behaviour which make fly fishing the sport that it is. If you ever get even the slightest feeling that you just might be spoiling someone else's enjoyment, then simply follow your instinct. The worst thing you can do is to drop the anchor in a prime drift being fished by another boat already in position. I saw this

happen in an English National eliminator and it caused some nasty moments.

Never ever motor up through a drift either you or others are working. Always go back up the wind in a wide arc before settling down back in line. It goes without saying that you must never motor within a hundred yards of a bank angler. You know what it feels like when you are bank-bound and a local hero races along filling your waders. Bank anglers too, can have their moments – there are those who believe that waders were made for crashing into

Take full advantage of bankside cover.

Long casting from the bank with a shooting-head often scores over traditional fly-line methods.

the water like a crazed hippo at every opportunity. If you must wade, do it quietly and steadily. If you don't, you are simply ruining your own sport and that of others around you.

FLY LINE COLOURS

The array of fly line colours staggers the imagination. I do know, though, that false casting with a bright peach coloured line will scare trout. I always stick to pale green, olive, ivory or mahogany and on the subject of nylon, I prefer misty green or smoke grey. The dark shades of some of the more expensive sorts are excellent fish frighteners!

ABOUT HOOKS

I must say that I do rely on the hand-made hooks made by Partridge of Redditch. Their Capt. Hamilton range of wet fly and nymph hooks really is superb. These flies have the perfect hooking bend. Among the less expensive machine-made hooks, Mustads are still pretty good and I have no complaints.

LONG CASTING

I am convinced that the ability to cast a long line is a major asset. Equally important is the need for watercraft and the skill to turn our offerings into as near life as is possible.

RETURNING FISH

Catch and release is bound to become important. There could possibly be a lower-priced ticket for those who love to catch trout but who don't want them for the table. As long as the fish are not badly hooked and not handled at all out of the water, they should survive. With this in mind, the picture sequence taken by Phil Bagnall shows just how it should be done.

Catch and release is not something which should be forced on to anglers, however.

Catch and release fishing should be practised like this. Play the fish firmly so as not to put it under undue stress.

As it tires, slide it to hand. Do not use a net.

Reach for the rear of the hook shank of the fly, gripping firmly with your thumb and index finger.

Your compressed barbed or barbless hook will ensure that the fish wriggles free quite easily.

Off the fish swims, none the worse for its experience, and will be there to provide sport for someone else.

'You takes your choice'. Small fishery stocked rainbows. . .

. . . or wild brown trout. I personally enjoy both.

Mr Derek Graham of Falkirk with the current British record rainbow trout of 21lb 4oz 4dm, taken from Loch Awe in 1986.

THE FUTURE

Many fly fishers were anxious when the first of the major fisheries left the hands of the various water authorities. In the following years, waters like Blithfield, Tittesworth, Rutland, Grafham, Queen Mother, Toft Newton and Ravensthorpe were proof enough that private management does work well and that the early fears were groundless. At the same time, others like Bewl Water, Pitsford, Draycote and Ladybower are still authority controlled and their fishing is excellent too. In short, I'll vote for whatever works best for trout fishing.

CONCLUSIONS

We all complain when poor stocking makes fishing too difficult but then again we moan if it is too easy. Casting to a moving fish will always be the fly fisher's first love but we all know that this cannot happen every day and if we want to catch fish, then we must alter our methods and approach. The wise and successful fly fisher is an all-rounder who will be able to draw on a wealth of experience.

Before closing, I must mention a few hobby-horses which somehow failed to slot into our calendar. Winter trouting could, for example, have been described in more detail, but I don't see the need, other than to include basic suggestions. Many rainbow fisheries stay open the year round, the water authorities making this possible when they finally agreed that rainbows do not, or very rarely reproduce in stillwaters. There were just three days last winter when I ventured out on to a trout fishery. Because the conditions were good, the fish obliged and were in reasonable shape but I put them all back. A particularly mild February day at Ravensthorpe was enjoyable I must admit. My advice, then, is to fish on mild days. Please don't go on an endurance test in cold winds and driving rain – it just is not worth doing.

Now let's take a look at the official records issued by the British Record (rod caught) Fish Committee.

BROWN TROUT

Weight	Date of Capture	Location	Captor
14lb	05.09.58	Lough Melvin, Northern Ireland	J. Talbot-Frith
17lb 8oz	10.09.57	Loch Poulary, Scotland	D. Grant
17lb 12oz	04.05.61	Loch Faskally, Scotland	R. N. Campbell
18lb 2oz	28.07.65	Inch Lagan, Loch Garry, Scotland	K. J. Grant
19lb 4oz 8dm	06.04.74	Lower Lough Erne, Northern Ireland	T. Chartres
19lb 9oz 4dm	03.08.78	Loch Quoich, Scotland	J. A. F. Jackson

Although Lt.-Col. Creagh-Scott held the rainbow record for so long with his eight-and-a-half-pound Blagdon fish, things have altered rapidly since 1974. From then on the rainbow's growth throughout the list was influenced and assisted by some form of pellet feeding.

RAINBOW TROUT

Weight	Date of Capture	Location	Captor
8lb 8oz	09.09.24	Blagdon	Lt.-Col. Creagh-Scott
10lb 4dm	—	Gooderstone Manor, Norfolk	M. Parker
12lb 4oz	24.05.74	Exe Valley	A. D. P. Berger
12lb 4oz	05.07.74	Exe Valley	I. L. Johnstone
13lb	13.07.74	Exe Valley	M. H. Lenthall
13lb 2oz	28.09.74	Downton Tannery	W. J. Drummond
14lb 4oz	22.07.75	Avington Trout Fishery	J. L. Farmer
18lb	26.06.76	Avington Trout Fishery	A. Pearson
19lb 2oz	06.04.77	Avington Trout Fishery	R. W. Hopkins
19lb 8oz	25.05.77	Avington Trout Fishery	A. Pearson
20lb 7oz 2dm	16.09.86	Avington Trout Fishery	P. Cockwill
21lb 4oz 4dm	04.10.86	Loch Awe, Argyll, Scotland	D. Graham

Index